The Art of Building a
Winning Football Team

Bill Polian
with Vic Carucci

TRIUMPH
BOOKS

This book is available in quantity at special discounts for your group or organization. For further information, contact:

Triumph Books LLC
814 North Franklin Street
Chicago, Illinois 60610
(312) 337-0747
www.triumphbooks.com

Printed in U.S.A.

ISBN: 978-1-60078-981-6

Design by Sue Knopf

All photos are courtesy of AP Images, except for pages 26, 64, 204, and 222, which are courtesy of Getty Images.

This book is dedicated, with much gratitude,
to the most important people in my life.
To Eileen, who is my wife and partner in all.
To our sons—Chris, Brian, and Dennis—
who have always made us proud to be their parents.
To our grandchildren—Annie, Will, Jack, Caroline,
Kate, Aidan, and Charlotte.
They bring sunshine to our life every day.
Most of all it is dedicated to our daughter, Lynn,
whose devotion and loyalty to all
through her selfless and optimistic approach to life
inspires every member of our family;
most of all her father.
—Bill Polian

To Emma, who is a constant reminder
of how blessed we truly are as a family. Love, Pop.
—Vic Carucci

Contents

Preface

THROUGHOUT MY MANY YEARS AS A COACH, scout, and club executive in college and professional football, I have learned incredibly valuable lessons from some of the all-time great influencers of this and other sports.

Chief among them from football are Marv Levy, Tony Dungy, Paul Brown, Don Shula, Bill Parcells, Jim Finks, George Allen, Paul Tagliabue, George Paterno, Joe Paterno, Norm Pollom, as well as two legendary figures from basketball, John Wooden and Bob Knight.

My primary motivation in writing this book is to share those lessons, which you will find sprinkled and woven throughout.

No sports executive succeeds or even exists without players and coaches. Every player on every team for which I have worked contributed to my success more than I ever have. Many are mentioned in this book. Space precludes mentioning them all. But to all: Thank you from the bottom of my heart. You are truly "the game."

I mention all of the assistant coaches and scouts with whom I have worked in pro football in the acknowledgments. That mention does not come close to sufficiently thanking them for all they have done for me. Their lessons, hard work, support, and most of all their friendship have made my career a joyride.

To all of the doctors, trainers, videographers, and front-office staff who have contributed to that success to my heartfelt thanks. I owe a special debt of gratitude to Toni Kirkpatrick Miller and Sue Kelly, who were my loyal assistants through the years. The same goes for Donna Montana, Connie Papa, Lisa Hatter, and Carol Constantine, who ably assisted those of us on the NFL Competition Committee.

To George Paterno, Jim Schaff, Paul Robson, Cal Murphy, Kay Stephenson, Norm Pollom, Ron Waller, Bob Ferguson, John Butler, Bill Munson, Ed Stillwell, Steve Champlin, Chris Polian, Tom Telesco, David Caldwell, Tom Gamble, Don Weiss, Joel Bussert, and Dom Anile, I give my undying respect and deepest gratitude.

Finally, a special salute to the men without whom this book and my career would not exist: Coach Bob Windish, who started me on this road, and supported me every step of the way...and Coach Marv Levy, my role model, my mentor, and my dear friend. He made this all possible.

Acknowledgments

THE AUTHORS WISH TO GIVE their heartfelt appreciation to the following for their contributions to this book: Tom Bast, editorial director at Triumph Books, for embracing the idea from the start and providing tremendous support throughout; Jesse Jordan, our editor at Triumph Books, for overseeing the project from start to finish; Mark Zimmerman, of Headline Media Management, for his assistance in putting us together; and Amy Jo Griffith and Danielle Lavelli, for their tireless work in transcribing many hours of interviews and for helping with research and other details along the way.

We would also like to give special thanks to Patrick Smyth, executive director of media relations for the Denver Broncos, and Avis Roper, senior director of communications for the Indianapolis Colts.

Additionally, we would like to acknowledge the coaches and scouts with whom it has been Bill's pleasure to work:

Coaches

Kansas City Chiefs: Bobby Ross, Frank Gansz, Kay Dalton, Joe Spencer, and Rod Rust.

Buffalo Bills: Ted Marchibroda, Walt Corey, Jim Ringo, Tom Bresnahan, Elijah Pitts, Don Lawrence, Ted Cottrell, Dick Roach,

Bruce DeHaven, Ted Tollner, Jim Shofner, Art Asselta, Charlie Joyner, Nick Nicolau, Dan Sekanovich, Chuck Lester, Rusty Jones, Hank Bullough, Joe Daniels, Dick Jauron, Chuck Dickerson, Joe Faragalli, Herb Paterra, and Ardell Wiegandt.

Carolina Panthers: Don Breaux, Blair Bush, George Catavolos, Billy Davis, Vic Fangio, Ted Gill, Cary Godette, Chick Harris, Jim McNally, Chip Morton, Joe Pendry, Brad Seely, John Shoop, Kevin Steele, and Richard Williamson.

Indianapolis Colts: Tom Moore, Howard Mudd, Mike Murphy, John Teerlinck, Ricky Thomas, Greg Blache, Rusty Tillman, Bill Teerlinck, Tony Marciano, Jay Norvell, John Pagano, Kevin Spencer, Gene Huey, Jon Torine, Todd Grantham, Richard Howell, John Hufnagel, Chris Foerster, Diron Reynolds, Jim Caldwell, Clyde Christensen, Ron Meeks, Russ Purnell, Alan Williams, Pete Metzelaars, Leslie Frazier, Rod Perry, Frank Reich, Larry Coyer, Ray Rychleski, Jim Bob Cooter, Ron Prince, David Walker, Devin Fitzsimmons, and Ron Turner.

Winnipeg Blue Bombers: Cal Murphy, Fred Glick, Mike Riley, Bob Yazpasiani, and John Gregory.

Scouts

Chink Sengal, Bob Ryan, Dave E. Smith, Elbert Dubenion, Bruce Nicholas, Bobby Gill, Les Miller, Dave Gettleman, Tom Gibbons, Dave W. Smith, Doug Majewski, A.J. Smith, Ralph Hawkins, Jack Bishofsky, Joe Bishofsky, Tony Softli, Boyd Dowler, Pat Martin, Bob Guarini, Malik Boyd, John Becker, Kevin Kelly, Kevin Rogers, Todd Vasvari, Clyde Powers, Byron Lusby, Bob Terpening, Matt Terpening, Jamie Moore, Mark Ellenz, Jon Shaw, Ryan Cavanaugh, Paul Rolle, Duke Tobin, J.W. Jordan, Andrew Berry, George Boone, and Mike Butler.

Foreword

WHEN I THINK ABOUT BILL POLIAN, the first word that comes to mind is *loyalty*. I'm not sure I've ever met a man who is more loyal than he is. He was loyal to me for the 14 years we were together in Indianapolis, and he has been loyal to me since.

I had three head coaches during my time with the Colts—Jim Mora, Tony Dungy, and Jim Caldwell—and I was very close with all of them. But I only had one general manager, and Bill was a great source of continuity during that time. I was honored to be drafted by him in 1998.

Bill and I had very open lines of communication. We always had visits after the season where Bill would kind of go through some things that he wanted me to do as a player, and then he would ask me questions about the team and what was happening in the locker room and get a perspective from there.

At the same time, I always appreciated his advice. Bill's a guy who has been around football for a long, long time. He has seen it all, he had great experience with Jim Kelly, so I always took to heart any insider coaching point that he might have had because Bill is an old coach and an old scout. He would always have something he wanted me to work on for the off-season as a player, as a leader, whatever it might be.

Obviously, in 14 years together, there are going to be some disagreements on some things. But at the same time, Bill's door was always open and he always answered his phone. If we had a disagreement on something, we would always continue to communicate until we came to some kind of resolution. We were on the same page.

That was true even though, after the Colts made me the top-overall pick of the draft, I went through some tough negotiations that would cause me to miss the first three days of training camp. I was 22 years old, and I had no idea how negotiations worked. I've since realized that it's not personal, that that is the business side of the NFL, and it's really one that the player needs to stay out of.

But here I was, a rookie, and I was very frustrated that I wasn't at Anderson University, where our camp was being held. I was very antsy. Once I signed, I didn't know how it was going to work. Was Bill going to be mad at me for missing three days? I was looking at him thinking, *Golly, maybe he doesn't think I'm that good of a player, because of some of the things he said to my agent.* I had all of these emotions going through me.

Finally, I signed my contract at the Colts' facility. My car was still running outside. I was trying to make it to the afternoon practice to avoid missing four days; I was looking to keep it to three-and-a-half days. And Bill said, "Hey, I'll ride up there with you."

I'm thinking, *Oh, my gosh! He's going to reprimand me for missing camp.* Then, after we got in the car, it was immediately clear that the negotiations were over. I was officially the Indianapolis Colts' starting quarterback. And Bill was my greatest ally. He was going to defend me, protect me, help me in any way that he possibly could.

For a young kid going into uncharted waters in professional football, it was a very comforting hour-long drive to Anderson with Bill telling me what I could expect from him and, at the same time, having some laughs and telling some stories.

I can hardly remember a practice in training camp or in season when Bill was not out there standing with the coaches behind the offensive drill or the defensive drill. He was always evaluating, seeing what players were going to make the team. Bill definitely had his finger on the pulse of the entire team.

Before the game, Bill was always walking through the stretch lines, shaking hands with all the players. With most general managers, you think about them running the draft and making some trades, but Bill was hands-on with everything.

I always knew that Bill was going to get the best players available to try to help our team. Other than the year that I was drafted, and when we had the fourth pick and the 11th pick, he was picking 20-something or lower every single year. It wasn't like we were getting the first or second pick of the drafts every five years. We had good seasons, so we weren't getting a top-10 pick.

But I always had great trust in him that the players he was picking in the first round through the seventh round were guys that were going to help us. You can't hit on every one of them, but Bill hit on most of them and most of them filled a need.

Nobody put more work in. Nobody studied players more. I just knew he was going to do everything in his soul to get us the right players to help us win.

I always loved Bill's toughness and his passion. Nobody loved to win more than he did. He was the first guy that you'd see coming into the locker room after a win to shake your hand and give you a hug. And any time you lost, Bill was going to be right there with you, too, feeling that same disappointment. He was still going to put his arm around you to say, "Hang in there. Let's regroup and get them next week."

You felt he was with you in the good and the tough times, and I always appreciated that.

—Peyton Manning,
Denver, Colorado, June 2014

1

Soggy Lunches and Validation

"We want to develop champions, not celebrities."

—John Wooden

"Discipline is knowing what to do, knowing how to do it,
knowing when to do it, and doing it that way every time."

—Bob Knight

ANYONE WHO HAS SPENT EVEN A LITTLE TIME around me has probably heard this phrase more times than they'd care to acknowledge: "What it takes to win is simple, but it isn't easy." I didn't coin it; Marv Levy, the Hall of Fame coach for the Buffalo Bills, did. But I learned it. To be more precise, I absorbed it into the very essence of my being. And, during my 24 years as a general manager— or senior executive—in the National Football League, I lived by it.

The simple part is having a clear organizational vision of your beliefs and staying true to them. It means never deviating from the concept that you build your team with players who have specific character traits. It means that the core of your roster won't necessarily include the biggest stars of their college teams. It means that who you draft won't always show up among the names that the "draft experts" place among their top-ranked prospects.

But none of that is easy. Finding those players requires considerable time and effort and discipline throughout your entire organization. Selecting them, even when more recognizable names are available, won't ever be the popular thing to do...but it's always the right thing to do.

Following that approach was, ultimately, the main reason that, on the night of February 4, 2007, I was sitting in one of the club-executive boxes assigned to the participating teams in Super Bowl XLI at what was then known as Dolphin Stadium in Miami Lakes, Florida. I was completing my ninth season as president of the Indianapolis Colts and watching, with great anxiety and nervousness, early in the fourth quarter as we clung to a 22–17 lead over the Chicago Bears.

I was sitting with my three sons—Chris, who was our vice president of football operations; Brian, who was an assistant football coach at Notre Dame; and Dennis, who was assistant athletic director at Tulane University—and director of football operations Steve Champlin, who, having been with me for 20 years, was like family.

Now, calling what we were in a "club-executive box" is an extreme exaggeration. It was a makeshift structure that more accurately could be described as a lean-to, not attached to the permanent press box in any way. For all intents and purposes, it was some pieces of wood that had been nailed together to form a box that enclosed some seats in the top row of the upper deck.

And it was definitely not built for the torrential downpour that lasted the whole game. It really did nothing more than prevent the rain from falling directly on us while keeping us slightly separated from the fans—the majority of whom in that particular area were rooting for the Bears—in front of us and around us, although there were no problems with our conflicting rooting interests whatsoever.

To get there, we had to walk through the stands and up the aisle, all the way to the top deck. If you had to use the rest room, you had to go all the way downstairs to the concourse. There was water up around our shoe tops. The boxed lunches that we received at halftime were soaked; we couldn't even eat them. We might have had some popcorn, but food, just as everything else that didn't have a direct connection with what was happening on the field, was the last thing any of us were thinking about at that or any point of the Super Bowl.

This marked the fourth time that a team for which I served as general manager or president had reached the Super Bowl. The first three were in consecutive years when I was with the Buffalo Bills, an historic run that began in 1990. That Bills team would play in the Super Bowl for a fourth straight year, after I was fired following the 1992 season, but given that most of those players were acquired on my watch, I might as well have been a part of that one, too.

I definitely felt as if I was. I know my wife, Eileen, did, too. At the time of that Super Bowl, I was finishing out the one season I spent as the NFL's vice president of football development and we watched the game from a box with some league officials. When the Bills came out for warm-ups, both my wife and I choked up. That was "our team."

All four of those games ended in a Bills loss, with each more excruciating than the previous one. Yet, even while going through all of that heartache and disappointment, we never strayed from the blueprint. In fact, sticking to it was precisely the reason we found ourselves with those multiple opportunities to take home the Vince Lombardi Trophy.

Then it happened—the play that would serve as the absolute validation of everything that I believed, everything that I had been taught, everything that all of us who had worked together for years knew would provide the ultimate payoff one day.

With 11:44 left in Super Bowl XLI, Kelvin Hayden, our second-year cornerback, intercepted a pass from Rex Grossman and returned it 56 yards for a touchdown. Hayden's first career interception would not only seal our 29–17 victory, it also provided as clear an example as any of why doing things the way we had done them for all of those years made sense.

The choosing of Kelvin in the second round of the 2005 draft was generally criticized. The common response was: "Who is this guy? He only played corner at the University of Illinois for one year after transferring from Joliet Junior College and after playing receiver for both seasons at Joliet. How can they take that guy in the second round?"

Kelvin played for a Fighting Illini team that hadn't had great success. He wasn't an All-American or recognized in any of the ways that would grab the attention of the average fan. He was not a household name by any means. Even people who studied the draft very, very closely didn't figure him as a second rounder and 60th-overall pick. They probably figured that he would be taken a round lower.

To borrow a term from our coach, Tony Dungy, Kelvin was the "Quintessential Colt." He was selfless, smart, hard-working, a self-made player in every respect. Kelvin also fit Tony's "Cover-Two" defensive system perfectly. The system emphasizes speed, so it consists mainly of smaller and quicker defensive linemen and linebackers, and it encourages passes to be thrown underneath the coverage and calls for runs to be spilled to the outside. Therefore, the cornerback not only has to be able to cover, but he also has to be a good tackler. He has to be physical and be able to mix it up, because he's going to be forced to make a lot of tackles in the short zone, both on passes that are completed in front of him and on running plays that come in his direction. He'll be one-on-one with the back on any number of occasions.

Kelvin was not a guy that was recruited by 72 schools or was a high-school All-American when he was a sophomore. He was just a blue-collar guy. That's what Tony wanted. That's what Marv Levy wanted. That's what Dom Capers, our coach in Carolina, wanted. That's what our program's been all about throughout the years.

Peyton Manning was the MVP of that Super Bowl, but Dominic Rhodes, whom we signed as an undrafted rookie free agent in 2001, could have been. We ran the ball exceptionally well that day. Dominic rushed for 113 yards and a touchdown on 21 carries, while Joseph Addai had 77 yards on 19 attempts.

Don't get me wrong. Peyton had a very good game, completing 25-of-38 passes for 247 yards and a touchdown, with one interception. He also did a remarkable job of handling the ball well under conditions that were torrential. But, overall, I just thought Dominic was equally deserving of the MVP.

The thing that stuck out about that victory was the fact that we had the best team in the league, really, or the best team in the conference, certainly, for the two previous years and hadn't advanced. So, when we rallied from a 21–6 halftime deficit to actually beat the Patriots in the 2006 AFC Championship Game at the RCA Dome, it was incredibly powerful. Our center, Jeff Saturday, was truly speaking for all of us when he said years later, during an interview on ESPN, "That was the most emotional win of all."

When you win the conference title in your own stadium, it's always pure because it's your fans, your team, your family, your team family that gets to share that with you. There are no outsiders. There are none of the hangers-on, none of the supernumeraries that seem to just envelop the Super Bowl. It's just you and the ones with whom you want to share something like that the most.

And it remains a vivid memory. The joy of having accomplished that and coming from behind and doing it in our building, after all we'd been through in the two previous years—losing to the Patriots, 20–3, in the divisional round in 2004; the 13 straight regular-season wins in 2005 and then we inexplicably lose to San Diego; the death of Tony Dungy's 18-year-old son, James Dungy, four days later and all of the heartache that we'd gone through, and then we lose in the divisional round of the playoffs to Pittsburgh by a field goal at the end—was overwhelming. It was the pure, unadulterated joy of having finally won the conference championship and going to the Super Bowl.

Just before we left for the airport to fly to Miami, Tony took all of the players and coaches to our indoor facility. He pointed up to the wall, to the banners for the five division championships the franchise had won in Indianapolis before we clinched the sixth in 2006. He then took note of the fact that there was a space for another banner—the one for the Super Bowl.

"Here's what we're going to do, guys," Tony said. "This whole week is about putting a banner up on that wall. That's what this is about. Now, let's get on the buses."

All I could say was, "Wow!"

Now, fast forward to June, to our organized team activity practice. The only players there were the ones who had been with the Super Bowl team. After the first team meeting, Tony walked all of the players out to the indoor facility, and he said, "Look up on the wall."

"There it is," Tony said, pointing to the new banner for our victory in Super Bowl XLI. "You did it!"

I watched in awe. We would have a ceremony to present the Super Bowl rings after the final OTA session in June, but the unfurling of that banner was, at least for me, the most emotional of the celebrations because it was just with the people who did it.

Taken in context, Kelvin's interception was the validation of everything we believed in, everything that we tried to build with the Bills, with the Panthers—when I was their GM from 1994 to 1997—and with the Colts. Here's a guy who's the typical product of our system making the play that won the Super Bowl. As Marv used to say, "Programs win, people don't."

The way our team was built, invariably a player like Kelvin Hayden was going to make a play like that, just as a player like Marlin Jackson was going to be the one to intercept a Tom Brady pass at our 35-yard line with 16 seconds left when we were up 38–34 on the Patriots, to end the 2006 AFC Championship Game and put us in the Super Bowl. Marlin was another cornerback we had drafted in 2005, a round ahead of Kelvin. He was better known than Kelvin, but he wasn't all that highly touted, either. Most people following the draft had him as a low-first- to upper-second-round talent.

But those two players were exactly what we needed and wanted, and they fit the profile that we established perfectly. Reggie Wayne, our standout wide receiver who I hope will go into the Pro Football Hall of Fame one day, was like Marlin and Kelvin. Reggie was the 31st-overall pick of the draft from the University of Miami, and it was another decision that prompted the second-guessers to say: "Why did they draft this guy? They don't need a wide receiver. They have Marvin Harrison."

Santana Moss was by far the more well-known receiver on that Hurricanes team, but Reggie was the more complete and NFL-ready receiver. *What it takes to win is simple, but it isn't easy.*

It's hard to find those kinds of people. Finding them takes a tremendous effort by a great many people and it has a great many levels. It starts with the core belief that you win with people that have great football temperament. Football temperament tells us that a guy has, number one, a real love for the game and all that goes with it, that football's important to him; number two, that he has a really good work ethic, is willing to do whatever it takes to win; and, number three, that he's a good citizen, both on and off the field.

When you have those kinds of people and when you have that kind of mindset in your organization, three things happen: One, you win. Two, you win in dramatic ways because you have incredible resiliency; you have that never-say-die spirit because it's kindled by this group of like-minded individuals—coaches, players, staff people, everyone. And, third, you do it in a way that makes you proud because, by and large, these are really good guys. They're people that fans want to root for.

Yes, you need a Peyton Manning. You need the Hall of Famers that we had with the Bills: Bruce Smith, Jim Kelly, Thurman Thomas, and Andre Reed. But you've got to have, as we did in Buffalo, all of those other players who fit the mold as well—guys like cornerback Kirby Jackson, who entered the NFL as a fifth-round draft pick of the New York Jets, was picked up by the Los Angeles Rams, and then by us; free safety Mark Kelso, whom the Philadelphia Eagles made a 10th-round draft pick from William & Mary and then released before we acquired him; defensive end Phil Hansen, who was not a well-known name when we took him with the second-to-last pick of the second round from North Dakota State; nose tackle Jeff Wright, whom we drafted in the eighth round from Central Missouri State; and linebacker Carlton Bailey, a converted nose tackle whom we drafted in the ninth round from North Carolina.

These are the kind of guys who become good players and some become great because they have that work ethic, that determination, that intelligence, that ability to say, "I'm a professional, I'm going to give it all I got, and team is what counts. I'm checking my ego at the door. I want to win. That's what's important."

If you have those kinds of people, and you put them around those game changers, that's what propels you over the top. You can't win without those kinds of players, because there are many more of them than there are game changers. You want all of your players to fit the same profile, but if you're lucky, four or five of them are going to be game changers. You have to have 24, counting the punter and kicker, who can go out there and perform at a high level and not be cowed by the pressure.

They're not worried about the extraneous, outside issues. They can focus and are smart and can make winning plays in tight situations. That's what you have to have throughout the team.

The NFL isn't the NBA. You hear people say the NBA consists of one or two or maybe, if you're very lucky, three game changers per team, and the rest are all "role players." They're rebounders or they're defensive players or they're guys who handle and pass the ball, but they're not game changers. That doesn't fly in football. Everybody has to do their job to the best of their ability.

Not that people in the NBA don't, but Michael Jordan, for example, could basically score on his own. He might need a guy to get him the ball on a rebound or a guy to set a pick for him, but not always. And he could beat anybody he had to one-on-one, so you could isolate him on the floor.

That doesn't happen in football, because even if you have top-flight receivers such as Marvin Harrison or Andre Reed that you could isolate on a corner, somebody still has to block for the quarterback. And somebody has to run a complementary route so that the defense can't double-team him. Then, the quarterback has to deliver the ball to him. Otherwise, he's useless. It's just a different game—the ultimate team game.

We followed a blueprint and it wasn't popular because it called for you to draft players who were not household names and they didn't fit the profile that draftniks think is good. But those players fit our system. They're the kinds of players the coach wants. The coaches can relate to them, they relate to the coach. It's what is now called "system fit." But what it's really about is getting people who are comfortable with your approach and getting people with whom you're comfortable.

That's what Marv Levy believed in, that's what I believed in. That's what Tony Dungy believed in. Dom Capers believed in it, too, although we did it with mostly veterans in Carolina. But they were all the same kind of people.

When you do it right, it's a beautiful, beautiful thing.

For me, winning the championship was not what people think it should have been. I wasn't thinking about the three Super Bowls we had lost when I was with the Bills, or the fourth in the year after I left. This was about something much larger than that. This was about all of those scouts, all of the Kelvin Haydens of the world, all of the Phil Hansens of the world, all of the Carlton Baileys, the Mark Kelsos, all of those guys who make you winners. It's not about *finally* winning one or *finally* getting a ring. It's about doing it the right way with the right people.

And that's the essence of what we were all about.

Deciding on the Decision Maker

"Failing to prepare is preparing to fail."   —John Wooden

"Plan your work and work your plan."   —Marv Levy

Hiring the right head coach is the most important piece to building a successful football team. Get it right, and you have a good chance of being successful for a long time. Get it wrong, and you will likely find yourself going backward in a hurry. It will cost you two things you never get back: time and money.

Simply put, there aren't nearly as many head-coaching candidates as players. If you make a mistake on a head-coaching hire, the cadre of replacements might not match up to the demands of the job. You've got to get it right, because as a general manager, you probably won't get to hire a third coach. And that presumes you get a chance to hire a second.

Either way, you always have to be ready with a list of candidates. George Young, the late and great general manager of the New York

Giants, used to say—and I never believed it until I lived it—that you should keep that list in your upper-left-hand drawer, because "you never know what is going to happen and you may be forced to go to that list at a time when you're least prepared to do it and you least expect to do it."

In the spring after the 2007 season—two years after Tony Dungy's son, James, died tragically—we were faced with Tony deciding he was going to immediately retire as coach of the Colts. After discussions with our team owner, Jim Irsay, and a lot of cajoling from me, Tony decided to stay one more year. I presumed that I'd be long gone from the Colts before Tony was, but it didn't work out that way.

Fortunately, and thanks largely to George's advice, I was prepared.

Another way that I helped enhance my readiness to hire a coach was to not limit my scouting to players. That was yet another lesson from the Gospel According to Marv Levy. He would always tell us, "When you're out scouting, make note of and tell me who the good coaches are that you see at the collegiate level. Tell me who the guys are who you think are really the up-and-coming stars, because we need to get those kinds of people on our staff."

Marv practiced what he preached, as I discovered when we were with the Buffalo Bills and had an opening for a receivers coach while we were at the East-West college all-star game, in Palo Alto, California. Marv was watching one of the teams practice on one field, and I was watching the other working out on another field. Afterward, as we were driving back to the hotel, he said, "I saw a good coach out there today."

"I did, too," I said. "Which position were you looking at?"

"Receivers."

"Yeah, me, too."

"Who is it that you liked?"

"Ted Tollner [who had just been let go as a head coach at the University of Southern California, but was working as an assistant at the East-West game]."

"Same for me."

We laughed, then after we got back to the hotel, Marv said, "Let's go interview him." We did, and we hired him.

Something I rarely, if ever, considered when hiring a head coach was how it would play with the fan base. In the short run, the hiring of a "name coach"—the so-called "winning of the press conference"—does help with ticket sales. And I'm not talking about a "hot coach" that some media guru has sprinkled holy water on. I'm talking about someone like Jeff Fisher. You hire a Jeff Fisher, you hire a Lovie Smith, you hire a Tony Dungy, there will be positive feedback at the box office.

Does it compare with drafting or signing a top name player? No. The economic impact is not the same. But there is an economic impact to signing that particular coach. How many coaches of that caliber are out there in any given year? Not a lot.

For the most part, the sole focus of a coaching search should be on finding someone who has the necessary credentials to lead your team to a championship. When I became general manager of the Carolina Panthers in 1994, I put together a club operational manual (which amounted to a compilation of everything I've learned throughout my career). In it I included a section called "guidelines for the selection of a head football coach." I used it to formulate the list of candidates and provide a structure for the interview process.

I've applied it, in one form or another, to the hiring of five head coaches for three NFL teams. The first was Marv Levy, with the Bills. Then I used it to hire Dom Capers, while I was with the Carolina Panthers. Then, with the Indianapolis Colts, Jim Mora, Tony Dungy, and finally, Jim Caldwell. I knew Marv the best, from scouting for him in the Canadian Football League and with the Kansas City Chiefs and from us working together with the United States Football League's Chicago Blitz (with Marv as coach and me overseeing our player-personnel department). But there were plenty of lessons gathered from our time together before and after he joined the Bills that I utilized with other coach hires.

My "guidelines for the selection of a head coach" are as follows:

1. Organization. That ranges from how he organizes his playbook to his practice plans, from year-round staff assignments to his off-season program. Each of those areas and many more must be laid out in writing and explained completely, step by step, especially with a candidate who has never been a head coach before. With someone like Tony Dungy, who had already been a head coach for six seasons in Tampa Bay and had spent two stints as a defensive coordinator in the NFL, I took for granted that he had it in writing. And he's such a great teacher that when he explained his program to me it was obvious that he was right on top of it. Today, every coaching candidate shows up for an interview with a "book" detailing all aspects of his program. But the book is only as good as the person reading it. You could put the book in front of a non-football person and it wouldn't mean a thing; it's just a book. You put that book in front of a football person, he digests it, he critiques it, he has questions about it.

2. Leadership. Does he have the philosophical approach, verbal skills, physical presence, stability, and courage to lead and motivate the coaching staff, the players, and the support staff?

3. Communication. Does he have good verbal skills? Does he listen? Does he respond to questions in a thoughtful way, or does he just tell people what to do? Is he open to suggestions? Can he interact with ownership, management, and other departments on their terms?

Can he sell his program to all of the team's stakeholders? Does he care and communicate that care to others or are they just numbers to him?

Can he teach or is he a lecturer? A teacher gets everyone involved. He is able to illustrate his lessons with real-life examples and sometimes funny parables. He gets his students invested and involved in what he's teaching. A lecturer just stands at the podium and spits out notes.

4. Emotional stability. Can he function well under pressure from players, staff, ownership, fans, and the press? Does he remain cool on the sidelines? Does he remain composed, organized, and does he take the lead at halftime? Does he use genuine anger as a motivational tool or does he come apart when he's frustrated?

Is he coherent in his remarks to the players, staff, ownership, and the press after a loss? Does a loss stay with him too long? Can he keep everyone in the program, including the general manager, focused by his own leadership when the "roof is falling down"?

5. Vision. This is the most important quality of them all. Does he have a clear picture of how he wants his team to look and play? Can he articulate it verbally and in writing?

Can he make long-term decisions in order to implement his vision when pressure is great for him to make a short-term, quick-fix decision? Has he organized the program in such a way as to implement his long-term plan?

What type of offense does he run? If, for example, you featured a power running game, à la San Francisco, then that would tell you that you had to invest in a certain type of offensive lineman such as Mike Iupati, a 6'5", 331-pound guard the 49ers drafted in the first round from Idaho in 2010. That, generally speaking, indicates more money. If you were more of a wide-open, one-back, three-wide-receiver attack—i.e. what we were in Indianapolis—then you really didn't have to invest heavily in power offensive linemen. The athletic linemen in the Indianapolis-style offense would be less expensive because they're smaller and more readily available.

Now, no matter what the system, you usually have to have a first-round left tackle, but the bottom line is the others in the more pass-oriented system can be smaller and, therefore, they're less in demand than the big guys. The same applies to defensive systems.

6. Strategy. Is he mentally prepared to make decisions on the sideline or does he react? Does he have direct responsibility for key strategic decisions? In other words, is he the guy making them or is he going to lean on somebody else? He's got to be the one to decide whether to go for it on fourth-and-goal. He's got to be the guy to decide whether he's going to kick a field goal or go for a touchdown.

As Marv Levy always used to say, "If we're penalized for having 12 men on the field, that's my responsibility." The head coach has to direct the strategy because everybody else has to believe that he's making the right decisions.

Although the offensive coordinator usually calls plays and the defensive coordinator calls the defenses, the head coach has to be the one to say, "Third-and-two, I want to run. You pick the run, but I want the ball run in this situation." That's a classic example of a strategic decision, because he wants time taken off the clock and he wants to force the other team to use a timeout.

Or the head coach might tell the defensive coordinator, "We've got to get the ball back, so give me some pressure here." And the defensive coordinator could respond, "Coach, they might hit a big one on us if we blitz." But the head coach will say, "It's alright, we'll take the chance. We need to get the ball back."

The head coach must be able to coherently explain the decisions he made during a game, because the press obviously is going to have questions. Ownership is going to have questions, too. And his explanation must demonstrate that he thought it all out.

7. Flexibility. Can he adjust to changing trends and rules, personnel, opponent schemes, personality or culture of players? And then I ask two rhetorical questions. First, can he change the nuts and bolts of his program to adjust to circumstances without changing his approach to the fundamentals? A perfect example that we experienced with the Colts was the sudden, unexpected, and shocking loss of Peyton Manning for the entire 2011 season. No one else is Peyton Manning, so you have to change your tactical approach. You become a much more run-oriented offense. We even thought of going to a two-back scheme, although we couldn't because we didn't have the personnel to do it.

Changing your tactical approach is not the same as changing your fundamental approach. You don't change your fundamental approach. For instance, even without a Peyton Manning, you practice the same way. You don't suddenly go to five-hour sessions to make up for the absence of a great player. But you have to alter your offensive or defensive system, depending on where the key player has been lost.

Secondly, can he be flexible and take advantage of circumstances or does he buy someone else's program, lock, stock, and barrel? In other words, does he say, "Oh, gee, Pittsburgh won using a 3-4; let's switch to a 3-4"?

Is he flexible enough to recognize that in the salary-cap era, because you're going to lose players on a continual basis, you have to have offensive and defensive systems that tend to be somewhat complementary? Does he understand that the 3-4 is more expensive than the 4-3 because: 1. Outside linebackers cost more than defensive linemen; 2. It's a heavy substitution defense, so on third down you're probably replacing two defensive linemen, a linebacker, and two defensive backs with better pass rushers and cover guys, so you have to have those players available?

And if it's a highly complex defense, you're going to need more veteran players who understand how to play it. Veteran players obviously cost more than younger guys, so how do you balance that on the other side of the ball?

8. Ability to judge talent. He's got to be able to see potential rather than just saying, "This is college player A and this is college player

B." He's got to be able to see what the potential of college player A is versus college player B.

Just before the 2012 NFL draft, after we had both departed the Colts, Tony Dungy was asked during a television interview who would he take between Andrew Luck, from Stanford, or Robert Griffin III, from Baylor. He said, "Now, most people would have said Andrew [whom the Colts would make the top-overall choice], but Bill Polian and I would have given careful consideration to RG3 [whom the Redskins would select with the second-overall pick that they acquired in a trade with the Rams] because Bill thinks outside the box."

What he was really saying was that, "Together, we recognized the potential of RG3 to affect defenses." Now, there's a downside to that, too, as evidenced by the injuries that RG3 would suffer because of all of the running he does. But Tony's point was that we both would have gone well beneath the surface in our evaluation. The coach has to be able to see that.

Can he identify and make use of role players who are not yet or will not be complete players?

His opinion about players matters greatly. And he can have an opinion while also being on the same page as the general manager, which is crucial and just happens as a matter of course. For instance, at the 1984 United States Football League scouting meetings, Marv Levy and I, as coach and de facto general manager of the Chicago Blitz, respectively, were sitting together when Mark Kelso's name came up at the safety position.

"Hmmm, William and Mary," Marv said when he noticed Mark's college. That's because Marv had coached there and always had a fondness for players from his previous coaching stops.

"Oh, he played for Jimmye Laycock, who played for me," Marv said.

"Yeah, and I've seen him and he's really a good player," I said. "He's small, but he's a smart, smart player."

We ended up not drafting Mark. The Philadelphia Eagles made him their 10th-round pick of the 1985 draft. Now, fast forward two years. The Blitz fold, I'm in Buffalo, and Mark is available as a free agent. I told our coach at the time, Hank Bullough, "This guy's really a great player." Hank had remembered him from that same '84 USFL scouting meeting; he was there as head coach of the Pittsburgh Maulers. Mark signed with Buffalo and had a marvelous career.

Another example of the coach and GM being on the same page involved another defensive back, Antoine Bethea, who was coming out of Howard University, a small school, for the 2006 draft. I took the tape of Antoine to Tony Dungy and said, "Tony, you've got to look at this tape. This guy's really something and he fits our defense to a T. Now he's at Howard University, so keep that in mind. But he's smart, he's their best player, everybody there raves about him. He's our kind of person, but I don't know where to put him. I don't know if he's a safety or a corner. He plays three-deep safety at Howard, but I think he has all the capability and physicality and size to play corner for us. But you make the decision. You know better than I. You invented the defense."

Tony looks at the tape, comes back to me, and says, "Oh, yeah, you're right. This is the kind of guy we want. I think we'll start him out at safety, because he'll feel more comfortable there and then maybe, by the second year, we'll move him to corner. He'll be a great corner, don't worry about that. But we'll start him out at safety."

We drafted Antoine in the sixth round. The first practice of minicamp, while lined up at safety, he made an interception. The second practice, which he also spent at safety, he got another interception. The third practice, again while it safety, he picked off a third pass.

Later that day, during a break, Tony walked over to me and he said, "I think we'll leave Antoine at safety." I just smiled. Antoine would go on to become a two-time Pro Bowl selection.

The coach also has to be able to articulate to the scouting department exactly what he wants in the way of players. With Marv Levy, Tony Dungy, and Dom Capers, it was right down to the letter. We had scouts with us in Indianapolis who had come from other organizations, in some cases who were holdovers, who had never heard that and never been through that dynamic where the head coach sits down and says, "This is what I want, A, B, C, D. This is how the three-technique defensive tackle needs to play. This is how the defensive end needs to play. This is what we want in a Will linebacker. This is what we need in corners."

Having the ability to spell that out and create the blueprint is how you succeed as an organization. It's not just, "Get good football players." Anyone can say that. You have to know specifically what you're looking for and be able to recognize it when you see it.

Once, someone asked Tony Dungy why he thought that he and I worked so well together. Tony said, "It's really pretty easy when you share a common philosophy of football and a common philosophy about how you want your team to look." That's the very definition of it.

Now, there are times when you'll have disagreements about whether or not a player fits the bill. But you have to be able to find your way to an answer that makes the most sense for the team. Invariably, a question you're going to face when your pick in the draft comes up is this: do we take player A because of his positional value or do we take player B because of systemic need? For instance, if you have a need for safety, and on the board is one with a similar grade to a three-technique defensive tackle, whom do you take?

There is no right or wrong answer. But the head coach needs to tell you what he would do and why. Tony Dungy would say, "Take the three-technique, because he's the hardest one to find." That's great logic, because it shows that he knows his system and understands the relative value of personnel within that system.

Do we invest in player A because of longevity and systemic value or do we let him go and replace him with a younger player because the dollars at stake outweigh his systemic value? There is no right or wrong answer to that one, either, but these are the tough decisions you face and what you want to find out is whether the coach can contribute to this discussion rationally.

These kinds of decisions, particularly regarding veteran free agents who have played well for you, are fraught with emotion. I plead guilty to allowing my emotions to get the better of me on numerous occasions.

There were many times during a personnel meeting just prior to the start of the free-agency signing period—when you're deciding which players to keep and which to let go—I'd get up and say, "Don't bring Player X's name up again. We're not cutting him." And then I'd leave the room. After the pro-personnel people allowed me to cool down awhile, they would knock on my office door and say, "Are you ready to continue the discussion?" My answer frequently was, "I would rather have a root canal or a colonoscopy...but, yes."

They're all tough decisions and you talk them through and ultimately arrive at a conclusion with which everyone can live. What you can't be is philosophically divergent. You can't have exchanges between the head coach and GM that go like this:

"I don't care that this guy has a big drug history. I think he's a difference maker and we should take him."

"Boy, oh, boy, I've just never had any success with these guys and they're frequently a problem, and they always get suspended and three years from now we'll be saying, 'Why did we take him?'"

"But he's a difference maker. We need him. We can handle the other stuff."

That's the sort of thing that can get you in trouble in a hurry.

The other part of it, at least on the general manager's side, is you have to recognize that the head coach and the assistant coaches have far more pressure than you do. They have weekly pressure, day-to-day pressure. Nowadays, the head coach has to face the press every day but Friday. That, in my view, is unconscionable, but he has to do it in accordance with the NFL's media policy.

It's up to the GM to make sure he is on the same page as the head coach. The head coach has to worry about coaching the team. He has to worry about getting the team ready to play. He has to answer for everything that goes on. Everybody else in the building has to support him. And that's especially true from the beginning of training camp until the end of the season. We strove to make sure that when we went to training camp, we had a team that everybody felt good about.

Cal Murphy, with whom I had the great fortune to work in Montreal and Winnipeg in the Canadian Football League and then later when he served as our CFL scout in Indianapolis, always used to say, "If you don't have it coming in, you won't have it coming out." That means, with rare exceptions, if you don't have a good team coming into training camp, you won't have it coming out of training camp.

During the off-season—the scouting season, the player-acquisition season—the head coach usually is going to defer to the scouting staff. Marv Levy put it best when he said: "During the off-season, the coaching staff is going to listen to the scouting staff, and they're going to have 90 percent of the input. During the season, the scouting staff is going to listen to the coaching staff, and they're going to have 90 percent of the input."

9. Public relations. Essentially, it boils down to, can he handle himself well in this media maelstrom that he's forced to endure these days?

I wouldn't disqualify someone if he wasn't good at that, as long as he was willing to work with a professional who could coach him up and help him get through what really is a trial by fire every day. We would then schedule his media availability when it's most efficient for him.

If he felt he wanted to do it before practice and wanted time after practice to meet with his staff and watch tape, that would be fine. Jim Caldwell did it that way with us in Indianapolis. If he felt that he did not want his day broken up by meeting with the media, we could do it after practice. Marv Levy did that in a much more benign media era, but his purpose was the same: be as efficient as you can be and don't let this sometimes onerous duty get in the way of efficiency.

Does he accept dealing with the media as an obligation or an occupational hazard? It is something that you have to do. If, intrinsically, you hate doing it, it's going to be tough to get better at it. So you have to accept the fact that you have to do it. I know very few people who like it, but you have to accept it.

Can he maintain a dignified approach under pressure? Can he articulate well under pressure?

Today's journalists want to put their subjects under pressure, whether it's by rapid-fire questioning or by over-the-top questioning. They're not trying to have a dialogue. There are a few who are trying to put the subject under pressure and shake them, much like a trial lawyer would do on cross examination. They're hoping that there's a blowup or something of that nature.

If you give the press material that they can run with, they create a narrative that "the coach really isn't good under pressure." Nobody challenges that. The fact is, while he might not be good under pressure from reporters asking him questions, he is excellent under game pressure.

Many times at ESPN somebody has said to me, "Well, that coach is not good under pressure."

Often, my answer will be, "You know what? He's one of the best in the business under pressure. The players would run over hot coals for him. That's the important thing."

Ultimately, you want to know whether the coach can sell his program and make some converts in the press. That's not as important as the other qualities, but if he can, that's a decided plus and some of that is personality driven. Marv Levy and Tony Dungy are genuinely nice people. It takes a lot to get them to become combative. There are other guys, like myself, that get combative right away. There's more than one way to skin a cat.

10. Player respect. Does his knowledge, leadership, teaching ability, approach to squad morale and discipline, and his personal habits and dignity earn player respect? Do they look up to him?

Is his approach to discipline fair? Do his personal bearing, conduct, and dignity—which encompasses work ethic, temperament, personal habits, etc.—generate respect from the players? Not liking, but respect.

11. Character. It boils down to one thing: do you want this man as a standard-bearer for your franchise? We know full well that we're all human beings and we all have flaws and we all have difficulties in our lives. We're not asking for Saint Francis of Assisi here.

I've had to refine these guidelines through the years. In fact, I have a whole other set of questions that apply to the salary cap, which was put in place in 1993. I was part of the process of formulating that system during the five years (1989–93) I spent working with the NFL Management Council. You have to make sure that the systems, offensively and defensively, mesh together both on the field and with the cap.

In 1998, when I became GM of the Colts, I already had five years of experience with the cap and realized the many little-known ramifications that would come into play. I also knew that we would be making a quarterback the top-overall pick of the draft that year and, in those days, that choice commanded a king's ransom in terms of guaranteed money.

The additional questions for coaching candidates come under the heading "Cap System Analysis," and they are as follows:

1. Does he have a firm grasp on how his offensive and defensive schemes will be impacted by the club's cap situation present and future, by the players at hand, by free-agent acquisitions available to implement the schemes, by the club's cash situation?

2. Which positions, on offense and defense, require superior athletes and therefore have to be paid at a higher level than other spots?

3. Which positions can be addressed through the draft, with players that will have minimal impact on your cap, as opposed to having veteran players that are going to consume more cap space?

4. How many highly paid players does the scheme on either side of the ball require? Fifteen superior players are probably impossible to acquire without massive cash expenditure and would certainly not fit under the cap.

• • •

One of the first questions you ask a head-coaching candidate when you get past the obvious preliminaries is, "Who do you have in mind as a coaching staff?" Usually, the very well-prepared one will say, "These are the men I have to have, these are the men I'd like to have, these are the backups if I can't get the people I want." The next question they'll typically ask the GM is if there is someone or a couple of coaches on the existing staff that you'd like them to consider, and in some cases they'll keep them.

I believe very firmly that you let the head coach pick the assistants. He has to have confidence in them and faith in them, and they in him.

If there's a guy I think highly of, I might throw him into the mix and say, "If you haven't made your mind up about this particular position, here's a guy that I think has a good track record." And in most cases they'll interview the guy and in some cases hire him.

When I worked with Dom Capers, our head coach in Carolina, he would ask me to reach out to certain assistant-coaching candidates before he called them to gauge their interest in joining his staff or to find out about their contract statuses. You sort of do what general managers do: handle the administrative chores for the head coach. Marv Levy firmly believed that the administrative side should do all administrative work, but the bottom line is that hiring assistants is the head coach's decision and absent some really, really strong issues, I would never involve myself in the discussion.

You'd also have to get into a discussion of how the offensive and defensive systems, which are in large measure carried out by the coordinators, fit your present salary-cap situation and what it might look like going forward. That, too, will impinge upon whether or not you choose the head coach.

For example, I believe the zone-blitz, 3-4 defense is more expensive than the Tampa Two. First, the zone blitz, while being a great defense, requires in large measure veteran players to execute it. Veteran players are, by definition, expensive. Secondly, it requires two excellent man-to-man cornerbacks. They are in short supply and, therefore, expensive.

It requires at least one, and ideally two, safeties such as Troy Polamalu, who are outstanding run defenders, blitzers, and pass defenders. (In Carolina, we used to refer to the strong safety position as the "Superman" position because he had to be able to do everything). It also requires two great outside linebackers who are not only great run defenders, but are game-changing pass rushers.

When you add that all up, it requires you to put a majority of your cap on the defensive side of the ball. I hasten to add that there's absolutely nothing wrong with that. If, however, you have paid a quarterback top dollar, the conundrum you face is how to provide him with weapons when you've committed a great many dollars to defense.

The Tampa Two, on the other hand, can utilize smaller, faster players who are, to use a phrase from the book *Moneyball*, "undervalued assets." Secondly, the system does not require outstanding man-to-man corners. As a matter of fact, Tony Dungy played with corners in Tampa that most would consider speed-deficient. The three, and only three, absolutely necessary exceptional players are the three-technique tackle, the weak-side linebacker, and the strong safety. Under Tony in Tampa Bay, that was Warren Sapp, Derrick Brooks, and John Lynch. Sapp and Brooks are Hall of Famers, and Lynch is likely to be one day.

Ironically, in Indianapolis, we never did find a long-term three-technique. Booger McFarland, who came in a trade from the Buccaneers, played the position for us very well in our world-championship year. Unfortunately, an injury ended his career prematurely. Bob Sanders, during his short but brilliant career, was Lynch-like. And Tony would tell you that our weak-side linebacker, Cato June, while not Hall of Fame material, was more than good enough, despite the fact that many people won't even recognize his name.

In addition, the Tampa Two is relatively simple to teach. As a result, you can play younger, cheaper players early, thereby increasing your cap efficiency. By the way, we made up for the absence of a Hall of Fame three-technique with two extremely "undervalued assets" who I hope will get Hall of Fame consideration: ends Dwight Freeney and Robert Mathis.

The kind of offensive system we had in Indianapolis—where you're throwing the ball roughly 60 percent of the time, and it's a constant check-with-me sort of situation at the line of scrimmage—requires very, very good receivers. It requires a running back that basically can make yards on his own. It requires pretty athletic tight ends, and more than one, because you basically play in two separate personnel groupings: two tight ends, two wide receivers and one back, and then three wide receivers and one tight end. That can get you heavily invested on the offensive side of the ball.

The salary cap was described by one of my colleagues many years ago as a "toothache that never goes away." It's a very complicated process that impacts your football team and the kinds of football decisions that you make in many different ways. But football decisions related to the cap should not be confused with cap management; they're two different subjects.

Cap management is not rocket science. It's fairly simple to manage the cap, because the rules are very clear cut. You either have room under your salary cap to acquire or retain certain players or you don't. Either you can create room by reworking existing contracts or you can't. What's hard is to fit the football systems and the types of players required to play those systems under the cap.

The idea that "capologists" would take over the game, which was a thought that made the rounds at the institution of the salary cap, has never proven true. It isn't a matter of "managing" the cap; that's an accounting function. Don't get me wrong. You have to check with the league every morning to find out how much room you have. You want to know how much room your competitors have. You want to make sure you're aware of and making use of any new contract terms that are being dreamed up by agents and clubs. But there is no breakthrough way to manipulate the cap.

You operate under the assumption that your talent level is relatively equal, meaning that the talent that you're paying from top to bottom is good enough to allow you to win. And, philosophically, you are either a person who believes that you always want a lot of room under the cap so that you have the ability to maneuver, or, if you have a good team, you're a person who believes that you want to try to retain as many players as you can, and that causes you to have less room.

Joe Banner is a former executive with the Cleveland Browns and Philadelphia Eagles, and he and I have talked about this many times. We worked on a lot of NFL committees together during the many years that Joe was president of the Eagles and I was with the Colts. Although we're friends and I have a great deal of respect for him, our views were divergent as to how to handle contracts. Joe believed that you sign players early and, therefore, you got them at lower prices and there was going to be some dead money involved. For example, if you give a player a five-year contract with a $5 million signing bonus, that signing bonus, for cap purposes, is prorated over the life of the contract at $1 million per year. It is almost always paid up front or very early in the contract. If the player, in this example, plays only three years and is then cut, the remaining $2 million of prorated bonus hits your cap the minute he is cut. That $2 million, which is now unusable, is called in the parlance of the business, "dead money."

I believed you let players go until the very end of their agreements so you had a very good benchmark of what they were and what they would become, and that caused you to sign them at higher prices. The closer you get to free agency, the higher the price, obviously, and that gives you less room.

We asked an independent service to do a study for us and when it was all said and done, it was about equal. Each of us, the Colts and the Eagles, won about the same amount of games. They had a better record of reaching championship games then we did. We reached two Super Bowls, winning one, and they reached one that they lost. It was really a wash. That convinced me more than ever that there is no arcane, secret cap-management formula that can put you over the top. It's the football decisions that you make that the cap impacts. The football decisions are the hard decisions.

The cap doesn't come into play at all if you're, say, Jacksonville, when the Jaguars entered the league as an expansion club in 1995. For the Jaguars' first three years, the salary cap didn't exist for all intents and purposes because they were starting from ground zero and building up. But if you're a middling team and you're looking to ascend or you're a team at the top that still believes that it's capable of remaining at the top, then an offensive or defensive system change and its cap ramifications would have an impact.

Wherever I've been, we always believed that we would make all cap-related personnel decisions before we went to training camp so that we would never ask the coaches to be the victim of the salary cap once we put the team on the field for the first training-camp practice. That didn't mean I agreed with everything the coach wanted to do in reducing the roster from the 90 players you have at the start of camp to the final 53.

My contract always gave me the final say on the roster, but it never was an issue because even when I believed the head coach was wrong about wanting to keep a particular player or I believed an assistant coach who was pushing for a particular player was wrong, I conceded to the head coach. It would have to be a very extraordinary situation for me to say, "No, we can't have this guy."

There have been a handful of occasions where I've said, "I don't agree with this, but I'll go along with you on it. But we're going to revisit this every week and if the guy is what I think he is, let's move him quickly. If you think he's got a chance, we'll give him that chance, but understand he's under a microscope." And in virtually all cases the head coach would say, "Yes, I understand."

People have often asked me what a general manager does in training camp. One of the things I did was mock cut the squad by position group every night. I did my own cut to 53 from about the second preseason game on, every single night, based on what I heard the coaches say in that night's player-personnel meeting. This way,

I could anticipate where there would be disagreements over certain players, and I would often sit down with the head coach before the last two preseason games and say, "We have a divergence of views here. I and the personnel staff feel a little different than the assistant coach does and the coordinator does. Let's play player X and player Y a lot in the fourth preseason game, so we've got a lot of tape to go on and a lot of information to make this decision."

I also wanted to make sure that I was covering everything, salary-cap wise, so that I could say to the coach, "There's no cap problem if we keep player A and cut player B." That's where you sit down with the cap-accounting people and say, "Tell me, exactly to the penny, what the ramifications of cutting player A are versus player B." You have a list already prepared with all of those ramifications, and then other permutations come up on a daily basis. Player C gets hurt, so now you're going to have to keep player D, who you didn't anticipate having to keep. You have to add somebody to the squad, and what if you keep him? It's a nightly exercise.

Only once in my career did I ever run across a situation where an assistant coach wanted a player to make the team who had done virtually nothing on the field in the preseason. The assistant coach was very honest and he said, "I just have a feeling that he's better than the guy that we're looking to keep over him." I said, "We don't have any tape to prove that." He said, "I know, it's just a feeling." I went along with the coach's opinion against my better judgment. The player performed poorly in our opener against a very important opponent, and we released him the next day.

The player did go on to play as a backup for several more years on several teams. That wasn't the point. I was angry at myself for not sticking to our decision process. We try never to make decisions based on feelings, but rather on concrete, provable facts.

3

Escape From the Storage Closet

"You can always sacrifice your pride. You should never sacrifice your dignity." —GEORGE PATERNO

"No one trades you anyone they think can help them." —GEORGE ALLEN

ON AUGUST 2, 1984, I took one of the biggest steps on the path toward becoming a general manager in the National Football League. That was the day the Bills hired me as their pro personnel director, my first operational position with an NFL team.

As is the case with so many of these opportunities, there was some fate involved. The man who had previously held the job suffered a debilitating back injury that left him incapacitated. Apparently, Kay Stephenson, who was the Bills' coach, and Norm Pollom, who was their vice president of player personnel, had fought very hard with the team owner, the late Ralph Wilson Jr., to get the position of pro personnel director created. They wanted to make sure that an unfortunate circumstance wouldn't eliminate it.

I had been the de facto GM of the Chicago Blitz of the United States Football League, which had begun play in 1983 and had a very uncertain future. Don Lawrence, who was the Bills' defensive coordinator and had been a colleague of mine when I was a scout with the Kansas City Chiefs, went to Kay and Norm and said, in reference to me, "I've got just the guy for this job." It turned out that Norm's daughter, Debbie, was my assistant with the Blitz, and she also had some good things to say on my behalf to her father.

Kay invited me to the Bills' training camp, where he outlined the job. We had a subsequent phone call to discuss the salary, which was very modest. Kay then had me meet with the Bills' general manager, Terry Bledsoe, at a preseason game against the Chicago Bears. Ironically, it was played at what was then known as the Hoosier Dome, where I would spend a lot of time many years later as president of the Indianapolis Colts. The game was part of the facility's grand opening.

Through his tone and body language, Terry made it fairly clear to me that he wasn't thrilled about my coming on board. I think he might have been worried about the expenditure for my salary or what Mr. Wilson would say about hiring a new person to replace a guy that Mr. Wilson had not wanted to hire in the first place. Kay told me not to worry about it. The next morning he called to tell me I had the job.

I later found out that Mr. Wilson wasn't told a whole lot about my being hired. Kay and others in the organization advised me to "kind of stay below the radar." That was pretty easy, given that my office in the Bills' administrative building in Orchard Park, New York, was the roughly the size of a storage closet. Besides, Mr. Wilson was based in Detroit, where he spent most of his time, and I was going to be out of town virtually every weekend during the season, doing advance scouting of upcoming opponents.

I had all of the basic responsibilities of a pro personnel director: scouting upcoming opponents, keeping track of players who were waived from other teams, and managing our free-agent tryouts. In addition, Norm assigned me college draft work. I would leave on Thursday to visit a college on Friday, do whatever college film work I had to do on campus, and then scout that school's game live on Saturday. Carrying a 16-millimeter projector on a plane was quite a workout, but it was the only way you could watch film on the road, usually using a wall in your hotel room. On Sunday, I would go to the game of the team we were scheduled to face next, and enter info into our standard form notes on virtually every position group, substitutions, strategy, etc. I would come back on Monday and go through the film of the game, which was delivered to our facility via the NFL's film-exchange service (now all of the video you need, including college games, is downloaded instantly to your computer or tablet), and grade all of the players on the opposing team in case one of them might become available for a future trade. Generally speaking, I would separate them into four categories: difference-maker, quality starter, starter, backup.

After I finished watching the game film Monday morning, I would have to write a summation of the tendencies and offensive and defensive systems of the opponent and maybe a short paragraph—or, in some cases a longer paragraph—on every player that played on that team. You might cover 14 on defense, about the same number on offense, and everybody in the kicking game. The report—which also included my stopwatch times for how long it took the opponent to get off punts, field-goal attempts, and extra-point tries—had to be on Kay's desk by Tuesday evening so that he could digest it and then have it ready to distribute for when the coaches met with the players Wednesday morning.

We were struggling on the field, but it was a great working atmosphere. It really was one big family. For instance, every Friday night in the offseason, Kay would have get-togethers with his assistant coaches and the spouses at a restaurant or his home, and he often invited Eileen and me to join them. One night, in 1985, I was seated next to our offensive coordinator and offensive line coach, Jim Ringo, the late Pro Football Hall of Fame center for the Green Bay Packers.

Jim had a face that looked as if it was chiseled from granite and usually wore an expression that could be pretty intimidating. He was as rough and tough as they come. He was arguably one of the toughest guys to ever play the game, because he played center at 205 pounds and won the bulk of his battles at the line.

So Jim, with a clear expression of skepticism, pointed to me and asked Kay, "Who's this guy?"

"It's Bill Polian, he's our pro guy. He'll help us win."

Jim was clearly unimpressed. He just responded with, "Eh."

The next day, Jim walked into my office and said, "I want a complete rundown on the defensive lines of everybody in our division. Give me a complete rundown, top to bottom. And have it ready by Friday."

"Okay, coach," I said, without batting an eyelid.

Off I went, working morning, noon, and night, to put together the most comprehensive report possible. In those days, there were five teams in our division, the AFC East, so I had to give a scouting report on four defensive lines. Now, to be fair, I had some carry-over from the previous season, but it still had to be written up and I had to get up to date on the film, so it was an arduous task.

On Thursday afternoon, I walked into Jim's office and I said, "Coach, here's the rundown." I then dropped a two-inch thick, bound stack of papers, the size of an average opponent's scouting report, on his desk.

"Okay," he said, without ever looking up.

The next morning Jim walked into my office, threw the stack of papers back on my desk and said, "You'll do." From that day forward we became fast friends, colleagues, and comrades. It was a tremendous relationship.

In training camp, Kay had me assisting our special-teams coach. I was working with the long-snappers, holders, and kickers. One immediate challenge I faced was my inability to get Dale Hellestrae, a long-snapper we had drafted from SMU in the fourth round in 1985, to stop snapping the ball to the holder with the laces facing the kicker. You don't want the kicker to hit the laces with his foot because that causes the ball to go off kilter. When that happens, it's called "giving the kicker a lace."

You have to snap the ball in such a way that the revolutions cause the laces to face the goal post when the holder catches it and sets it down. The holder was our punter, John Kidd, who had great hands, but you don't want him to have to spin the ball around after he catches the snap because that takes time, thus increasing the chances for a block. The extra move can also cause the kicker, who is looking only at the ball and nothing else, to be distracted.

At dinner one night, I said to Jim Ringo, "I've got a real problem with Hellestrae. I can't get him to stop giving John a lace, and I don't know how to straighten it out. Would you mind taking a look?"

"Yeah, I'll come over after practice."

When practice ended the next day, Jim came walking over to us. With an ever-present cigarette in his mouth, he told Hellestrae, "Alright, go ahead, snap a few." Hellestrae snapped three or four balls. Gesturing with the cigarette in his hand, Jim then said, "Okay, move the lace about a quarter turn when you grip the ball." Hellestrae did as instructed. Boom, no lace.

"Okay, just do that," Jim said. Then, he walked away.

For 15 years in the National Football League, Dale Hellestrae rarely gave the kicker a lace, helping him to become one of the greatest long-snappers the game has ever seen. And all it took was a two-minute fix by Jim Ringo.

• • •

Thanks to our 2–14 record in 1984, the Bills owned the top-overall pick of the '85 draft. And thanks to a trade we made with the Cleveland Browns, we wound up with two first-round choices that year. The Browns wanted to sign Bernie Kosar, who was coming out early from the University of Miami. Bernie not only was a top-flight quarterback, but he was also from Youngstown, Ohio, and had grown up a Browns fan.

Ernie Accorsi, Cleveland's GM at the time, had figured out that if Bernie entered the NFL's supplemental draft—which would be held in July of '85, a few months after the regular draft—he could make a trade with us for the rights to the No. 1 pick, which we also held because of our league-worst finish in '84. NFL commissioner Pete Rozelle had given Kosar the option of applying for the regular draft or the supplemental draft, and he wisely chose the supplemental draft.

With Mr. Wilson's blessings, Kay and Norm decided that we would trade the first pick of the supplemental draft to the Browns in return for linebacker Chip Banks, a third-round pick in the '85 regular draft, and first- and sixth-round choices in the 1986 regular draft. (The first-rounder would replace the one we were giving up by sending the supplemental pick to Cleveland.)

Before the deal was completed, I got a call from a friend with another team who said he had it on pretty good authority that Banks didn't want to play in Buffalo and might refuse to join the team if we made the deal. If Banks didn't play for us, he wouldn't play, which was his prerogative. But we would still be out what was the major component of the trade.

Consequently, I advised Kay to consider building a contingency in case Banks chose not to report to us. Kay dispatched Elijah Pitts, our running backs coach, to Atlanta to meet with Chip to see if the information I had received was valid. Chip provided the answer by not opening the door to his apartment after Eli arrived there. Chip sort of spoke with Eli through the door, but wouldn't come out. Playing for the Bills simply wasn't in his plans.

We then re-structured the trade so that if Banks didn't report to us, he would go back to Cleveland and the Browns would instead give us their first-round pick, seventh overall, in '85. The trade was executed, Banks didn't report, and we ended up with the Browns' first-round picks in the '85 and '86 drafts, their third-round pick in '85, and their sixth-round pick in '86. That was a classic example of why you'd better turn over every rock before you make a trade.

I've been criticized through the years for being slow or even loathe to make trades, and it's because, as I discovered in our dealings with Chip Banks, there's a lot that can backfire.

Not long after the deal became official, I told Kay, "We could probably trade these draft picks for good, viable veteran players, and that might do more to save your job than any rookies we might draft. Because let's face it, we may be drafting players that somebody else is going to benefit from after we all get fired."

"Yeah, that's true and I appreciate you bringing it to my attention," Kay said. "But ultimately, we have to do what's right for the franchise. And we'll get a player with the top-overall pick that can turn this franchise around and we won't ever get that opportunity to get that kind of player again, so we've got to do what we've got to do for the franchise. That's what Ralph is paying us to do. We're going to draft people who are going to win with this franchise."

That just solidified in my mind what a great and selfless person Kay Stephenson was and what an honor it was to work with him.

Having the top-overall choice meant we could actually begin negotiating a contract with the player we intended to select. Norm and Kay believed that player was Bruce Smith, a defensive end from Virginia Tech who had won the Outland Trophy as the nation's top interior lineman. I was a little bit of a mixed bag at the outset. I had tremendous regard for Bruce's talent, but I thought Ray Childress, a defensive lineman from Texas A&M, was more ready to play in the NFL. Norm believed that Bruce had much more upside than Ray did.

Interestingly, in a fan poll in the *Buffalo News*, 72 percent of those who responded said we should use the No. 1 pick on Doug Flutie, a Boston College quarterback who had won the Heisman Trophy and had made himself an icon by pulling off a miraculous, last-second victory against the University of Miami. Another 16 percent said we should draft "someone else," and of the players in that category, Bruce Smith was the second-favorite choice behind Bill Fralic, an offensive tackle from Pitt. I found the poll results a little amusing.

That reminds me of another "Marv-ism." If you let the fans dictate your choices, you'll end up sitting next to them.

Bruce had everything you look for in a dominant defensive end: size, long arms, explosiveness, speed, and strength. He was hampered as a collegian by the fact that he was close to, or slightly above, 300 pounds. In fact, I had seen him play early in the season at Clemson in a battle that was billed as a "heavyweight championship" between Bruce and another highly touted defensive lineman, William "The Refrigerator" Perry. It was an unusually hot September afternoon, even for Clemson, South Carolina—90-plus degrees and serious humidity. To say the heat wore both guys down is an understatement. After long drives, both had difficulty reaching the bench. As it turned out, Norm Pollom, as he very often did, correctly assessed Bruce's rare ability to rush the passer.

When Bruce got down to 265 pounds in his third season, he became virtually unblockable for the remainder of his career. Thanks to Norm, I learned a very valuable lesson: big guys occasionally take a play, or two, off. It's tough to haul those 300-plus-pound bodies around, especially under difficult weather conditions. Ray Childress went onto have a terrific career with the Houston Oilers, who of course would become notable rivals to our Bills teams. But Bruce was the one who went to the Hall of Fame.

In the winter of '85, it was time to begin the process of signing Bruce. With it, came a dilemma that no one could have ever anticipated. Terry Bledsoe, our GM, had a heart attack and was hospitalized. It was very serious and he was out of the office for a long time. I immediately began taking on the contract-negotiation task, so to speak. Not that there was a lot to do in those days because there wasn't unrestricted free agency, but I was signing guys off the street and things of that nature.

Mr. Wilson had a close friend, Pat McGroder, function as his eyes and ears in the Bills' offices. Pat had a highly successful liquor business, and was a leading citizen of Buffalo. He was very instrumental in Mr. Wilson putting the team there in 1959, as a founding member of the American Football League, after he was unable to work out a lease agreement with the Orange Bowl in Miami. Pat had even served as the Bills' interim general manager in 1983, between the time Stew Barber was let go from the job and Terry was hired. Pat saw me in the office one day and we started chatting. I know he liked the fact that there was "another Irish kid" in the building, and we quickly developed a friendship.

Along the way, I also got to know Dave Olsen, who was the Bills' treasurer, pretty well. As I understand it, Pat, who wintered in Phoenix, called Mr. Wilson when he heard the news of Terry's heart attack and said, "Listen, there's a guy over there that works in pro personnel named Bill Polian. He's capable of handling the Bruce Smith negotiations." Kay echoed Pat's sentiments.

At the same time, Dave, who worked side by side with Mr. Wilson in Detroit, went to the boss and essentially said the same thing. Finally, Dave summoned me to Detroit. In our first formal meeting, Mr. Wilson explained how he felt about the importance of signing Bruce and his overview of the economics of the National Football League. He also asked about the Baltimore Stars, who had Bruce's territorial rights in the United States Football League. Bruce was born in Norfolk, Virginia, so that would have been pretty close to home. I knew the Stars' president, Carl Peterson, who had been the player-personnel director for the Philadelphia Eagles, would be a formidable adversary. The Stars had a fair amount of money, so this would not be your average, everyday first-round signing.

"It's going to cost a lot," I warned Mr. Wilson.

Without flinching, he said, "Let's do it."

Dave and I embarked on what would be a week-long trip to Virginia to negotiate the deal. I had never done a first-round contract before, let alone the top pick in the draft. And never in a competitive marketplace, where it's one league against another. And never against an opponent like the Baltimore Stars, who had had a lot of money and had already won a USFL championship. I had played poker before, but not at these stakes.

I knew one of Bruce's agents, Brig Owens, from my time with the Chiefs. Brig had been a defensive back for the Washington Redskins, and we had a pretty good rapport as a couple of guys who knew football. A local attorney from Newport News, Virginia, was also involved. After about a day and a half of negotiations, it became clear he was representing the Stars' point of view. He just made no secret of the fact he was leaning toward Bruce going to Baltimore.

Together, Dave and I made a great team. He was tremendous in terms of massaging the numbers, which wasn't my strength. At that time, I would have been totally out of my element trying to deal with things such as how the signing bonuses would be paid, and getting that information translated back to Detroit, where all of the team's finances were managed. But Dave was just superb at it.

I was the football guy, so I was able to speak the same language as Brig when it came to explaining our vision for Bruce, the defense, and the team. I also knew exactly what the USFL could afford to pay, what their top end was. Kay was helpful, too, suggesting certain points about the team to highlight.

Putting the deal together was a two-stage process, with the first stage being the sales pitch. We had to convince Brig and Bruce's other representative that the Bills were a viable franchise, in hopes that they would then convey that message to Bruce. The team was struggling on the field and at the box office, so there was a real question of viability. Were the Bills going to stay in Buffalo? Were they going to be sold? Were they going to fold?

Obviously, the other side was gilding the lily a little bit to make our job tougher, which was to be expected. Brig would say, "This is the worst team I've ever seen. Why do we want to consign Bruce Smith to this when he can go to a team that's already won a championship and is probably going to be better?"

"We have a plan to win," I told him. "We recognize we're not very good now, but we're going to be better. And Bruce Smith is part of that."

I also put on my chamber-of-commerce hat and said, "Buffalo's a great place to live and a great place to play. It's not what you think it is. It isn't Siberia. It's a great football town, it's a blue-collar town. It's probably a heck of a lot similar to, or maybe even better than, Baltimore, because you'll never replace the Baltimore Colts in another league; you just simply won't.

"You'll be an appendage in a league that isn't guaranteed to last. The reason I left the USFL was because I didn't have a guarantee that it was going to last. That's why I'm in Buffalo now. This is a solid franchise. Mr. Wilson has every intention of keeping it there. We have a wonderful stadium, much better than what you would play in in Baltimore. We've got a nice practice complex, which Mr. Wilson is committed to making better. You'll like it in Buffalo."

Stage two was focused on money. The position of Bruce's agents was that he was going to be playing close to home in Baltimore and the Bills were a lousy team with no chance to win, so we were going to have to pay a premium for them to even consider us. At that point we talked about what we were willing to do and how it could be done. They made counter offers, and Dave's position was, "We can do this...we can do this...we can do this."

And I kept coming back to, "Look, it's wonderful to be with the Baltimore Stars, but ultimately you may only be with the Baltimore Stars for a year and a half, and are you going to get all the money that they promised you? This is not a stable situation. We're very stable."

"Well, prove to us how stable you are," they replied.

And that was when we presented them with four-year contract worth $2.4 million. Back then, those were mind-boggling numbers. They won't resonate with a lot of people now, but those were the days when a $500,000 contract was enough to choke a horse. I mean, you're talking about millions of dollars when no player had made that in the history of the NFL up to that point. The point was made, the deal accepted.

I had done contracts before, but that experience showed me for the first time what a high-stakes negotiation looked like. If you went to graduate school for three years you couldn't learn as much as I learned from Dave in a month. Through his example and by osmosis, Dave taught me a series of lessons, the most important of which were: do your homework and be prepared.

Know all of the numbers. Know what the parameters of the contract are. Know your adversary. Understand the landscape (which refers to what's happening around the negotiation, what's happening with the other team involved, what's happening with the other teams in the league). Understand the marketplace (the going rate for players of Bruce's caliber, and there weren't many of those around).

Another lesson from Dave was to keep the negotiations civil. I'll be the first to admit that I didn't learn that one well enough, certainly, but it was extremely valuable nonetheless. Dave also taught me to listen to the other side and to let the other side know that your word can be counted upon, which is absolutely the case with him.

If Dave Olsen told me that the sun was going to rise in the West tomorrow, I'd pull the blinds on that side of the house.

We lost our first six games of the '85 season. After the fourth, Kay Stephenson was fired. Hank Bullough, who had been our defensive coordinator, became the head coach. I had no prior relationship with him, and I presumed that at the end of the season he would do what every new coach does and make a lot of changes—including sending me packing. When we proceeded to finish 2–14 for the second year in a row, I was certain of it.

Before facing what seemed to be my inevitable fate, I sat down and wrote, by hand, a three- or four-page letter to Dave Olsen about the team, despite its dreadful record, being salvageable. It was mostly a case of reiterating much of what Kay and I had already discussed with Dave. The first step had already been taken by drafting and signing Bruce Smith. That removed, at least from a football standpoint, the black cloud that had hovered over the Bills since the departure of standout running back Joe Cribbs after the Bills lost a court battle to prevent him from signing with the USFL. That was a terrible blow to the team, especially because it had resulted from questionable legal advice Mr. Wilson had received regarding language in the Bills' contract with Cribbs that presumably would have prevented him from leaving but fell short in the eyes of a U.S. District Court judge.

I also wrote, "Andre Reed, one of our fourth-round picks in 1985 from Kutztown State, is here and he's going to be a good player. Frank Reich, a third-rounder in '85 from Maryland, may or may not be the quarterback of the future, but he's certainly good enough to get us by until and unless Jim Kelly comes on board from the USFL. If, in fact, the USFL is headed for demise, we'll get better players."

With three games left in the '85 season, Hank brought Jim Valek on board as an administrative assistant. Soon thereafter, Jim came to see me and he said, "You report to me now." He also made it clear that: A, I wasn't his guy, and B, he wasn't thrilled with the work I'd been doing. That just reinforced my assumption that I would soon be gone.

Dave Olsen then asked me to come over to Detroit and meet with Mr. Wilson to discuss that letter I had written. I didn't think much of it. The three of us went out to dinner, at which time I reviewed my letter with Mr. Wilson. He asked questions like, "Do you think this turnaround is really doable? Do we have the players on board? Where do you see us improving?"

I returned to Buffalo the next day and wrote Mr. Wilson a note thanking him for the meeting. After that, I headed to the Blue-Gray college all-star game in Montgomery, Alabama. While I was there, I told a former colleague with the Chiefs, "It looks like I'll be out of Buffalo in a couple weeks." He responded the way I hoped he would by asking if I wanted to go to work for the Chiefs again.

"Yeah, that sounds great," I said.

While I was in Montgomery, I had a phone conversation with Terry Bledsoe. I don't remember what we talked about, but I do remember telling him, in reference to our 2–14 finish, "The best thing about this season is that it's over." He responded with, "Yeah, you're right." I remember thinking that it was a poor choice of words on my part. And I felt even worse about it when I learned, soon thereafter, that Terry had been released as the Bills' GM.

The next thing I knew, I got a call from Dave Olsen asking me to come to Detroit. I didn't think any more of that than I did the previous trip there. I presumed, having let Terry go, they were going to say to me, "Well, hey, we didn't get a chance to say goodbye to you and thank you for what you've done." It turned out to be much more than that. And I was astounded.

"We think you're the person to lead us into the future," they told me. "Hank Bullough will have final say on the roster, but you've got enough football experience and enough operational experience to fill the job. You can work with Hank and with Norm Pollom. And we'll pay you $75,000 a year."

I gladly accepted. I felt prepared. I felt confident that I could do the job because of my experience in the CFL, the USFL, and doing that high-profile negotiation on the Bruce Smith contract. Additionally, Kay Stephenson had kept me involved with every single football decision and every single football operational issue while he was there. I worked concomitantly with Norm on the draft. I had led our drafting when I was the personnel director with the Chicago Blitz. And when the Blitz no longer had an owner and was being run by the United States Football League, I was, in conjunction with Marv Levy, appointed by the USFL to run the franchise.

I'm sure that Pat McGroder put in more than a few good words for me when the general manager's job opened up. Truth be told, Pat McGroder was probably the reason I was the GM. I know he liked me personally. He saw me work. He just got a feeling that I was a competent person.

Soon after I returned to Buffalo, Pat called me from his winter home in Phoenix.

"Alright listen, you're my boy and I know you're going to do a great job," he said. "I told Ralph you could do it. And when I get back, I'm going to take you by the hand and I'm going to introduce you to everybody you need to know in town."

"Sounds great, Pat."

What I didn't realize was that Pat was suffering from lung cancer and would pass away about a month later. To this day, I am profoundly saddened that we never did get to make those rounds together.

Searching for Something to "Shout!" About

"Every day you come to work, five things will happen you didn't anticipate."
                                        —Bill Parcells

The first thing that happened the day the Bills appointed me GM was that Jim Cipriano, the team's longtime ticket manager, came to the office and said, "As of today, we have 12,000 season tickets renewed in an 80,000-seat stadium."

Not knowing exactly how to react, I said, "Okay...thank you very much?"

I wish that had been the end of the bad news.

"I don't know how many more season tickets are going to be renewed," Jim added. By the tone of his voice and look on his face, I didn't get the sense that he was optimistic about us seeing a surge at any point in the near future.

Soon thereafter, Don Hartnett, the league security representative, gave me a briefing that curled my hair. It turned out we had players who were involved with drugs. We had a number of players whose lifestyles were not conducive to what you would consider to be upstanding NFL citizens.

That was sort of my welcome to the job.

But I didn't have any second thoughts at all. Those were part of a long list of challenges that had to be met. In order to win football games, we had to get everything else around the team right. If we didn't, it would get in the way of winning. Without those fixes, Vince Lombardi would have had a hard time succeeding, especially in an era when there was competition from another league.

I knew what needed to be fixed, football-wise. I had the blueprint for that. I did not know what the blueprint was for fixing the infrastructure of the franchise. That was where our vice president of operations, Bill Munson (who was often called Muns), came in.

The picture he gave me was not pretty. We had cost overruns in virtually every area of the stadium operation. As we soon would discover, there were some things going on within the organization that really were beyond the pale. Much of it had been concealed from the Detroit office.

It was clear there were people in the building who flat out didn't care whether the team won or lost. In fact, a number of them showed disdain for the coaches and players. The attitude was, "Ah, the hell with these guys. They make too much money anyway."

Employees are teammates, not fans. They have an obligation to support the club's efforts, everywhere, 100 percent of the time. Criticism of coaches, players, or team decisions is both unprofessional and unacceptable.

We had a series of—and this was Bill Munson's term—fiefdoms on the non-football side, run by people who were interested in their own agenda. We set about to try to change that. We did a lot of internal work, just hour after hour after hour poring over spreadsheets, trying to find where we could increase profit, decrease cost, and make sure that everybody was being responsible. The spreadsheets were scattered all over the floor in my office. Muns and I were literally crawling around on our hands and knees, trying to figure out where things were wrong and where we could make things better.

On multiple occasions, I would tell the front-office staff, "Listen, every dollar we save that we do not waste in the non-football operation goes to sign Jim Kelly or Bruce Smith or some other football player that can help us win. And then we'll all win by doing that."

But that fell largely on deaf ears with some people that had been there for a long time. To them, I was just another in a long line of guys that occupied that GM office. Sooner or later (and probably sooner), they knew I'd be heading out the door, just like the others.

I shared our findings with Dave Olsen, our treasurer, during his periodic visits from Detroit and our lengthy daily phone conversations, and he translated to Ralph Wilson everything that we were uncovering and facing. At one point, there was a phone conversation where Mr. Wilson said, "You have my permission to go ahead and do anything that you have to do to make sure that we make this organization as good as we can make it." He was 100 percent supportive.

Through Muns's diligence and hard work, we were able to create a series of plans that allowed us to clean up the stuff that had been going on and then move forward in a positive vein. It involved letting people go. Now, we didn't want to let people go just on a whiff of impropriety, or because we didn't think their attitudes were what they ought to be. We had to have documentation and that took time and effort and a lot of hard work.

After that, it was a matter of putting people that we trusted—and we knew had the integrity and the desire to excel—in positions that were needed and that allowed us to stanch the bleeding, so to speak.

One was the late Ed Stillwell, who took over security. A retired senior investigator for the New York State Police who had been working for the Marriott Corporation, Ed made sure that we had the right interface with league security, and he had his thumb on what was going on as far as what our players were doing in the community and what bad apples might be hanging around the team.

Right after that we brought in Steve Champlin, a former Naval officer and academy graduate who had worked under Ed at Marriott, to run the stadium. When we took Steve and his wife, Mary, out to dinner, we were really recruiting hard.

Maybe, as it turned out, a little too hard.

"You know, Steve, honest to goodness, I really believe that we can build this thing and we're going to win the Super Bowl," I told him. "That's our goal here. We're going to have an organization that can win the Super Bowl, and you're going to be a big part of that because unless we get this stadium part right, we won't have the resources to get it right on the field."

I found out later that Mary had told Steve, "That guy's crazy. Why would you want to go to work for him?"

We had to modernize greatly in strength and conditioning. Fortunately Hank Bullough recommended Rusty Jones, with whom he had worked with the Pittsburgh Maulers of the USFL, to become our strength-and-conditioning coordinator. Rusty was as important a hire as anybody because he brought with him a brand-new way of looking at strength and conditioning. Simply put, he was the forerunner of everything that exists today in strength and conditioning at the pro and college levels.

Rusty created an individualized program for each player. He created the scientific, nutrition-based approach of helping players elevate their performance level. He created the low-weight, high-rep style of lifting. He created the idea that rest and recovery were critical to getting the team on the field on Sunday in the best shape and in the best frame of mind.

For a long time, NFL training tables mostly consisted of players loading up on big steaks. Teams would feed them as much protein as possible, along with potatoes, bread, and butter. Once Rusty came aboard, we started serving players a lot of chicken and fish. His focus was on lean weight versus fat weight.

Rusty had to convince players and coaches that a player with lean weight was more efficient and durable than a player with fat weight. It took some convincing, but Rusty's belief in his system and his ability to get it across to players in a positive way allowed him to get us to where we needed to be in that regard.

Once we had the right people in those critical front-office roles, we turned our attention to the issue of fan engagement, or lack thereof. We weren't connecting with the fans in any way. I remember one weekend, when I was out with my sons, I was struck by the fact that the only logo of a Buffalo sports franchise that I saw on kids' hats belonged to the Bisons, the city's Triple-A baseball team.

We weren't doing enough to get the fans on our side, to make them recognize that we really were trying to win and intended to get it right. We also were at the low end of the totem pole in terms of sponsorship, which was then just beginning to be a factor in the National Football League.

Bill Munson and I began to brainstorm and the first thing we said was, "Let's get out and meet people, face to face." We didn't have any money to have a focus group or anything like that. We couldn't hire an ad agency or invest in any of the conventional methods businesses use to get customer feedback. So we said, "We'll do it ourselves."

Bill estimated that we must have made about 200 appearances, at various community breakfasts and service-group gatherings around western New York during that first winter. We would ask people to tell us what they wanted and what we could do to improve their game experience. Invariably, we heard the same two things: "Better ticket availability and better security." They would share stories of taking their kids to the game and having to put up with awful language and people being drunk and fights going on.

Read any business book, and you'll find that the things you need to correct are right in front of your nose. Most times, even though you have to change culture to do it, it's a relatively easy correction.

Ultimately, out of that interaction with fans came a marriage with Marine Midland Bank to make tickets available at its nearly one hundred branches all across western New York. People 30 years of age or younger won't identify with that, but in those days most people did their banking at a branch. Marine Midland also wasn't charging a premium as the secondary-market ticket services did, and was providing the best tickets available not sold on a season-ticket basis. In addition, we created a premium program where, if you opened a checking or savings account, you could get Bills hats and stocking caps at a discount.

We also wanted all of the bank's tellers and managers to feel as if they were our teammates and partners. And we did that by having meetings with them and hosting special days for them at training camp and minicamp. I met such a person in the spring of 2014 at a charity golf tournament in Dunkirk, New York. She remembered fondly and vividly her visit to the stadium and her interactions with our staff. You can't put a price on that.

Then, we got together with the creative people at Marine Midland and talked about the need to have something that identified us, that would take us up from a team that underperformed, from the stumbling, bumbling quasi-minor leaguers that so many people had labeled us, and give the fans something to rally around (today, they call it branding). The bank and its ad agency came up with "Shout!" as our theme song. The minute we heard it was a eureka moment. Everybody said, "That's it. That's our theme song."

The bank bought the rights to it from the Isley Brothers, who released it in 1959, and then the agency redid the lyrics to say:

The Bills make me want to shout
Kick your heels up and
Shout!
Throw your hands up and
Shout!
Throw your head back and
Shout!
Come on now
The Bills are making it happen now
Stand up now come on and shout
Yeah, yeah, yeah, yeah
Say you will
Shout it right now, baby
Say you will
Come on and come on
Say you will
Come on and shout
Yeah, yeah
Shout!
Buffalo's happening now
Shout!
We're on the move now
Shout!
The Bills are happening now
Shout!
They're making it happen now

Shout
We've got the spirit
Shout
A lot of spirit, yeah
Shout!
We've got the spirit
Shout
Just watch it happen it now
Hey, hey, hey, hey
(Repeat chorus)
Let's go Buffalo
(Repeat chorus)
The Bills make me want to shout

When we scored and those fans started singing, "Let's Go Buffalo (Shout)," the place rocked. It was unique. It also managed to get under the skin of some of our opponents. I remember, after Miami beat us at home, Dolphins linebacker Brian Cox standing at the mouth of the tunnel after the game and yelling, "Shout now, you [bleeps]! Shout, now!"

The song gave rise to a whole line of "Shout!" merchandise. And it's still going strong to this day, and not just at Ralph Wilson Stadium. I've been in a lot of stadiums, including some college stadiums, that play the original version of "Shout!" after the home team scores.

Gradually, we began to change that atmosphere to where now the Bills were considered, at least in the general landscape of western New York, something that was positive. The lesson to be learned here is as follows: define the problems. We did that on the field, we did that in the front office, and we did that in the stadium operation. It took some time, but we did it.

Once you define the problems, you then have to determine what the solutions are. Some can be proactive selling. Some can be the creation of an image, which was what "Shout!" and the ability to reach out to fans through the Marine Midland ticket offices did.

In any franchise, you have to have an infrastructure that is dedicated to helping put the best possible team you can on the field because, ultimately, that's the only thing that counts. Yes, proper salary-cap management counts. Yes, concessions and merchandising count.

But if you don't win, all of that becomes just excess baggage.

What it takes to win is simple, but it isn't easy. Straight from the Gospel According to Marv Levy. So is this: "The whole has to be greater than the sum of the parts." That comes about because you have players who are smart and, because they're smart, they get better over the course of their careers and they can accept coaching and, therefore, play as a unit on a week-to-week basis better than their opponents do and better than their talent, individually, would indicate.

You have to have players who think team and win first, "we" and "us" instead of "I" and "me." You have to have individuals who are willing to sacrifice for the good of the team. You might not catch as many balls as you think you should, but if that's important for the team to win, then that's a sacrifice you have to be willing to make. You might not get to carry the ball as much as you like and you might not get as many sacks as you would want, but none of that matters if the team wins. Team goals supersede individual goals and as a result, you end up with the whole being greater than the sum of the parts.

After that, you need players who are dynamic difference makers, as many as you can get. You can't get a lot because of the draft and the salary cap and all the other league-wide rules that essentially disperse those difference makers over various clubs. But you try to get as many difference makers as you can.

Then—and this is the hardest part because it's not really quantifiable—you want to get people who are "winners." You want people whose background indicates that they have a high propensity for winning. I learned this lesson from Kay Stephenson when we were discussing what we looked for in quarterbacks.

"How much does arm strength and physical stature factor into it?" I asked. "Because there are some guys that I've seen that play well, but they don't have great arm strength and they don't have great physical stature."

"Let me tell you about one of the worst quarterback workouts I ever saw," Kay said. "It took place in Los Angeles, and this guy was so skinny that if he turned sideways, he looked like an exclamation point. He was not muscular; he didn't have a lot of definition to him. His release was fine, but his arm was clearly below average. And his athletic tests, while good, were not exceptional; I'd say a little bit above average. Generally speaking, it was a very poor workout, maybe the worst quarterback workout I'd seen in a while because you expect a quarterback in his workout to light it up. You expect him to throw rockets. Then I thought to myself, 'What I've seen in person does not match up with what I know about this guy's performance.' So on my way back to Buffalo, I stopped off at the school and I went through all the film and I gave him a performance grade. And if my grade on the workout was C-plus—and I was probably charitable doing that—my grade on the performance on the screen against opponents was A-plus. I came back and told Chuck Knox [the Bills' coach at the time] and Norm Pollom what I had seen. You have any idea who the quarterback is?"

"No, I'm stumped."

"Does the name Joe Montana ring a bell?"

"Yes, it does."

"What's the moral of the story?"

"The moral of the story is that the intangibles and the propensity for winning and the ability to perform under pressure against an opponent in tight situations far outweigh the tangible things that you can measure at the quarterback position."

There's an old saying, and I can't remember where I heard this, but winners find a way to win.

Rocky Bleier, the former running back for the Steelers, is another example. When I was scouting for the Chiefs, I wrote three paragraphs on him, which is really a lot for a pregame report, but I ended it this way: "This player, while he is not imposing, is the guy that finds a way to win. And he's the guy that they believe will find a way to win. And when the game is on the line, Rocky Bleier is going to find a way to win. At clutch time, he's the guy you have to stop."

Sure enough, at the game I was scouting, the Steelers came from behind, and Rocky scored two touchdowns in the fourth quarter to beat us. That's what winners do. And if you're a good scout, you recognize that and understand that. There's value to that.

Doug Flutie. Too small, can't play in the NFL. The guy just wins and he wins everywhere: won at Boston College, won in the Canadian Football League, won with Buffalo, won with San Diego.

Roger Staubach. Maybe the greatest winner of all time. Now, he was prototypical from the standpoint of physical gifts and mental gifts, but nonetheless, a winner.

After that, you want people who have very, very good football temperament. That describes a person who loves football. It ought not to be just a way to make a living or just a way to make a tremendous windfall financially. It ought to be something that he really enjoys, something in which he loves to participate.

Football temperament describes a person who has a great work ethic and who has great football intelligence. That doesn't mean you have to be an A student, but you have to have a good understanding of how to play the game and of all of the responsibilities that go with playing your position.

Football temperament also describes a person who is a good citizen, living his life on and off the field in a reasonably good manner in what you would expect of the average American citizen. And it describes a person who has the ability to will himself to win.

When a player first gets to the National Football League, he's simply happy to be there. He feels that he has reached the end of the rainbow, that he has made it to the top. And then he realizes very quickly, a couple of weeks into his first season, that, "Boy, this is an awful place to be if you don't win." So then he begins telling himself, "Hey, I've got to win. I've got to do everything I can to win in order to keep my job, in order to have a good experience in the National Football League."

And once you begin to win, you begin to recognize that you're never really satisfied until you've reached the top, unless you're winning championships. That's what you're looking for in players: people who have that hunger to progress, that hunger to succeed.

In the mid-1980s, we had some difficulties in Buffalo with the way some of our players comported themselves on and off the field. We had people there that, to borrow a phrase from Donnie Walsh, former president of basketball operations for the New York Knicks and Indiana Pacers, "When you got on the plane and you looked in the back where the players sat, you weren't too thrilled about it."

There were questions about whether our players were dedicated to winning, whether they were the kind of people that you wanted, whether they believed that the whole was greater than the sum of the parts. We had to find a better way to identify them. It's not just measuring athletic ability. It's not just determining football acumen. It's personality and it's psychology.

We began to ask ourselves, "How is it that we have all of this physical information on guys, but we don't have anything from the psychological side?" Bob Ferguson, who joined the Bills as assistant director of player personnel in 1985, and I talked about it and we decided to look into it. At that point, we were just giving college prospects the Wonderlic test, which is still a very valid measure of basic intelligence. But we had no psychological test, and we were relying on interviews that we, as general managers and coaches, were conducting and they were haphazard, at best.

I actually heard a coach say "I can look into that guy's eyes, and I know if he's a football player." Well, I couldn't, and I presumed since I was not the dumbest guy ever to come down the block (close, but not the dumbest), there were a lot of other people who couldn't, either. When I asked around, almost everybody had the same feeling. So I asked my sister, Regina, who has a degree in psychology, and she said that there are tests that you can give. "You are way behind the times," she told me. Ralph Wilson's wife at the time was a practicing psychologist, and after getting Mr. Wilson's permission, I also spoke with her on the same topic.

After more research, we became one of the first teams in the NFL to institute a psychological test. We chose the 16PF (the initials stand for personality factors). We had two psychologists from Canisius College interpret the results for us.

The 16 traits that the test evaluates are: warmth (which indicates friendliness toward others and willingness to participate), reasoning (which is indicative of cognitive ability and intellect), emotional stability (which refers to the candidate's ability to adapt while under stress and whether they are easily upset), dominance (which addresses levels of aggression, assertiveness, and cooperation), liveliness (which indicates whether the person is likely to be cheerful or expressive as opposed to introverted or serious), rule-consciousness (which conveys attitudes toward authority and likelihood of obedience), social boldness (which refers to whether an individual is likely to be timid or shy as opposed to being uninhibited or outgoing), sensitivity (which measures whether the candidate is compassionate and sympathetic to others or if they tend to be more objective), vigilance (which specifies how trusting, accepting, or suspicious the individual may be around others), abstractedness (which can refer to being imaginative or solution-oriented, but at the higher level can also suggest being impractical), privateness (which can indicate how forthright or non-disclosing an individual might be), apprehension (which indicates whether someone may be more self-assured or insecure), openness to change (which is regarded as flexibility and a liberal attitude as opposed to being attached to the familiar), self-reliance (which identifies how self-sufficient or group oriented an individual might be), perfectionism (which refers to self-discipline and precision as opposed to impulsiveness), and tension (which conveys the likelihood of being time driven or impatient instead of being relaxed and patient).

As the program grew and we changed jobs, moving to Carolina and then to Indianapolis, the psychological assessment was a huge part of the evaluation process. So much so that in Indianapolis, if we thought a player didn't fit from a psychological standpoint, we'd take him off our draft board.

I do not believe that NFL players ought to be held to a higher standard than other people. I recognize that it contradicts the belief of a person that I feel tremendous affection and affinity for, NFL Commissioner Roger Goodell, but we're all held to the same standard as citizens. We've got to obey the law, we've got to treat people well in our daily lives, we have to do things that help us succeed in our work.

We had a number of people, not the majority but a number, who did not share that value system. And the results spoke for themselves with our 2–14 finishes in 1984 and '85.

You start every scouting season with 5,000 names. You try to winnow that down to 150. Getting there requires the ability to identify the players who have what it takes to play in the NFL and those who don't. There is a discipline to being able to do that, and also some talent involved.

You can be a very competent scout if you just learn the discipline and you work very hard at it and you learn how to study tape. Then there are people like Bobby Beathard and George Young and Dick Steinberg and Norm Pollom, the greats of the business, who are great because they have the talent for it. I think the Lord blessed me with talent for it, too. Now, as noted author Malcolm Gladwell says, "You have to put the 10,000 hours in, too."

Lord knows we all did that. But I think you have to have a talent for it and if you have a talent for it, you like it. I found out pretty early that I had a talent for it and that I liked it very much.

During the mid-1970s, when Marv Levy was coach of the Montreal Alouettes of the Canadian Football League, his player personnel director, Bob Windish, asked Marv if he could pay a few people expenses to provide some additional scouting reports on American players. Coach Levy was good with that, and Bob hired me to be one of those part-time scouts. I played on the football team that Bob coached at New York University in the mid-1960s.

I had also coached at Manhattan College, Columbia University, and the U.S. Merchant Marine Academy , where I worked for George Paterno, brother of the legendary Joe Paterno. In that capacity, I prepared scouting reports on recruits and did advance scouting of our opponents, although that doesn't happen anymore at the college level. That taught me the basics of how to put together a scouting report.

Over the years, I had talked with Bob and with George Paterno, who had been head coach at the Merchant Marine Academy, about what it took to be a good player and gotten to know some people in the National Football League just to say hello to them and heard them speak at clinics and things like that. Bob, who had been an NFL scout, put together guidelines for personal qualities, athletic qualities, and position-specific grades, and then asked each of us to write a paragraph explaining what the player is all about and how he can help our team.

We were grading mostly pro players who were going to get released from the National Football League and so my typical report might say the following about a player: "Good stature for the position in the CFL...Bright...Coaches describe him as coachable and is a quick study...Very functional at his position...Probably going to be a little small to make it in the National Football League...Good explosion...Really good football temperament...Likes the game... Plays hard and will be a good addition to the team...If he's released he's one that we ought to put on our "neg" list (which refers to the negotiation list on which you place names of NFL players for the right to offer that player a contract to play in the CFL).

In a nutshell, what you do in evaluating talent was captured by something that the late Bill Walsh told me many years ago when he said, "When you're evaluating scouts, what you really want to do is latch on to the guy that can tell you what a player can do and how he can help you as opposed to what he can't do." It's much easier to say, "This guy can't play," than it is to say, "He's too small to play 3-4 defensive end for Bill Parcells, but I think he has the qualities of football temperament, explosion, speed, and athletic ability to play for us as a 4-3 defensive tackle in the Canadian Football League."

One day, Marv read a set of reports from me that caught his eye. He liked the fact that I was able to distinguish between what mattered and what was fluff.

One report in particular that Marv noticed, ironically enough, was the one I prepared on Tony Dungy, who was a quarterback at the University of Minnesota at the time. In the report, I said, "Everyone at the University raves about him as an individual. Exceptionally smart, exceptionally dedicated, exceptionally high character, a born leader. He will not make it as a quarterback in the National Football

League because he's too short and his game is a lateral movement game—rollouts, quarterback runs. His arm probably is not as strong as you would like in the National Football League, but he will be a star in Canada. Very similar to Condredge Holloway and others who have had great careers in the CFL."

In 1977, the Alouettes put Tony on our "neg" list, but he turned us down because Tom Moore—who would later serve as Tony's offensive coordinator with us on the Colts—was an assistant coach for the Steelers and convinced Tony, whom Tom had recruited to the University of Minnesota, to sign a contract as an undrafted free agent with the Steelers. Tom told Tony he was going to convert him from quarterback to defensive back. As luck would have it, 25 years later, Tony and I would get together in Indianapolis for one of the great runs in NFL history.

Finally, Marv called Bob Windish into his office and said, "I would like to meet Bill Polian." Bob brought me up to Montreal soon thereafter. I met with Marv, and he basically treated me as he would a full-time member of the organization and explained his personnel philosophy, and how I should do my job in the context of that philosophy. Who would ever think that a person of Marv Levy's stature would take the time to think about what this obscure guy that he never met was doing somewhere in the East? But he did. That's among the many things that set Marv apart.

We formed a relationship that lasts to this day and is responsible for virtually all of the success I've had in the game. When people ask who's been my greatest influence, I tell them all that I know about pro football and most that I know about life I learned from Marv Levy.

Scouting has become more of an elimination game, which I do think is a good thing because as a club operator, I think you want to deal with as few people as possible so that ultimately the final choice that you're making is a really, really educated choice.

Scouting also has become more homogenized, which is a bad thing. It started in 1963, when the Detroit Lions, Philadelphia Eagles, and Pittsburgh Steelers combined their scouting efforts. That led to the formation of LESTO, which was an acronym for Lions Eagles Steelers Talent Organization. A year later, the Chicago Bears joined the group, and it became BLESTO. The Vikings and other teams joined the group as the years passed. BLESTO took a scout from each club and assigned him to the combine with the understanding that there would be open disclosure. Whatever one scout knew would be shared with everyone else in the group.

They would be able to cover far more schools, at lesser cost, and each member of the combine would receive virtually every piece of basic information they needed to know about a player: height, weight, speed, forty-yard dash time, college record, injury history, a grade looked at by an area scout, who is assigned to a specific part of the country, and then ultimately a cross-checker, who travels around the country to double check the assessments of the area scouts.

At the same time BLESTO was formed, another group called CEPO, an acronym for Central Eastern Personnel Organization, was created. It included the Baltimore Colts, Cleveland Browns, Green Bay Packers, and St. Louis Cardinals. It would later expand with the additions of the New York Giants, Atlanta Falcons, and Washington Redskins and eventually became known as the National Football Scouting Organization.

In the days before the information explosion, a lot of the data was closely held and was not readily available. So, if you did not make a really big investment in scouting as an organization, you were behind the eight ball because you would only get the basic information that the combine to which you belonged provided, leaving gaps in what you knew about players. Back then, many teams didn't use psychological testing of players, choosing instead to allow coaches to handle that, and they, of course, weren't qualified to do so. Many did not do background checks.

The quality of your scouting staff meant a lot back then. How good was the area scout? How well connected was he at the schools that he serviced? What kind of information could he ferret out that others could not get? We truly competed with each other. And as a member of the NFL's competition committee and then later as the vice president of football operations for the league, George Young constantly crusaded for that competition to remain sacrosanct.

"We compete on the field and an extension of competition on the field is competition in scouting," he would say. "We ought not to share every piece of information."

In 1977, the clubs decided to consolidate and conduct examinations of the top 250 or so college players. And then they said, "Well, you know what? We ought to share the medical data, too. This is not information that everybody's worried about being proprietary. And, by the way, while the players are there, we can time them in the forty, we can measure them in the vertical jump, and we can do some position drills."

And that was how the annual event, known as the NFL Scouting Combine, came into existence in the early 1980s. It started in New Orleans, then moved to Dallas, then to Tempe, and eventually found a permanent home in Indianapolis, first at the RCA Dome and then at its current location, Lucas Oil Stadium.

It has now grown into a monster that threatens to devour us all. And it has absolutely no relationship whatsoever to the original intent of the founding fathers of the combine. It has been taken over by the league and does not resemble what it was in the early days when it was truly a scouting function. It is a media event for my two employers, ESPN and SiriusXM NFL Radio, and for NFL Network and for hundreds of writers and broadcasters from around the country.

I will say that it is managed a lot better than it used to be. Early on, it was the Wild West, especially when it came to the interviews that each team wanted to conduct with players. We would literally kidnap players and take them place to place and hide them from other teams so they couldn't get the interview.

I remember a time when I corralled a player that we were interested in as soon as he left his previous interview. I took him by the arm and began steering him across a rather lengthy hallway to our room, all the while explaining who I was and why I was taking him to a new destination. Not 10 steps into the journey, I was stopped cold by a very angry scout from another club who said, "He's ours! We made an appointment with his agent." My response was, "Well, we didn't, but I wasn't aware that you had to do that." The player stood there dumbstruck as we argued with one another.

In the end, we agreed that fair was fair and he would go with the other team with the proviso that they would bring him back to us as soon as they were finished. They didn't.

Now, teams can arrange interviews with up to 60 players before the Combine. The scheduled interviews—which are published for all team representatives to see—are limited to 15 minutes and an air horn signals when time is up. They are conducted at the Crowne Plaza and Convention Center in Indianapolis. Each team is assigned a hotel room, from which the beds have been removed. Chairs are set up, light refreshments are available, and there's a white board for diagramming plays. And in this tiny space, up to a half-dozen men congregate in a circle to find out as much as they can about a player in 15 minutes.

Most players are taken aback by the experience, and I can't blame them. It's more like a detective squad interrogation room at a police precinct than a setting for a job interview. As a result, with the Colts, we decided to leave the interview process to our team psychologist, Dana Sinclair, a former Canadian Olympic field hockey player and a PhD in psychology from Cambridge University who specializes in sports psychology. We believed, with the exception of quarterbacks, where you put them on the white board and talk Xs and Os, she was far more qualified to conduct the interviews and elicit the appropriate information than we were.

As a general rule, clubs provide players with extensive and valuable club gear as inducement to be fully engaged in the process. It turns out that it really wasn't necessary in our case. The player grapevine being what it is, we soon found out that players at the Combine were anxious to meet "the lady psychologist," whom they not surprisingly found very attractive.

As a result of the information explosion—including the explosion of people like me and like former Washington Redskins general manager and Houston Texans GM Charley Casserly, who have background and standing to offer opinions on players in the media—all of that data on players is now public. With very, very little effort you can sit in your office and get a pretty good picture of what a player is like.

Unfortunately, there are those in the hierarchy of NFL teams who rely a bit too heavily on that information. I've actually had club presidents who really involved themselves in this process, yet who didn't understand the process, say to me when I was a general manager, "Would you take this guy?"

And my answer would be, "Yeah, I don't see anything wrong with him."

"Well, you know, this reporter told me that on his big board he's hearing that this guy has some problems off the field."

Then, I said to myself, "Why would you believe that guy as opposed to your own scouts?"

When you get that sort of question from your team president, it means one of two things: either you don't have good scouts or you don't trust them. That's sort of a snapshot of what scouting has become.

Anyone can pretty much predict who's going to go in the first round and even well into the middle of the second round. Now, what we can't predict is what teams they're going to. But you can predict who's going to go because all this information is out there and when you put it all together, even if you don't have a good understanding of what it takes to make a good football player, you basically know what the consensus is.

More and more, the draft is trending toward the consensus, which is leading to more mistakes. As a general manager, my instructions to our scouting staff were, "Don't go with the flow. Let's mine our own data, let's be our own people. We're not afraid to make a controversial choice. Because if we're making the choice, we believe it's the right choice. I don't care what anybody else thinks about it."

5

The Prodigal Quarterback Comes Home

"The best result of a negotiation is when both sides win—a win-win. The next best is when both sides are a little disappointed with the result. This means it was probably a fair deal." —Paul Tagliabue

"Leave a little on the table for the other guy. You will probably have to do business with him again."
—Paul Tagliabue quoting his father

There are parts of Buffalo Bills history that are almost too bizarre to believe. And there's one part that I can say I'm particularly glad to have missed.

It happened in early June 1983, while I was working in the Canadian Football League. Two months earlier, the Bills had made Jim Kelly, the star quarterback from the University of Miami, the

14th-overall pick of the draft after using the 12th choice on a tight end from Notre Dame, Tony Hunter (who would spend only two years with the Bills and four in the NFL before suffering a career-ending leg injury with the Los Angeles Rams).

Jim was the third quarterback selected in the now-legendary Quarterback Class of '83, after John Elway (who was selected first overall by Baltimore but later traded to Denver) and Todd Blackledge (No. 7 by Kansas City) and before Tony Eason (New England), Ken O'Brien (New York Jets), and Dan Marino (Miami), who amazingly was the next-to-last pick of the first round.

Jim made it clear from the start he wanted nothing to do with playing in Buffalo. He went so far as to instruct his agents to get the best offers they could from the United States Football League's Chicago Blitz, which had drafted Jim, and the CFL's Montreal Concordes, who also expressed serious interest in signing him. Jim even made a visit to Chicago and, not surprisingly, came away very impressed with the Blitz's coach, the late, great Hall of Famer George Allen.

Nevertheless, the Bills, with Pat McGroder serving as their interim general manager after replacing the departed Stew Barber, were undeterred. They kept negotiating with Jim's agents, Greg Lustig and A.J. Faigin, and finally put together a four-year, $2.1 million deal that Jim was going to sign.

Or so it seemed.

As the story goes, Jim and his agents were in Pat's office, with Jim literally on the verge of putting pen to paper. All of a sudden, a phone call came in and a secretary, sitting outside the office, picked it up. It was from Bruce Allen, George's son and the general manager of the Blitz, asking to speak with A.J. Faigin.

For whatever reason, she put the call through.

Allen was on a three-way connection that included the late John Bassett, principal owner of the USFL's Tampa Bay Bandits and one of the most influential voices of his league. About a month earlier, Bassett had invited Jim, his agents, and one of Jim's closest friends and former Hurricanes teammates, fullback Mark Rush, to a Bandits game to give them a feel for the quality of play in the USFL. They spent several days at Bassett's plush condo in Sarasota, where they were treated like royalty.

Allen and Bassett told Faigin to hold everything with the Bills, and that Faigin and Lustig should exit the building and meet them at Bassett's home in nearby Toronto to listen to an offer that would blow them away. They walked out, leaving behind a glaring blank spot on the contract where Jim was supposed to have signed his name.

Later that night, Allen and Bassett informed them that the USFL was so determined to land Jim, he could have his pick of any of its teams. Allen said he would gladly trade Jim's rights to the team of his choice and he and Bassett promised that he would receive far more money than the Bills were offering. As a sweetener, they also extended the pick-your-USFL-team proposal to Mark Rush, who had been a fourth-round pick of the Minnesota Vikings, and assured Jim that any USFL club would sign them as a package deal.

The two of them put together their wish list of teams, and to no one's surprise, they were all warm-weather cities: Tampa Bay, Jacksonville, and Houston. Soon thereafter, Dr. Jerry Argovitz, the Houston Gamblers' owner and a dentist, invited Jim and Mark to Houston, where he would have the attractive opportunity to throw passes in the Astrodome.

Before making a contract offer, Argovitz wanted to make sure Jim's shoulder, on which he had undergone surgery after severely separating it during his senior year of college, was fully recovered. Argovitz took Jim to a park and asked that he throw him some passes as he ran routes. Not quite sure of what to make of the owner of a professional football team running pass patterns for him, Jim, who had one of the strongest arms of any quarterback to play the game, figured he should take it easy to enhance Argovitz's chances of catching the ball.

But Argovitz told him he wanted more velocity on the throws.

"Okay," Jim said. "If that's what you want."

The next pass wound up breaking the ring finger on Argovitz's right hand.

Right after that, Argovitz, after receiving Jim's rights from the Blitz in exchange for four draft picks, signed him to a five-year contract worth $3.5 million, including a guaranteed signing bonus of $1 million. That made him the USFL's second-highest player after running back Herschel Walker.

Jim would go on to have two brilliant seasons in Houston. Working in the run-and-shoot scheme, he threw for 9,842 yards and 83 touchdowns. He completed 63 percent of his passes with an average of 8.53 yards per attempt. In 1984, Jim was MVP of the USFL, setting a league record by throwing for 5,219 yards and 44 touchdowns.

The run-and-shoot essentially evolved into today's spread offense. It consisted of four wide receivers—two wideouts and two slots, and no tight end. The slots were little guys; they were the forerunners of Wes Welker and Brandon Stokley. All four receivers could fly. The Gamblers would spread the defense by lining up in a four-receiver set. They had a big running back who could pass protect and a big, pass-protecting line that could also move you off the line of scrimmage.

The quarterback would take the ball from under center, drop straight back or sprint right or left, stop and throw. In most cases, it involved five guys running patterns, with the back going out late as a check-down guy or as part of half-field patterns. They could also run the option on the goal line.

Jim proved that he was an extremely talented quarterback in every respect: athletic ability, arm strength, accuracy, field-

THE PRODIGAL QUARTERBACK COMES HOME

generalship, leadership, toughness. He was a 10 in every category. To this day, and with all due respect to Peyton Manning, Jim Kelly is the greatest long passer that I've ever been around. He can drop a pass in a five-gallon bucket at 75 yards.

You could not have lived in Buffalo during that time and been unaware of how the loss of Jim Kelly affected the perception of the franchise. It was viewed as just an absolute, outright stumble. And it felt doubly worse due to the earlier loss of a talented running back, Joe Cribbs, to the USFL because the Bills had allowed it to happen with incorrectly worded language in his contract. So they lost two players who arguably would have reached marquee status because they didn't have enough acumen to get the job done. That was just another example, in the public's mind, of the bumbling Bills.

The Bills became fodder for Johnny Carson's late-night monologue. They were considered such an embarrassment, such a non-professional organization that, at one point, the late Larry Felser, a longtime sports columnist for the *Buffalo News*, wrote that the city just might be better off without them. That was a stinging commentary from Larry, who heavily influenced sports opinions in western New York.

And the perception by players from other NFL teams and those coming out of the college ranks was: "These guys are minor-leaguers. This is an awful place to play, it's not a good place to work, it's not a good place to live." There was a malaise that surrounded the franchise that resulted from the losses of Jim Kelly and Joe Cribbs. Those weren't losses on the field. Those weren't because of injuries or poor coaching or anything that you could correct. They were because of poor business acumen, the inability to get the job done, or so people assumed.

In 1986, a potential trade materialized for Jim's negotiating rights, which we still owned. It would have involved some pretty high draft choices, and I thought it was something that Mr. Wilson should at least consider. For one thing, it could have netted us, at the very minimum, a decent quarterback, along with allowing us to fill other positions. For another, Jim was going to be difficult for us to sign, because his price tag would be high for that time and he already had made it clear he had no desire to play for the Bills, so I thought we needed to look at a fall-back option.

"No!" Mr. Wilson said emphatically. "We're not going to do it. We're going to sign Jim Kelly."

"Jim Kelly is going to cost a fortune to sign," I reminded him.

"I know. We're going to sign Jim Kelly."

It was easy to understand why. In addition to being supremely talented, Jim was also a known quantity. It was as if you were getting a guy from another NFL team. Forget about the USFL. Jim was a proven professional in any league.

In my mind, having actually seen him up close and personal for a whole season in the USFL, there was no question that he was going to be a great quarterback in the NFL. There were no questions about him physically, none about him mentally, none about him emotionally. He was so big, so strong, so tough, I honestly thought that we had a weapon that nobody else had. Guys like that are rare in professional football. They're rare in professional sports. They make everybody around them better, and that's what Jim did.

He made the offensive line better because he would hang in, deliver the ball, then take a shot rather than being skittish and running out of the pocket. His linemen would say, "Hey, we know where he is, we know he's going to be back there. All we have to do is just steer everybody by him." When you're playing with a guy as tough as that, you become tougher. You want to reach that standard.

Jim made his receivers better because of his ability to make every possible throw there was. He rarely hung receivers out to dry with throws that were off-target or didn't have enough steam on them. That ball came out of there a hundred miles an hour and it was catchable and in the position where the guy didn't have to stretch for it or lay out for it.

There was no question in my mind that there wasn't any risk at all in signing Jim. We were getting the guy that was going to take us to the Promised Land, no question about it.

On July 29, 1986, at the end of an 11-week trial in U.S. District Court in Manhattan, a jury awarded the USFL all of one dollar in its $1.7-billion antitrust suit against the NFL. That was trebled to three dollars. But the hollow nature of that "victory" was based on the fact the jury rejected all of the USFL's claims that the NFL's contracts with the television networks broadcasting its games constituted a monopoly, which was the very essence of its case.

Five days later, USFL commissioner Harry Usher announced that the league was suspending operations until 1987 (although it would never resume play), and a week later, the NFL announced that more than 600 USFL players were available to NFL teams. Soon thereafter, Al Davis, the late owner of the Raiders (who were in Los Angeles at the time) called me and said, "I'll give you any seven players on our team for the rights to Jim Kelly. Name the players."

So I named Howie Long, an eventual Hall of Famer, and virtually every other star that they had. He said, "Well, I'll call you back."

He never called back.

Greg Lustig then called me to say he wanted to meet. After receiving permission from the NFL office, I called Lustig back. The first thing he said was, "We don't want to go to Buffalo. We didn't want to go to Buffalo in the first place. We have no intention of going to Buffalo now."

All Lustig wanted to talk about was convincing us to trade Jim's rights to the Raiders. I told him that he wasn't necessarily in a position to make that demand, but that I thought it was still appropriate that we get together.

"Let me talk to Jim about what we have going here," I said.

I had a week to prepare. My plan was to sell Jim on the Bills, making sure that he understood we weren't as bad as our record or reputation said we were. In another life, I had been a college recruiter, so I knew a little bit about how to do that and how to put our best foot forward.

We agreed to meet on August 14, 1986, in New York, at the Helmsley Palace Hotel, which happened to be right across the street from Saint Patrick's Cathedral. I remembered being there as a little grade-school boy, touring that magnificent church. I considered that a good omen.

I opened the meeting by sharing an anecdote of being with the Chicago Blitz while Marv Levy and I were on the sideline of a game against the Gamblers in the Astrodome. In the second half, our safety, Doug Plank, was blitzing. Doug was one of the toughest guys in the game. He was the guy after whom the "46 Defense," made famous for its dominance on the 1985 Chicago Bears, was named. Doug came after Jim and he popped him right under the chin. It was a hit that in today's NFL would get you ejected and suspended. You could see that he opened a gash in Jim's chin, yet, with blood pouring out, Jim stood back there and delivered a strike for a touchdown.

Marv and I looked at each other and we both went, "Holy cow!" or words to that effect.

I told Jim, "It was that play, more than any other, that convinced me that you're the kind of quarterback we need with the Buffalo Bills. I didn't need to see anything other than that play." That was probably a little bit of an exaggeration, but it did carry a lot of weight with me.

Jim laughed and said, "Oh, man, Plank really hit me with a good shot."

I also reminded him of when he beat us in a Saint Patrick's Day blizzard in Chicago. I'm talking about 17–18 inches of snow. I said,

"Heck, you played in a blizzard in Chicago. Why are you worried about a little snow in western New York?"

We were just two guys talking football. For a moment, it stopped being a business meeting and became more of a casual conversation. I think it put Jim at ease a little bit, allowing me to gain some trust from him.

After that, I went into my recruiting speech.

I told him about Andre Reed, an extremely talented receiver that had been drafted from Kutztown State the previous year. I told him about Pete Metzelaars, who we had acquired in a trade with the Seattle Seahawks in '85.

"We've got Bruce Smith on defense," I said. "We got some guys who can make plays on this team. This is not the mediocre outfit that it was when you were originally drafted in '83. It's a new, young team that you're going to grow with and we're committed to building through the draft."

I then showed Jim a diagram that I had drawn of the offense. It was a typical pro formation for those days: a tight end, two wide receivers, two running backs. "With Jerry Butler and Chris Burkett, along with Reed and Metzelaars, we have a group that is very different from the little guys you've been throwing to with the Houston Gamblers," I said. "And we've got a decent offensive line.

"This whole thing has been built with you in mind. This is not an offense that we dreamed up out of whole cloth and we don't care who the quarterback is. This is an offense that requires a quarterback who can lead, who can make throws down the field, who can do the kind of things that are necessary to have a top-flight passing game. And we think that that's possible in Buffalo."

At some point the idea of a trade to the Raiders came up and I said, "Well, Jim, here's the issue: we control your rights. They belong to us unilaterally, and there's no place that you can go of your own volition without our agreement. And I'm quite sure that we would never agree to trade you."

"Well, what if I didn't come to Buffalo?" Jim asked. "What if I just refused to play?"

"Well, if that happened, I guess at some point in time we'd be inclined to maybe entertain a trade, because what skin is it off our nose if you don't play? We would be no worse off than we are now. But I can assure you that we wouldn't trade you to the Raiders, under no circumstances. It's not happening. Take it to the bank. It's just not happening."

I then proceeded to make him understand the realities of my situation, and how it would impact his situation.

"I'm a new GM," I said. "So I can't have my pocket picked or I'll be dead in the water before we get going. The Raiders are looking to pick my pocket, so if we did end up trading you, I would insist that we trade you to the worst place possible, which would probably be Green Bay [at that time, the Packers were really down in the dumps]. And I'd take a bag of balls from them before you would go to the Raiders. I just have to draw that line. And I know Mr. Wilson feels the same way.

"We recognize that you're a premium player and that you're going to command big money, but we think that we're on the road to success here and we've got the right blueprint and you're an important part of that. We think that this is the right place for you and you're the right guy for us, so we want to make this work.

"This franchise has a cloud over it because we didn't sign you. Conversely, when we do sign you, that cloud will be lifted. Those gray skies will disappear, and there'll be nothing but blue skies proverbially. The fans of Buffalo will welcome you with open arms. You're not just another football player coming to Buffalo. You're the prodigal son coming home to lead us to the Promised Land."

Jim seemed to take everything I was saying in stride. He thanked me, said he would think about it, and have Greg call me back.

I didn't feel any pressure, really, because you're either going to get the deal done or you're not. You give it your best shot and if it doesn't work, you move on. There's always tomorrow. That's sort of the way I've always looked at things. Now, I did know that if we didn't get Jim signed, the results probably weren't going to be good for me or anybody else, but that comes with the territory. When you get in this business, you expect that. You just live with it.

But I had confidence. Maybe it was just bravado or maybe I didn't know any better, but I was confident we would get it done. I left the meeting with a positive feeling. For whatever reason, I think Jim was intrigued. My sense was that he was thinking, *Well, this may not be as bad as I thought it was going to be.*

On the morning of August 15, 1986, I was at the airport in Buffalo, ready to head to Houston, where I would meet with Jim Kelly's agents later that day. It just so happened that the next night, we would be playing a preseason game against the Oilers in the Astrodome.

I felt all along that we had to move quickly or the deal wasn't going to get done. I was absolutely convinced of that. We were getting a second chance at bat. We had struck out the first time. You rarely get a second chance and we were getting a second chance. We couldn't strike out. We couldn't let it drag on. We had to close the deal.

Western New York knew that this was the opportunity to right the original wrong and if Jim became the quarterback and came "home," so to speak, everything would be looking up for the team and the community. I got to the airport, and people there knew I was on my way to Houston to do the negotiations. There were actually children from a Catholic church in a northern suburb of Buffalo that brought along a little scroll, which was essentially a group of prayer thoughts for me.

"We're praying for you when you go to sign Jim Kelly," a nun told me.

Only in Buffalo where the Bills are civic priority One every day of the year!

But when you're preparing for a negotiation of this magnitude, you have to put all of that emotion and peripheral stuff aside and focus on the bottom line. You can't allow anything to cause you to lose sight of the fact you have a job to do. Nothing else matters.

The flight to Houston gave me a fair amount of time to think about the negotiations and make some notes. I was focused on comparable deals, at least as Jim's agents saw them. At the time, there were two. One belonged to Joe Montana, whom the San Francisco 49ers had made the highest-paid quarterback in the NFL. The other belonged to Steve Young, then of the Los Angeles Express and the highest-paid quarterback in the USFL.

The negotiations would be held in a suite at a hotel separate from where the team would stay for the preseason game. The suite was large enough to contain two caucus rooms, one for each side to privately discuss strategy or to simply cool off when things got a little bit heated. We agreed to keep the hotel's location a secret because of all of the media attention the negotiations were drawing. I had decided before leaving Buffalo that I wasn't going to go anywhere near the team hotel, because I knew that there would be plenty of reporters there from western New York and I had no intention of providing any progress reports about the talks.

I arrived for our first session with my briefcase that contained two Jim Kelly files—one with football information (scouting reports, long-term plans for the team, statistical research, notes about our division) and the other with a lot of economic background (mainly financial data on the top-paid quarterbacks in the NFL and USFL)—and the legal notepad (in my trusty Wilson NFL football-type leather binder) to write down points they were making and sometimes points that I wanted to make.

When you're dealing with non-football people—and I learned this from the Bruce Smith negotiation—oftentimes lawyers will make a statement that is untrue, and just saying to them "it's untrue" doesn't refute it to their satisfaction. You have to have the documentation handy to say, "No, here's exactly what the issue is, here's where you're wrong, and here's why you're wrong." Of course, they have scouting reports and financial data of their own, which is all the more reason why you need all of that reference material at your fingertips.

In the first meeting, you're setting the parameters. You're building a theoretical fence around the negotiations. The other side is saying the fence covers six-and-a-half acres. You're saying, "No, my fence covers about half of that." The first day is all about staking out your respective positions and making the arguments back and forth. I'm listening to what they have to say, and trying to rebut it. They're listening to what I have to say, and trying to rebut it.

People think negotiations go around the clock. They don't. Once you get beyond five hours, it becomes really exhausting and you have to take a break. I think the first day we went five to six hours and the discussion was focused on the Montana and Young contracts. I was trying to figure out what their "magic number" was. By the end of the day, I got to the point where I was pretty confident in saying to myself, *I think a million a year is the magic number.* By today's salary standards, that would be laughable for a backup quarterback, but it was unheard of for anybody in the National Football League at the time.

At this point, Jim was not involved in the talks. As is the case with the vast majority of pro athletes, he left the negotiating to the people he hired to do it for him. Whenever a player was involved in negotiations, which was rare, my approach wasn't the same as it was with an agent. Number one, because I never wanted to offend the player if that was even remotely possible. Number two, because that guy is your player, he's your teammate, he's why you exist, he's why I have that job in large measure. You serve at the sufferance and pleasure of the owner because he pays you, but the players are the ones who draw the people. There wouldn't be any other employees if there weren't players.

I've always believed players needed to be treated with dignity and with kindness and with care. Sometimes you can say things in a negotiation that can be misconstrued, that people can feel has been said out of spite. Body language comes into play as well. Nick Saban, one of the finest coaches in the history of college football, is fond of saying, "We all see the world through different sets of eyes," and he's exactly right.

Whenever a player came in to talk about something that had to do with his contract or negotiations, a business issue, I was very different than I was with the negotiators. The negotiators are there to get the most for their client. They don't play by the Marquess of Queensberry Rules, so you have a different demeanor with them.

Now, you try not to be nasty. You try not to be combative if you can avoid it. That's not easy for me to do because I see the world through my own eyes. You're representing your owner's point of view. You're his agent. Your responsibility is to represent his interests and follow the marching orders he's given you.

You look at a negotiation as a series of small agreements that lead to a large agreement, with lots of discussion around each small point. You enter them with the following principles:

- Number one, know the landscape that surrounds the negotiation. Who's the decision maker? What are the aims of those you're negotiating against? What is their point of view about your situation and what you have to offer? What are the outside forces that may or may not play a role here, either positive or negative?

- Number two, know the economics. When I first met with Mr. Wilson in Detroit prior to the Bruce Smith negotiations, he said, "Remember this, in pro football, economics always wins out." You have to know what you can spend. You have to know what form it can take. You want to know what is appropriate. You want to know what the comparable deals are. You need to understand what kind of a contractual precedent you might be setting in the industry , and, more importantly, on your team.

- Know the other side's hot button. What's really important to them? What's really important to you?

- And, finally, go into it understanding that it's a two-party negotiation. The best negotiation—and this should be engraved in stone for every general manger—is a win-win. You need to know what is a win for you and what is a win for them. It isn't a zero-sum game.

That said, whenever Greg Lustig and I would make some progress, A.J. Faigin would try to walk it back by saying things like, "No, that's not true. No, your team isn't very good." Or, "No, Jim Kelly will be hurt by playing in the harsh Buffalo winters." Over the course of several hours, that got a little tedious. But it was clear that Lustig was going to be the good cop and Faigin was going to be the bad cop.

Faigin was trying to say, in essence, "I hear all your comparable numbers, but you're going to have to pay more because your team is bad and you're a rookie general manager; you won't be able to draft anybody that can play. You've got poor players and you have a bad coach. Buffalo's a bad place to live and has an awful climate." I saw his negotiating tactic for just what it was: to create an impression that we were somewhere south of a Class-D, minor-league baseball franchise, and as a result we were going to have to pay a large premium to get Jim.

The next day, Faigin pushed me too far. He kept talking about how bad our offensive line was and that Jim was going to get hurt behind it. I told him that wasn't true. Then, I talked about the linemen we had. I talked about our offensive line coach, Jim Ringo, a Hall of Famer. Did we have to add a guy or two? Yes, but we were committed to doing that. Lustig would try to change the discussion, but Faigin would come back to it again.

Finally, I got up and I walked over to him. He was sitting in a chair over by the window.

"Look, if you know so much about offensive line play, why don't you get out of that chair and show me how you would like your offensive tackle to block a wide-nine rusher," I said, while standing over him. "Show me how you would do that. Then show me how you would block a bull-rusher. Teach me how to play offensive line."

"I don't have to do that," he said.

"Well, you're such an expert on offensive line play, so show me what you know. Show me what you know! Because I don't think you know anything!"

Lustig jumped in at that point and said, "Stop! Enough is enough."

The negotiation went kind of downhill from there. Every time Faigin would come in with a monkey wrench, I would say, "Pipe down. It's pretty obvious that you don't know what you're talking about." It had gotten to the point where I was unwilling to talk with him anymore. As a negotiator you do have to create some perameters on your side of the table. When the other side gets too obstreperous, you just say, "Stop!" And that's what I did.

Finally, Lustig called Jim and said, "You'd better come over here."

Jim showed up a short while later to lay down the law.

"Look, this is a negotiation," he said. "I want this to be as fruitful as it's supposed to be. You've got to get along. A.J., don't be jumping into Bill's stuff. Treat him with respect. He knows what he's talking about. Bill, you've just got to understand they've got a job to do. They represent me."

Faigin's goal was not to prevent us from reaching an agreement. His idea was to try to get me upset in an effort to drive the price up, reinforcing the idea that we would have to pay so much more because we were so lousy.

We called it a day. Our game against the Oilers was that night, and Jim attended as Ralph Wilson's guest in his suite at the Astrodome. Mr. Wilson approached it with the same sense of urgency that we were approaching the negotiation. It was going to be a full-court press. We were going to use every piece of ammunition to get this done. I was at the game, as well, but I steered clear of the media. I wanted to be as unobtrusive as possible. But I heard afterward that Mr. Wilson did a great job of selling Jim on the Bills and Buffalo.

The next day, Dave Olsen and our treasurer, Jeff Littman, joined me at the bargaining table with Jim's agents. There was a change in attitude on the part of the agents. Whether it was because of Jim's laying down the law the day before or his visit with Mr. Wilson at the game, his agents were more receptive to what we were offering, which was a five-year deal worth $8 million, including a $1 million signing bonus. That made him, at least briefly, the highest-paid player in the NFL.

I actually began to have a little bit of trepidation. The numbers were really high. We were breaking new ground. Through this whole process, I was like, "Whew, man, this is a big number! How did we get here?" But Dave provided some perspective, saying, "We have to take into consideration the value that Kelly will bring to us off the field." Mr. Wilson, who had returned to Detroit after the game, adopted the same kind of tone.

"Listen, we've come this far," he said. "We said we're going to sign him."

Then, Mr. Wilson started to laugh and said, "Now, don't go any higher than you are now, but get it done." We were both laughing over that one.

"Okay, boss," I said.

Around eight o'clock at night, Faigin said to Lustig, "We need to get Jim over here. He's got to sign off on this." Jim showed up soon, and he and his agents caucused for a long time. Then there was some discussion of the payment schedule for the signing bonus. They caucused again, and we used the time to call Mr. Wilson and tell him we were closing in on an agreement.

Finally, around midnight, they said the words we'd been waiting so long to hear:

"We have a deal."

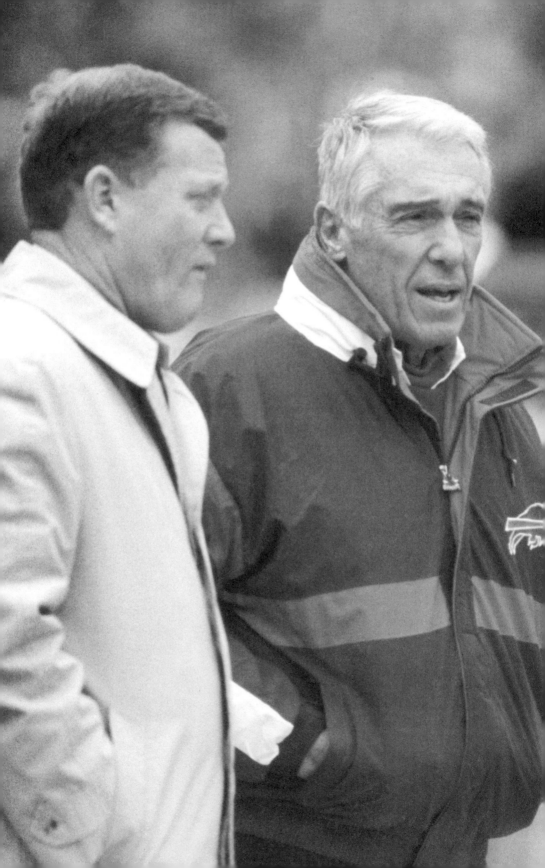

6

Setting a New Course

*"A prepared team is a confident team. A confident team is
a motivated team."*
— Marv Levy

After our hug to celebrate his long-awaited signing with the
Buffalo Bills, I attempted to explain to Jim Kelly what was ahead for
him. "You're not going to believe the response this is going to get
in Buffalo," I said. I could tell Jim was a little skeptical, thinking that
what I was telling him was an exaggeration. I assured him it wasn't.

"Believe me, you're not going to realize how important this is
until you go through it," I said. "So, prepare yourself."

At the crack of dawn on August 18, 1986, I called Bill Munson,
our vice president of operations, and he began making arrangements
with people at Mr. Wilson's Detroit office for a private plane that
would get us from Houston to Buffalo for the official announcement
later that day.

"Where should we have the press conference?" Muns asked.

"Where's the biggest place in town?" I asked.

"The grand ballroom of the Hilton Hotel."

"Okay, book it!"

Then Muns wanted to know if it was necessary to have a large police presence at Prior Aviation, the private airport in Buffalo where we would be landing. I told him we should, saying it was better to be safe than sorry.

After we landed and the plane taxied to the terminal, we could see through our windows what Muns's idea of a "large police presence" looked like. There was a small army consisting of state police, sheriff's deputies, and local police. I remember someone on the plane joking, "Do we have John Dillinger aboard?"

After we got off the plane, Jim walked over to a bank of cameras and made a couple of remarks. I did the same. A TV reporter brought a football that he asked Jim to throw to him so that the reporter could say he caught Jim's "first pass as a Bill." Fortunately, Jim kind of lobbed it, just to help make sure that first pass was a completion, which it was. Then, we climbed into a stretch limousine that was part of a motorcade—complete with press and camera cars that you see traveling with the president of the United States—which took us to the press conference.

As it turned out, the significant police presence was justified. Besides the huge media gathering, there also was a fairly large crowd of fans along the driveway leading out to the street. It was even a little shocking for me to witness. As the motorcade—led by numerous squad cars with their lights flashing—turned onto Route 33, the main artery leading to downtown, Jim looked at me and said, "Woo! You weren't wrong about this."

People were pressed against the chain-link fences on the overpasses, waving and holding signs that said, "Welcome to Buffalo," "Welcome Home," "Our Day Has Come," "We Love You, Jim." They parked their cars on the shoulder of the road, and got out to acknowledge Jim as we drove by. Some literally hung out of the windows of homes along the route.

Jim couldn't believe his eyes, either. At one point, he just shook his head and said, "Holy smokes!" Or words to that effect.

Hundreds of people jammed the lobby of the Hilton, and as soon as they spotted Jim, they began chanting, "Kel-ly! Kel-ly!" Shortly thereafter, they chanted, "Super Bowl! Super Bowl!" The level of enthusiasm and optimism was beyond comprehension.

Inside the grand ballroom was a massive dais, where Jim would be joined by his parents and agents, Mr. Wilson, Coach Hank Bullough, the late Mayor Jimmy Griffin, County Executive and former Bills receiver/quarterback Eddie Rutkowski, and yours truly. We had also arranged for a phone call from Governor Mario Cuomo, who had been a part of our recruiting efforts by writing Jim a letter that encouraged him to "play for New York's only professional football team." As we gathered in a holding area, Denny Lynch, our public relations director, walked up to me and said, "We're going to have to get this thing moving because the network television affiliates are preempting the 6:30 national newscasts to broadcast this live."

Of course they were. For their audiences, nothing more important could have been happening elsewhere in the country or the world, for that matter. The Bills are 24/7/365 in Buffalo. They are, as Eddie Rutkowski used to say, the barometer of life of western New York. When the Bills win, the barometer's up; when they don't, it's down. Everything the Bills do is news and, in this case, the news was a signing that lifted the dark cloud that had existed for three or four years and was inflated by other events, such as the Blizzard of '77 and the terrible downturn in the steel industry.

It gave people hope. The prodigal son had come home.

I understood that, at least symbolically, it was much more than getting a football player's signature on a contract. It was a civic endeavor. It was about how the citizens of western New York viewed themselves. Not that it should have been, because they are the greatest people in the world. They are the most industrious people in the world. Buffalo wasn't going to fold up and go away if we hadn't signed Jim Kelly.

But there's no denying the Bills are a huge part of the fabric of their life and, until they could celebrate a Super Bowl, this would serve as the franchise's greatest triumph since winning back-to-back American Football League championships in 1964–65.

The best line of the day came from Mr. Wilson, when he opened the press conference by saying, "I don't have a prepared speech because attorneys have to read those to make sure everything's okay, and attorneys cost a hundred and fifty dollars an hour. And for some reason, we're kind of low on funds today."

The next morning Jim passed the requisite physical examination he had to undergo before the contract became final and was on the field at Fredonia State College for his first training-camp practice in the afternoon. At that moment, the suit-and-tie-wearing mega-celebrity who had been given a reception befitting a president was in his own element. Finally, after all of the negotiating and posturing that is all a part of the business of football, Jim Kelly was able to get down to the business of playing football.

Given that Jim had only gotten a peek of the playbook for about an hour after lunch, Bob Leahy, our quarterbacks coach, told him that he didn't have to go in the huddle and could just throw some passes along the sidelines. Jim had other ideas. Not long after the practice began, he jumped into the huddle and started calling plays. They were fairly basic, but it was impressive to see him running an offense he barely knew.

With every player that you draft or you sign, even though you have seen him in person before in some other context, you always want that first practice to go well. You want everybody watching to say, "Wow!" and not, "Oh, my God!"

Thousands of people lined the fences around the field. It was, at the time, thought to be the largest crowd ever for a training-camp workout in the history of the team. There was no doubt they were there for one reason: to get their first up-close glimpse of the "messiah" in action. If they didn't get to see Jim perform an actual miracle, they were certainly looking for him to demonstrate he was capable of doing so.

And then Jim cut loose with about a 60-yard bomb that he threw down the sideline to a wide receiver named Jimmy Teal, who was many steps ahead of the free safety. Although there was a pretty brisk wind in his face, Jim launched a beautiful rainbow of a throw and dropped it right over the receiver's shoulder, right down the chimney. I can't remember who I was standing next to, but I turned to him and said, "Yeah, okay, we're good. We got the guy we thought we were getting."

Still, I knew, for multiple reasons, it wasn't going to be an easy transition for Jim. I made sure that I shared that with Mr. Wilson.

"We are going to have to help him along here," I said. "He is going to face more media and more outside pressure than he's had before. He's going into an offense that's completely different than what he's played in for the last two years. He may be a little frustrated by it, so we have to try and help him through it."

Compounding the challenge was that we really hadn't established an identity as a team; we didn't know what we wanted to be or what we could be. Hank Bullough was a former defensive coordinator and his focus was on defense. He was trying to get the message across that, in order to win, we had to play good, sound defense. Now, all of a sudden, Jim Kelly comes along and the focus, at least among people on the outside, was "throw the ball on every down." To them, no matter how much you threw it, you weren't throwing it enough.

Jim, for whatever reason, didn't click with Bob Leahy. Not that there was any bitterness or fighting there, but it just wasn't the kind of marriage that you would like to have between coach and quarterback. And that's an important relationship, especially for a young quarterback. Through no fault of his own, Bob hadn't gotten to know Jim all that well. To throw Jim in there on the eve of the season and say, "Hey, you're the quarterback, it's your team" was a tough situation for everyone involved. It was particularly hard on the coaching staff, but that was the circumstance.

At that point, we were not a team where the whole was greater than the sum of the parts because we really didn't know what the whole should look like. We had acquired a very critical part in a quarterback who I believe is among the greatest and most accurate long passers who have ever played the game, and among the two or three toughest quarterbacks in the history of the game. But everything around him was sort of discombobulated. Jim truly had a linebacker's mentality, which you would have thought would have meshed perfectly with the philosophy of a defensive-oriented head coach, but it didn't. There was a disconnect there.

We were trying to build a defense that could be reliable and we didn't have the parts to do that. We had a future Hall of Fame end in Bruce Smith, but he was still very much in his NFL adolescent stage and unconfortable with what Hank and the coaches wanted him to do. We had another future standout in outside linebacker Darryl Talley, but he also was still in his NFL adolescence and he and Hank didn't hit it off, either. You had a couple of pretty good players on the front seven in Fred Smerlas and Jim Haslett, but several other members of that unit were either journeymen or nearing the end of their careers. We were an average to poor defense with an offense that was also struggling because it didn't know what it was trying to be.

As a result, guys on both sides of the ball got really frustrated. Don't forget, there were many players who had been through a lot of losing before this, including the 2–14 finishes of the previous two seasons, and now they were facing another losing season. It got more and more frustrating for the players, it got more and more frustrating for the coaches, and by the time we hit the last half of that season we were struggling badly.

I don't put the blame on anyone but myself for that. The ultimate responsibility for us not having all that we needed to be successful was mine. I knew what to do in terms of how to set the organization on the right path. I knew how to sign players and how to put together a roster. What I didn't focus on was what an architect does, and that was get together with the head coach and draw up a blueprint of what this was going to look like at the end. We were in a situation where we really didn't have a blueprint, and I'm not sure that the players had anything they could buy into and say, "Here's how we are going to win."

After a loss to New England put our record at 2–6, I was summoned over to Detroit for a meeting. The consensus was that we probably needed to make a head-coaching change. There was friction between Hank Bullough and some of the players. A specific situation had arisen that had to do with Hank criticizing a player in front of the team. It was serious enough to draw the wrong kind of attention from the owner.

"Mr. Wilson, you need to talk with Hank about this, man-to-man, and explain to him that he needs to get this right," I said. "And the way to get this right is for him to sit down with the player and just explain to him that what he was doing was for the good of the player and for the good of the team. For lack of a better term, he has to smooth it over."

Mr. Wilson agreed. He called Hank and they had a long conversation, which was cordial, but didn't go anywhere.

Afterward, Mr. Wilson said to me, "If this continues, we probably are going to have to make a change. And if that's the case, who would you recommend?"

"Marv Levy," I said, without hesitation. "I don't think there is any question that he is what we need at this point in time, if we are forced to make a change."

There ensued a somewhat lengthy discussion about Marv's 31–42 record in five seasons as head coach of the Kansas City Chiefs. Dave Olsen questioned me a lot about his values and why I thought they would fit the Bills.

"You are very close to this man," he reminded me. "Now, let's make sure that we are making the right decision for the right reasons, not because he is your friend." Dave was really playing the devil's advocate. He made me defend my beliefs, which, of course, was the right thing to do.

Both Dave and Mr. Wilson brought up Marv's controversial decision to run the Wing-T offense with the Chiefs. Marv took a lot of grief for using a scheme that had only been utilized at the collegiate level and media critics said had no business in the NFL, where defenses were too athletically gifted to let it get the better of them. The Wing-T revolved around the running game. It was a way to run the football with both power and deception that was actually quite good. Tubby Raymond was running it at the University of Delaware. Marv even tried to hire Tubby as his offensive backfield coach, but he elected to stay at Delaware.

Marv wanted to run the Wing-T because he did not have a quarterback that he felt we could rely upon. We had a rookie in Steve Fuller who turned out not to be what we had hoped. Marv thought that the Wing-T would be different and give us the ability to eat some clock, keep our defense off the field, give opponents some preparation problems, and be suited to the personnel that we had until such time as we could build the personnel up to where we were a true, wide open pro-style offense.

I explained to Dave and Mr. Wilson that at the end of that first season, Marv felt that the Wing-T wasn't the right way to go so he abandoned it. Eventually, we gravitated to a more wide open, pro-style offense and that's the way it was for the remainder of his time in Kansas City. Yet, the Wing-T label stuck just as so many other labels are inaccurately attached to people.

I had hired Marv to be the analyst for our preseason telecasts, because I knew he would do an excellent job. But I also wanted to have him around as a sounding board for me. Once the season began, we spoke by phone once every two weeks or so. I wanted to get his opinions on the team. I asked him where he thought our strengths and weaknesses were. He gave me player evaluations. Marv has always been loath to criticize another coach, so he wouldn't go anywhere near what he thought our blueprint ought to be. Not as an outsider. I knew it would be far different if he were our head coach.

This team needed direction and inspiration. It needed a leader who the players could follow, who they believed, ultimately, would take them to the Promised Land. And that was Marv Levy.

I go back to my first year in Kansas City as a scout and we were on the practice field during training camp at William Jewell College in Liberty, Missouri. The next day, we were going to practice against the Houston Oilers at the Arrowhead Stadium. Marv called together all of the rookies and young backup players, most of whom would be going against another team for the first time in the NFL.

He didn't address them in a professorial way, which is what people would assume because he went to Harvard Graduate School. He spoke to them the way that an inspirational officer would speak to his troops.

"Listen, I know that you want to do your best tomorrow," Marv said. "I know you have been working hard at camp to reach this day, and tomorrow is the first step along the road to making a career for yourself in professional football. Now, there are some things that you have to do, beginning with tonight—make sure that you get your rest. Most importantly, make sure you pack your AstroTurf shoes because we have been on grass here all week and now we are going on AstroTurf. Don't leave it to the equipment manager. Double-check your bag before you leave the locker room tonight and make sure you have your AstroTurf shoes.

"Because, not only do you want to do your best, we want you to do your best. You have invested a lot of time and effort here. We are proud of the work you put in and we want to see you have the opportunity to do your best. Is everybody with that? Good. Let's go!"

I said to myself, *Holy mackerel! I never heard anything like that in my life. I'd walk through fire for this man.*

That's Marv, that's who he is. None of it's contrived, none of it's theatrical. It's what he does to get you to reach and do more than you think you can, and he does it in an inspirational way—in a way that makes you feel good about yourself, about your teammates, and about your mission. He is the quintessential leader. From that day forward I was a true believer.

The average reader will say that's a very mundane thing, but the delivery and the message, which was positive and uplifting, is what we needed. Of course, Marv did much, much more of that over the course of his career in Kansas City and were it not for the tragic drowning of star running back Joe Delaney, while he was attempting to save a child, or the divisiveness of the 1982 players' strike, I'm sure he would have gone on to have great success in Kansas City. The late Lamar Hunt said many, many times that the greatest mistake he made as owner of the Chiefs was letting Marv go.

Was I a true believer? Yes. Was I a Marv Levy disciple? Yes. I just knew that what he had was exactly what the dysfunctional Bills' locker room needed.

I wasn't thinking about, *Oh, if I'm wrong about my recommendation of Marv, I'll lose my job.* What I was thinking about was, *Let's get this team as good as we can get it and then we'll worry about taking on Don Shula and company and all the others that we have to beat.* I approached it exactly the way Marv would have approached it if he were in my shoes, because everything I know about pro football and everything I believe about pro football is reflective of his beliefs.

Then, ultimately, I said to Mr. Wilson, "You don't need to take my word for it; you need to satisfy yourself. Here's Marv's number. Give him a call." And he did. I think they had a rather lengthy conversation. I found out later that Mr. Wilson called Mr. Hunt as well, who also gave Marv a glowing recommendation.

I think it's safe to say that there was a faction of players who felt that a change was necessary. They were, as players go, relatively vocal about it in the press and you could read between the lines. And the issue of whether or not Hank could resolve whatever disagreement he had with a player festered a little during the week as we were preparing for a game at Tampa Bay. By the end of the week, Mr. Wilson called me and said, "I'm really thinking about making a change."

We laid an egg in the first half against the Buccaneers to fall behind 20–0. We were just awful. At halftime, Mr. Wilson called me to his private box. He told me he was really upset because we had played with no effort, the players weren't giving their best, and that he had made up his mind to fire Hank after the game. Dave Olsen told me to call Marv and tell him to get ready to come to Buffalo. Marv was getting ready to go to Montreal to rejoin the Alouettes as their general manager, so the timing proved to be fortunate on our part.

We did end up rallying in the second half, and actually had a chance to win the game. But on the final play, with the Buccaneers holding a 34–28 lead, Jim Kelly threw a pass that running back Robb Riddick, who was wearing a cast to protect a broken bone in his left wrist, dropped at the goal line.

The next day, we relieved Hank and hired Marv. As expected, media and fans pretty much gave a ho-hum reaction to Marv's hiring, but I didn't do that. As far as I was concerned, there was no other candidate.

Naturally, questions came up within the team about the kind of head coach we were getting in Marv. Our offensive line coach, Jim Ringo, and Jim Kelly and Darryl Talley each came up to me and, referencing Marv's record in Kansas City, essentially asked, "Can we believe in this guy? Is this the guy who can take us where we need to go?"

"Trust me, believe me, you're going to love him," I said. "He's the right guy for the job."

I remember Jim Ringo saying, "Okay, but he's still got to prove it to me."

I said, "He will. Don't worry about it."

Two days later was the first team meeting with Marv as head coach; it was the Wednesday before we were to face the Pittsburgh Steelers at home. I introduced Marv, giving a brief version of his biography—including the fact that he began his professional coaching career as one of the NFL's first special-teams coaches—and then explaining why this hire should be as exciting to them as it was to me.

"I am convinced that he will do for us what he did for the Kansas City Chiefs," I said. "We were one step away from the playoffs there; we can take that final step here. The people in this room are going to have a lot to do with it, but Marv's the guy, as you will find out very shortly, who knows how to help you get to where you want to go."

I turned the podium over to Marv, who proceeded to set the agenda while quoting straight from the "Gospel According to Marv Levy."

"Men, we have one goal and that is to win the Super Bowl; that's what we are here for," he said. "What it takes to win is simple, but it isn't easy. And here's what we need to do to be a winning team. First, we have to run and stop the run. Now, that doesn't mean forcing the running game. It means that, at the end of the game, we need to have run for more yardage than our opponents. And if you do that, you are going to win 90 percent of the time.

"Secondly, we've got to win the turnover battle. We need to take the ball away and we need to make sure that we don't give it away; don't give the opposition any gifts. And if you win the turnover battle, you're going to win 90 percent of your games.

"We have to have great kicking teams, because kicking teams are a third of the game and they eat up the most yardage and they make the biggest difference in the game. A blocked kick is highly correlated to winning. A great kickoff or punt return has a high correlation to winning. Field position has a high correlation to winning.

"And we have to be smart. We don't want to be dumb and we don't want to be dirty. Our goal is to be among the top five in the league in fewest penalties.

"Finally, you have to make sure that the people in this room and their efforts are geared toward the whole being greater than the sum of the parts. If everyone does his job to the best of his ability, then the whole will be greater than the sum of the parts.

"I don't have a lot of rules; in fact I only have three: be on time, be a professional in everything you do in and outside this building, and be a good citizen. If you do those things, we are going to do what it takes to win...Now, let's go beat the Pittsburgh Steelers!"

All of the players and coaches in the room jumped up from their chairs and began applauding. It was clear, from the moment he opened his mouth, that Marv had the team in his hand. I never saw anything like it.

I said to myself, *Well, we've just taken the first giant step down the road to success.* It was as though we had suddenly become a new team.

Now, the coaches and players who were feeling a little uncertain about Marv a couple of days earlier were coming up to me, one after the other, and saying, "Wow, did you make the right pick!...Man, oh, man, we've got a guy who knows how to win!"

How serious was Marv about the importance of playing "great special teams?" On November 8, the day before we were to face the Steelers, we acquired Steve Tasker off waivers from the Houston Oilers and immediately made him active for the game. Steve was a backup wide receiver, but an extraordinary special-teams player. He would go on to be the best "gunner," the primary tackler on punt coverage, that the game would ever see. He also was a hell of a punt returner—and a good receiver, as well.

The Oilers weren't looking to part ways with Steve. He had been on their injured-reserve list, and they were trying to bring him back onto their active roster. Under NFL rules, he first had to clear league-wide waivers before being activated. The Oilers purposely chose to waive him on a Saturday before a Sunday slate of games on the assumption that most teams would have their rosters pretty well set at that point. They also figured that a reserve player who had been hurt and mostly spent time on special teams since they made him a ninth-round draft pick in '85 would have a good chance of sliding through the waiver process. Furthermore, they were counting on all of the teams to follow the unwritten rule that says when another club is trying to activate a guy from IR, you don't put in a claim for him.

But what they didn't count on was that we knew all about Steve from his days as a player at Northwestern. Marv and I, having worked for the Chicago Blitz in 1984, scouted Northwestern—which was one of our territorial schools—along with John Butler (who would join the Bills in 1987 as personnel director) and had reports on him and on a great punter named John Kidd (whom the Bills drafted in '84) in the files. I had also gotten a good look at Steve during his rookie season with the Oilers when I was assigned to scout a game between Houston and Seattle because we were planning to trade for Pete Metzelaars, a tight end for the Seahawks, right after that and I was the last set of eyes to verify that Pete got through that game healthy. Steve absolutely shined on special teams, so I made a note on my charts that he was a guy that we really would have great interest in as a special-teams player—especially as a return guy—if he became available.

What the Oilers also didn't count on was our extreme desperation at the time. We were the lowest of the low. We were fighting for our survival, so honoring an unwritten rule wasn't going to be much of a priority—especially when, because of our league-worst record in '84, we had the first opportunity to claim a player off waivers. And as soon as Marv and I saw Steve Tasker's name appear on the waiver wire, we claimed him.

About a month later, at the winter scouting meetings, I ran into the late Mike Holovak, who was executive vice president of the Oilers. Mike was a wonderful, wonderful man and a guy who had been terrific to me when I was a scout. And as soon as he saw me, he ripped into me, saying, "Don't you have the courtesy to let a guy go through waivers from the injured-reserve list? That's terrible!" He really let me have it.

I really felt bad, because, number one, you never want to offend someone you think highly of and, number two, it really was kind of the rule of thumb in those days that you didn't do it. I kind of shrugged my shoulders and said, "Mike, I wish it were anybody else but you that was involved, but we are so darn desperate that we have to get players wherever we can get them."

"Well, he's going to be a good player for you," Mike said. "I can guarantee you that."

Steve stood only 5'9" and weighed 185 pounds, but he was an incredibly gifted athlete and an extremely good tackler. I remember returning from a jog one day and I noticed, as I walked down the tunnel into our stadium, a television crew at work on about the 40-yard line. They were filming Steve doing standing back flips for a commercial. He must have done about 20 while I was watching. The director would just say, "Okay, that's pretty good, but let's get another take." And Steve would do more. Rather than getting mad and saying, "What are you doing here with one of our most valuable players?" I just shook my head and walked away.

Then, there was our Bills basketball team, which would play charity games against teachers and civic groups at various high schools. Every once in a while, I would go with them and referee and just have some fun. Some of the most fun would be watching, right at the end of warm-ups, when 6'7" Pete Metzelaars, an All-American basketball player at Wabash College, would throw one off the backboard and Steve would come flying in and jam it—and the crowd would go wild.

Steve was more consistent in changing games than Devin Hester (who established himself as one of the game's best kick-returners during eight seasons with the Chicago Bears) because Steve would cause a fumble on a punt return or he would cause a fumble on a kickoff return or he would make a big return himself that would change a game or he would block a field goal. Steve did more game-changing things on special teams than any player I've ever seen, including Deion Sanders.

Sure enough, everything that Marv had said in that team meeting was driven home against the Steelers. The game was played on November 9, Veteran's Day weekend, which as anyone who has lived there knows is the unofficial (or maybe the official) start of winter in western New York.

It was nice and sunny at kickoff, and then the wind picked up to semi-gale force as the game went on. Neither team could throw the ball because the wind, gusting up to 40 miles per hour, was just too strong. So it became a day for running...and stopping the run...and making decisive plays on special teams.

We scored the game's first touchdown, in the opening quarter, but the extra-point attempt failed after the snap was blown off course. We reached the end zone again in the second quarter, and this time the PAT was good to give us a 13–0 lead. The Steelers came back with two third-quarter touchdowns, but wind-influenced blunders by holder/punter Harry Newsome didn't allow them to convert either PAT, and they trailed 13–12.

Steve Champlin, who headed up our stadium operations, had monitored the weather closely before the game. He advised Marv to be sure to take the wind in the first quarter so that the Steelers would be going into it in the fourth. But for some reason, the Steelers didn't call a timeout before a punt just before the end of the third quarter, their last with the end at their back. Therefore, Newsome had to kick into the teeth of a wind that our center, the late Kent Hull, would later say had more velocity than he had experienced during hurricanes in his native Mississippi.

Predictably, the ball traveled a mere 20 yards to the Pittsburgh 48. With the help of a running game that would produce 172 yards to the Steelers' 53, we proceeded to drive 36 yards to set the stage for Scott Norwood to kick a 29-yard field goal that secured our 16–12 victory.

Years and years later with the Colts, Tony Dungy and I and a few others were sitting around at dinner during the season and everybody was telling stories. Then, we started kidding Tony about how the players thought he had the ability to control the weather, because he had a direct pipeline to God.

"You know, there is something to that," I said. "Marv's first game against the Steelers ..." And Tony, who had been the Steelers' defensive coordinator at the time, finished the sentence, saying, "Yeah, we couldn't get the ball snapped and down on an extra point because the wind was blowing so hard. We outplayed you guys seven ways to Sunday, and we couldn't get the extra point because of the darn wind. Can you imagine that?"

I just laughed.

I would love to say that what happened against the Steelers that day was an omen and we would go on to win all or even most of our remaining six games. We didn't. We won only one more, which gave us exactly as many wins as we had through our first nine games.

That provided a clear reminder that Marv's presence alone wasn't going to be enough to turn the team around. We had to help him, and the best way to do that was to get more of the kind of players he was looking for.

7

Managing a Strike...
and Striking Gold

"Pro football doesn't build character, it reveals it."

—MARV LEVY

"When you win, say little. When you lose, say less."

—PAUL BROWN

AS SOON AS THE 1986 SEASON ENDED, I met with the scouts and coaches to evaluate the existing roster and begin the process of finding the kind of players we needed to win.

Knowing exactly what Marv Levy wanted, I was now in a position to be proactive rather than reactive. I was able to go to Norm Pollom, our scouting director, and to the scouts, and list the qualities that Marv sought in a player: someone who is smart, football savvy, is a hard worker, has a love for the game, will buy into what we're doing, is a solid citizen, and has a great work ethic. We weren't going to take a lot of chances on players who were character risks or work-ethic risks.

Leading up to the 1987 draft, the public outcry was, "The Bills need a wide receiver to make the most of Jim Kelly." When we had our first organizational meeting to discuss our approach to the draft, Marv said to Mr. Wilson, to me, and to the scouts the same exact thing he'd said to the media: "The best way to help Jim Kelly is to build a dominant defense."

On the outside, that was met with a resounding chorus of boos, but people inside the building were on board with it. We understood that defense was where we needed the most help and where the draft had the most talent. We understood that if we could improve significantly on that side of the ball, Jim and the rest of the offense would benefit from working with a shorter field and having less pressure to score.

Thanks to our 4–12 record, we had the third-overall pick of the draft, which figured to put us in good position to get a top defensive player. As we were finishing our board—our ranking of all of the prospects from one through about 350—Marv gave all of us explicit instructions regarding a highly touted defensive lineman from the University of Washington, Reggie Rogers, who had a history of off-field trouble.

"Take his name off the board," he said. "I don't want him. He's not our kind of player."

"Now, Marv, wait a minute," Norm said. "Reggie Rogers has a chance to be a Pro Bowl player for a long time." Norm was correct, ability-wise.

Marv wasn't budging. He banged the table, which I don't remember him doing very often. It was so out of character for him. Then he said, "I don't want Pro Bowl players. I want Super Bowl players."

I had gone out just before the draft to look at a lot of tape on Rogers and came away with a different opinion than Norm's. It had to do with work ethic. He was extremely talented, but he didn't play hard all of the time. He played hard only some of the time. I got what could be termed mixed reviews from some of his coaches at the University of Washington.

Now, no college coach is ever going to talk badly about one of his own kids, but what you want a college coach to say is, "You should take this guy and don't look back. He is going to help you win a championship just like he helped us win a championship." And if the college coach knows you and knows what you stand for, he'll say, "Listen, this guy is your kind of guy, this guy is going to thrive in your program, this is the guy you want." When I was with the Colts, college coaches that I knew used to tell me, "He's got the horseshoe stamped on him."

I didn't hear anything like that about Rogers. What I heard was, "Boy, he's got a lot of ability and when he puts it all together, he can be a dominant player." That's not what you necessarily want to hear, especially with a high pick.

For the first time really in my career, I was responsible for managing a draft. Fortunately, I had learned a lot from studying one of the great general managers in the history of the game, the late Jim Finks (with the Vikings, Bears, and Saints) and I learned a ton from Kay Stephenson and Norm in terms of draft management—knowing who might go where, how to put together intelligence that informed that knowledge, how to differentiate between what was rumor and fact, how to determine which teams were positioning themselves where.

Intelligence is gleaned from three sources: that which is readily available in the media; that which you acquire from human sources, meaning people who are very, very knowledgeable and in a lot of cases "plugged in"; and, finally, that which you can determine based on what you know from sources one and two.

The first thing you do when you're preparing for a draft is put together a list of all of the other teams' needs. In the old days, I did that on a couple of sheets of 8½x11 paper. These days, the pro personnel department of virtually every team produces a Needs Book, something I believe we were among the first to do in Indianapolis. That was the brainchild of my son, Chris, who was our assistant GM. That book is very closely held, circulated only to the head coach, general manager, scouting director, and owner. You study it to determine what the landscape is.

Of course, in today's world, every team will have made some moves in free agency, disgorging players and adding players from other teams. Therefore, the mosaic of what teams were at the end of the previous season is not what they are as you approach the draft. You would use the needs book as the starting point, but then you would seek updated information from what was readily available in the media.

In Indianapolis, we refined the process to the point where every football decision maker every day would receive a clips package containing articles written by the beat reporters of the other teams in the league. In the days before Twitter and live coverage of the pre-draft college Pro Days, that was how we kept an eye on which players were visiting which teams, which players teams had worked out, and things of that nature. There would be some significant information that would come out of those reports. For example, if the head coach with an offensive background went to a particular defensive player's workout, and the defensive coordinator wasn't with him, that might be a smokescreen or he might be looking at someone else. If a particular defensive player was working out and the defensive coordinator and the position coach were in attendance, you could be pretty sure they had strong interest in him.

As time went on and the amount of available information continued to grow, simply reading the clips wasn't enough anymore. So Chris would assign certain teams to a college scout or a member of the pro-personnel staff to update us every day on what they were doing in advance of the draft. For instance, when you find out the Jets have signed Michael Vick as a free agent, as they did during the 2014 off-season, you ask: "Does that mean they're going to be in the market for a quarterback?" At the end of the day, we would call in the pro-personnel staffer we assigned to the Jets and ask him how he saw the situation. And he might say, "Vick's going to be number two behind Geno Smith. Maybe he's going to be 1A. They've said on numerous occasions that they wouldn't pass up a stellar quarterback in the draft, but I would tell you it's probably not a priority." That's the kind of human intelligence you get from someone who is an expert on that particular team.

I had those same duties during my days working on the pro-personnel side. You were expected to be an expert on the teams that you covered. You knew that a move a team made in one direction would beget two or three other moves in the other direction. For example, when the Jacksonville Jaguars made multiple free-agent moves on defense during the 2014 off-season, if you were an expert at watching how they were constructing their team, you would say the odds were pretty good that they were going to go offense in the draft, as they did by picking a quarterback in the first round (Blake Bortles of Central Florida), two wide receivers in the second (Marqise Lee of USC and Allen Robinson of Penn State), and a guard in the third (Brandon Linder of Miami).

In addition, when assistant coaches go to on-campus workouts and to the Combine, they talk with other assistant coaches. They are, perhaps, the most talkative group of people in any business on earth. I always cautioned our assistant coaches with a phrase that Dom Capers taught me and taught our staff in Carolina: "Give a little, get a lot." If you're good at it, you can give a little information about your team while getting a lot about someone else's.

David Caldwell, the Jaguars' GM who scouted for us in Indianapolis, did a magnificent job keeping everybody thinking they had no intention of taking Blake Bortles. And that was our approach, too. Do little in public view and say less. Stay with your process in-house. Don't give out any information whatsoever. Don't give out any signals whatsoever. And don't try to blow smoke because, sooner or later, people will figure it out.

That didn't mean I refused all calls from media members. But the ones with whom I spoke knew enough not to ask me about our team because they knew I wasn't going to tell them what we were doing. They would ask me about what I saw the people around us doing. And they get what you're going to do from other people around you.

There were members of our scouting and coaching staffs in Buffalo, Carolina, and Indianapolis who were great intelligence gatherers. They weren't information gatherers; they were intelligence gatherers. You would learn very quickly who those guys were, and you could rely on them. If there was something that cropped up, you could say, "Okay, let's talk to Chink Sengel"—a longtime Bills scout who had played for Bear Bryant at Kentucky. Chink was a legend in the scouting world. To say he was well connected is the understatement of the century.

I always used the last two weeks before the draft for what I called "draft management time." There's a big difference between setting your board and managing the draft. As part of the draft management, I would go through our plan for a week with only a couple of others from the college-scouting staff so that we had a clear picture of what we thought would take place. After that, we would bring in the head coach and our pro personnel director and start going through scenarios. The conversation would go something like this:

"Here's what we think Dallas is going to do in the first round. Do we feel good about that?"

"No, not so good. I don't think the guy that they're talking about drafting in the first round is going to be there."

"So they're possible trade-up candidates."

We would then mark them down in the "trade" column on our board. And we would go through all 32 teams trying to pinpoint who might be in the trade-up market, who might be in the trade-down market, and which players they were targeting that fit their needs.

When we were at Indianapolis, we asked our computer people to take five mock drafts done by analysts in the media—such as the ones from my ESPN colleagues, Mel Kiper Jr. and Todd McShay—and give us the first two rounds based on the average of their picks. This was done on the assumption that they were using information gathered from talking with people from other NFL teams to come up with their choices, so we saw it as a way of looking into how other clubs saw the draft unfolding. We took a tongue-in-cheek approach by calling it the "Guru Board."

You know everybody's not telling them everything, but the fact of the matter is you're getting bits and pieces of intelligence that, if put together in a cohesive form, gives you an interesting picture. You turn over every rock.

Two days before the draft, our work would be buttoned up and done. If we hadn't made a final decision on our order of players we would select with our first-round pick, we would leave it open. If somebody wanted to sleep on it, if somebody wanted to ruminate on it, if somebody wanted to discuss it, no problem. Otherwise, we were locked in.

In the 1998 draft, we knew we wanted to make Penn State's Shane Conlan, who would be a sure-fire starter at inside linebacker, our first choice, but we were confident we could select him lower than the third slot. Our plan was to trade down and, in the process, acquire an extra second-round pick with the goal of drafting two starting cornerbacks in the second round. We put out feelers before the draft for trades. And, bingo, we got a bite from the Houston Oilers, who had the eighth pick, where we still expected Shane to be available. The Oilers wanted to move up to No. 3 to get Alonzo Highsmith, a running back from Miami.

The day before the draft, Mr. Wilson came to town and I explained to him what we were going to do.

"Are you sure we're going to be okay with this?" Mr. Wilson asked.

"Yes, as far as I can tell," I said. "I think we're in good position because I don't see anybody else taking an inside linebacker before we do."

We completed the trade with the Oilers, who gave us a second-round pick for the swap of first-rounders. Then, an hour or two before the draft began, another trade was announced: Cleveland worked out a deal with San Diego for the fifth-overall pick of the draft. The Browns had jumped in front of us by giving up outside linebacker Chip Banks, their first-round pick (24th overall) and a second-round pick for the Chargers' first- and second-round choices.

Marv and I looked at each other and said, "Uh-oh! Uh-oh!"

Mr. Wilson was upset.

"Did you guys know about this?" he asked heatedly.

"No, sir," I said. "We did not know anything about it."

"How could we not know anything about it?"

"The Browns did a great job. It's [then-GM] Ernie Accorsi. He did a great job of disguising his intentions, and he pulled the trigger now."

We began to talk about whether we should trade ahead of the Browns. After much hand-wringing—and I was probably the chief hand-wringer—we finally settled down. Marv said, "We made a good decision, we made a good trade. The odds are with us. We don't have to go up." We ultimately concluded that the Browns had made the trade so that they would be able to get Rod Woodson, a cornerback from Purdue and a future Hall of Famer, and not Shane Conlan. We also decided that if we were wrong and the Browns took Shane, then we would get Woodson, whom we liked as well.

The draft began and we were sweating as we watched the television. Tampa Bay started it off by selecting Miami quarterback Vinny Testaverde. After that, the Colts picked Cornelius Bennett, an outside linebacker from Alabama. As expected, the Oilers used the third-overall choice on Highsmith. Green Bay then went with Brent Fullwood, a running back from Auburn. Now, it was the Browns' turn...and they chose a linebacker, alright...Mike Junkin, an outside linebacker from Duke.

We were ecstatic. "Whoa-ho, we got our guy!" we shouted. We knew that St. Louis and Detroit, the teams picking sixth and seventh, respectively, would not pick Conlan. And they didn't. The Rams selected Kelly Stouffer, a quarterback from Colorado State, and the Lions landed Reggie Rogers.

And Marv's instincts about Shane and Reggie Rogers were also right on the money. Shane would start on our first three Super Bowl teams, and would also appear in three Pro Bowls. The Detroit Lions wound up making Rogers the seventh-overall pick. However, he only played six games as a rookie because of a series of emotional problems that led to him spending time in counseling.

Rogers' second season ended after only five games when his car struck another vehicle, killing three teenagers. Rogers was found to have a blood-alcohol level of 0.15, almost twice the legal limit of 0.08. He also suffered a broken neck, and the Lions waived him the following summer. A year later, he was convicted of vehicular homicide and sentenced to 16 months in prison. Afterward, he had brief stints with the Bills and Tampa Bay Buccaneers, and was out of football completely by the end of the 1992 season. Sadly, Rogers was found dead at his home in Seattle in October 2013.

We then made a trade with the Buccaneers, giving up a fourth-round pick, to move up in the second round, and that allowed us to get Wisconsin cornerback Nate Odomes. Nate would become another fixture on those Super Bowl teams. We used our other second-round selection on Texas Tech cornerback Roland Mitchell, although he didn't turn out to be as good as we had hoped.

But the rest of that draft did give us more of the solid pieces that would go a long way toward helping to round out the sort of team Marv wanted to build: fullback Jamie Mueller (Benedictine) in the third round, defensive end Leon Seals (Jackson State) in the fourth, tight end Keith McKeller (Jacksonville State) in the ninth, and last—but certainly not least—6'6" 352-pound offensive tackle Howard "House" Ballard (Alabama A&M) in the 11th.

Considering that Howard would go on to play in four Super Bowls and two Pro Bowls in six seasons with the Bills, his selection was one of the greatest draft coups of all time. Through some of his close contacts on the Alabama A&M coaching staff and research of league rules, Norm Pollom had found out that "House" was draft eligible, but intended to go back to school for another year and, therefore, wouldn't be available to us or any other NFL team until 1988. So we waited and waited until the 11th round of what was then a 12-round draft, when Norm finally said, "Go ahead and pull the trigger!" Howard stuck with his plan to return to school and then, at the end of the season, we signed him for the equivalent of a fourth-round contract, which still turned out to be an incredible bargain for the kind of talent he possessed.

"House" was the right tackle on a line that included a great left tackle in Will Wolford, a highly talented guard in Jim Ritcher, and a tremendous center in Kent Hull, whom we signed from the United States Football League in 1986. With the USFL breaking up, there were lots of players either to whom we had rights or players who were simply free to sign with the NFL. Hull, who had been with the New Jersey Generals, fell into the latter category. And he was someone we thought would be a perfect addition to the Bills.

No NFL team had drafted Kent, because when he was coming out of Mississippi State, he weighed all of about 245 pounds. But he joined the Generals and was an instant starter. I'll bet he didn't weigh 270 pounds then, but he was quick and he was aggressive and he was tough. You could tell that he was still growing, that there was going to be more growth potential for him, but his quickness and his toughness jumped off the film at you. Kent was a big reason why Herschel Walker broke the pro football record for single-season rushing yards with 2,411 in 1985 with the Generals.

The USFL background that Hank Bullough and I shared made us well aware of Kent and other players from that league. Hank and I spoke with Mr. Wilson and we explained who Kent was. We explained that we thought he had an opportunity to be a great center in the NFL. We told Mr. Wilson that the money he would command would equal that of a second-round draft choice.

He gave us the go-ahead to sign him, and we did—right at the time we signed Jim Kelly. Nobody knew Kent Hull at all and, of course, everybody knew Jim Kelly. Kent liked to tell a story that while Jim rode to his first training camp practice in the back of a limousine, Kent rode in the back of an equipment van.

But as the team grew and progressed and went on to achieve great things, the two of them ended up being the cornerstones and leaders not only of the offense, but the entire team. Kent died far too young, but his legacy of toughness will live on forever. He was John Wayne. Or, as someone said at Kent's funeral, "John Wayne wishes he was as tough as Kent Hull."

Essentially, most of the guts of those four Bills Super Bowl teams came from the drafts of 1985, 1986, and 1987. In '85, we got Bruce Smith, obviously, but we also picked up a Hall of Fame wide receiver in Andre Reed and a tremendous backup quarterback in Frank Reich.

The selection of Frank was necessitated by the fact that Jim Kelly was in the USFL and Joe Ferguson, who had been the incumbent quarterback, was near the end of his career and wanted to move on from Buffalo. It also involved much more drama than any of us anticipated.

I first became aware of Frank while on a scouting trip to the University of Maryland. The Terrapins' head coach was Bobby Ross, who had been the special teams coach for the Chiefs when I was scouting for them.

"You really ought to take a hard look at our quarterback, Frank Reich," Bobby said. "He's an exceptionally smart guy, he's a great leader. He doesn't have the arm talent that Boomer Esiason had, but he's absolutely a clutch guy, and he's exactly what you guys are looking for."

I looked at Frank's game film, and it was very impressive. Frank, of course, had led the greatest comeback in college history when Maryland beat the University of Miami Hurricanes. When I returned to Buffalo, and I told Norm Pollom and Kay Stephenson, "I think Frank Reich is really a guy that has a chance to be pretty darn good for us."

They agreed, and we had a consensus that he was someone we should draft, but we thought we could probably get him in the third round. He was not a household name and there wasn't nearly the detailed background information about draft prospects then that there is now.

We were in the draft room, and Mr. Wilson, who was getting ready to leave for Buffalo from Detroit, called. Norm told me to answer, and Mr. Wilson said, "We've got to take Frank Reich in the second round."

"I'll pass that information along," I said. "But what makes you think that?

"It's what I heard," said Mr. Wilson, who had people around him who studied the draft.

I shared what Mr. Wilson said with Norm and Kay. We had two picks in the second round, and one of them was earmarked for Mark Traynowicz, an offensive guard from Nebraska. Norm was absolutely sold on him. Norm was fine with using a later pick on Frank, per Mr. Wilson's orders, but he told me we couldn't make the pick unless we reached Frank by phone first to make certain he hadn't signed with the Baltimore Stars, who owned his territorial rights in the USFL and were still smarting from the fact we had already signed Bruce Smith.

I tried and I tried and tried, but I couldn't reach Frank. Just before he would board his flight to Buffalo, Mr. Wilson called again.

"Did you draft Reich?" he asked.

"No," I said. "We can't get hold of him. I don't know where he is. And we can't draft him if the Baltimore Stars have already signed him."

"Well, find him!" Mr. Wilson said pointedly.

I resumed my pursuit of Frank by phone. Meanwhile, as Mr. Wilson was in the air, we used both of our second-round choices on Traynowicz and receiver Chris Burkett from Jackson State. I finally tracked down Frank and discovered he had not signed with the Stars. Our hope at that point was that he would still be around for our pick at the top of the third round.

The moment Mr. Wilson walked into the draft room, he asked, "Did you find Reich?"

"Yeah, but it was too late for us to get him in the second round," I said.

Mr. Wilson was upset.

As we sat at the long table in the draft room, Mr. Wilson didn't say a word to me. I made certain I was sitting at the far end—as far away from everyone as possible. The draft had reached the bottom of the second round, and as each name was called, I sank deeper and deeper into the chair, to the point where I was almost under the table, as my career flashed before my eyes.

With the draft having reached the bottom of the second round, I heard someone say in the background, "Oh, man, Reich's likely to go right here." It felt like someone had just stabbed me in the spine. I literally thought to myself, *I'm just going to get up and walk out, pack my office, and leave. If he's picked one or two picks away from us, it's over.*

Now, with me slouched so far down in the chair that my head was barely over the table, came the final pick just in front of ours, by New England. It seemed as if an hour passed as the Patriots contemplated their choice. When it was announced the Patriots selected Ben Thomas, a defensive end from Auburn, I leaped out of my chair and screamed, "Ahhh! Thank God!"

Mr. Wilson then looked at me with that wry "Ralph smile" of his and said, "You know, sometimes it's better to be lucky than good."

Frank, of course, turned out to be the best backup quarterback in Bills history and arguably among the best in the NFL history.

In '86, we added Will Wolford, who would begin his career at offensive guard but soon become a dominant left tackle; defensive lineman Mark Pike, who would go on to become one of the game's very best at kick coverage; and tight end Butch Rolle, who would prove to be a virtual touchdown machine in the red zone.

At that time, there was no unfettered free agency, so you had to build your team through the draft, and we were doing exactly that. If you were concentrating, as we were, on getting guys who were really solid people that you could count on, we were able to put together not only a team for the ages but a team that was perfectly suited to the way Marv coached. His coaching style was always positive and always focused on fundamentals and what it took to win.

Marv believed that rather than doing a lot of things in a mediocre fashion, you should do a few in an extraordinary fashion. And do them in a way that eliminates fatigue, both mental and physical, on the part of the player. What that meant was that the players were going to have less time in practice in pads and on the field, more time in the classroom, and, frankly, more time for rest and recovery.

That was revolutionary. Not many people believed in that back then. When you really stop and think about it, in the NFL, the only coaches who approached it that way were Marv, Bud Grant, and Bill Walsh. At first, media and fans didn't grasp the concept. They would derisively refer to the Bills' training camp as "Club Marv," where the quarterbacks were able to skip lunch and play nine holes between practices. It was only after seeing us become a consistent Super Bowl contender that they realized the benefits of Marv's philosophy.

Marv got the idea from Bud Wilkinson, who won three national championships as head coach at the University of Oklahoma. When Marv was a young assistant coach, he spent a whole year listening to Bud speak at coaching clinics around the country. At one point, Bud said to him, "Every time I give a talk, you're in the front row."

Marv introduced himself and they became fast friends. The main point that Bud impressed upon him was this: "Given a choice between an overworked team and an underworked team, I will take the underworked team every time because I want them ready to go and give maximum effort on game day."

Therefore, it was incumbent on the players to use their time wisely and properly and dedicate themselves to the job at hand. If you have players with the characteristics Marv sought, you don't have to use physical punishment as discipline for them. You don't have to give them 50 reps in practice because they understand what they're supposed to do in 10. You don't have to preach to them every day about what it takes to be a good citizen. The players know that and they react positively to it. The more you simplify things for them, the more confident they'll be. And the more confident they are, the better they'll play.

I can't tell you how many times I've heard Marv say: "A prepared team is a confident team. A confident team is a motivated team." He always talked about preparation. Preparation is what makes a team confident. Preparation is what motivates a team. And Marv knew he had the players who didn't need to have pep talks, although you'd pay to hear one of his. The whole idea was if you have these kinds of players, you can prepare them in such a way that you get to Sunday raring to go physically, mentally, emotionally, because you haven't beaten the living daylights out of them in training camp or in the practice week.

Sometimes finding them was a case of trial and error. You're never going to be right 100 percent of the time. You're going to miss. The best of us in this business bat about .565 in player selection. And that's based on 24 years of evaluating drafts.

We knew we had a great player in Bruce Smith, but he did have some rough edges that Marv took steps to eliminate early on. Bruce was suspended for the first four games of the 1988 season for violating the NFL's substance-abuse policy. In 12 games that season, he had 11 sacks, which was pretty impressive, as were the 12 he had in the same number of games in 1987 and the 15 he had in 1986 after finishing with only six-and-a-half as a rookie.

Yet there seemed little doubt that he could be a far more dominant defensive end, capable of historic achievements, if he were only more disciplined and focused on maximizing his immense talent and more committed to the whole-is-greater-than-the-sum-of-the-parts mentality. Marv was at the end of his rope. He believed the time had come to deliver the clearest message possible to Bruce that it was time to shape up.

After the '88 season, Marv called Bruce in for a critical meeting. He asked me to be a part of it as well, but only to watch and listen. Marv would do the talking.

"Bruce, this is a turning point for you," Marv began. "You can be one of the greatest players in the history of the game or you can fail. Sack numbers aren't everything; it's what you contribute to the team, it's how you prepare, it's how you take care of your own body, it's how you conduct yourself.

"Now, this is not an idle threat. Unless you improve and unless you show us what you are capable of, I will not hesitate to trade you."

It was a Marv that Bruce had never seen before, and I had seen only briefly and intermittently during my career. But I didn't have any doubts that Marv meant what he said. When Marv makes a decision along those lines, he has done it for good and principled reasons, because he's the most accommodating of people. When Marv's not accommodating, it means that he has made up his mind and that isn't going to change.

Bruce was shocked by what he heard.

"I don't want to be traded," he said. "I love it here. I think we can achieve great things here, and I want to be a part of that."

Marv told Bruce that he wanted him to work with Rusty Jones, our strength-and-conditioning coach, and get his weight down and stamina to the point where he could perform "at a hundred percent" on every down.

"I want you to work on your technique," Marv continued. "It isn't just rushing the passer from the outside. You know you have the play the run, too. You have to do all the things that we need you to do in order for you to be a force."

Bruce was shaken, but I could tell he was immediately on board and very much wanted to be with the program. He proved that beyond a shadow of a doubt in the ensuing years. I would point to that meeting and the tutelage of our excellent defensive line coach, Ted Cottrell—who would eventually become the Bills' defensive coordinator and later work in the same capacity with the New York

Jets, Minnesota Vikings, and San Diego Chargers—as two of the biggest reasons Bruce is in the Hall of Fame.

The 1987 season would prove to be as important as any on the path to becoming a playoff contender. We took two major forward steps while dealing with a huge backward step in between: a work stoppage by the players.

We had opened the season by losing to the Jets, but won our second game, against Houston, after storming back in the fourth quarter. It was a victory that energized our entire team. That is, all but one guy...running back Greg Bell, who had been taken out of the game because of a mistake. As we staged this marvelous comeback—scoring three touchdowns in the final 8:37—everybody was up off the bench screaming and hollering and waving towels...with one exception. Greg was just sitting there, with his head down.

Although we knew NFL players would be going on strike two days later and that the league mandated that all teams continue with the regular season with "replacement" players, everyone was on cloud nine in the locker room. Marv made a little speech, saying, "That's the way to stay tough, believe in yourselves, keep fighting. We will see you all tomorrow morning."

As Marv and I walked together into a small dressing room just inside the entrance to the locker room, Marv said to me, "We need to do something with Greg Bell."

"I hear you," I said, realizing it would be something that would have to wait until after the strike. And no one had any idea how long the strike would last.

That was the bad news. The good news was that in a practice leading up to the Houston game, as our offense was working against the scout-team defense, I witnessed what I believed was evidence that our program had turned the corner. A rookie made a dumb mistake that would have been a penalty in a game, and a few of our linebackers who were kneeling on the sideline—Scott Radecic, Shane

Conlan, and Darryl Talley—yelled in unison, "Don't be dumb and don't be dirty!"

I couldn't wait to share the story with Marv after practice.

"You know what?" I told him. "They're on board. They've bought in. They hear you. We are on our way. They know what it takes to win."

"That's great," Marv said with a laugh. "We're getting there, we're getting there."

The next day, Marv and I met with the team for what would be the last time until the end of the strike. Once they left the building, they would not be allowed back as long as they were still striking. Marv and I remembered all too well the nightmarish experience from the strike of 1982, when he was the Chiefs' coach and I was one of their scouts. Marv and I had decided that while we were going to do whatever the league told us to do to the absolute letter of the law, we were not going to make enemies of the players as had happened in 1982.

The '82 strike lasted more than two months and caused the 16-game schedule to be reduced to nine games. We split the first two games, and then the strike came. After the strike, we lost five of our last seven. The players were completely divided and distracted. By the time Marv got them back, it was too late and we lost our jobs.

I said to Marv, "You set the stage and I will talk about the specifics because you shouldn't have to get involved in labor stuff; that's not your job."

Marv proceeded to talk about what a great victory it had been against the Oilers and how bright the future looked for the team once the strike was over. Then, he called me up to explain to the players what the coming days would bring and to try to put to rest some of the many concerns they had in connection with our signing other players to take their place during the work stoppage.

"Labor situations always end; let's start there," I said. "No matter how contentious they may be, no matter how much incendiary language you may hear, no matter how much table-pounding one side or the other does publicly, eventually they all end. And when they end, we need to make sure that we are together as a team.

"We can't let any outside force, be it management or labor—it doesn't matter whom—destroy what we showed the world we have yesterday. So, along those lines, we're forced to put a replacement team on the field, and we are going to do that, but we're not going to give them guaranteed contracts. And unlike what you may have heard, they are by and large not going to wear your numbers and they aren't going to use this locker room because you earned the right to be here, fair and square.

"You are our team. You are the Buffalo Bills. You are the team that we are proud to be associated with, and the fans are so proud of the way you played yesterday. So when this ultimately ends, I want you to come back, and Marv wants you to come back as a group that is every bit as together as you were yesterday and let's not let any of this outside stuff—which ultimately will be settled by others—get in the way of what we are here to accomplish. Whatever we do, let's do together and remember that whatever is said or done, you are our team and we will be back in this locker room together, and we are going to win championships together."

They did stick together and we put the worst replacement team in the league on the field because we didn't skirt the rules. We didn't go sign players right at the end of training camp, in anticipation of the strike. We didn't have replacement players practicing on some secret field somewhere. Our approach was that guys like Jim Kelly, Steve Tasker, Bruce Smith, Darryl Talley, Nate Odomes, Andre Reed, and Shane Conlan were our team and that's who we cared about. If we lost some games during the replacement period, that would be okay. We would live with that.

At the start of the season, we were given our marching orders by Jack Donlan, head of the NFL Management Council, that included the following strictures: "You may not contact players until the strike is called...you may not work players out unless they're being worked out for the the existing team...you may not sign players to futures contracts...you may not sign any guaranteed contracts whatsoever." The NFL Management Council didn't want teams to be exposed to possible sanctions from a federal court. The strategy of the players' union was to get through federal court what it couldn't attain through collective bargaining, and we didn't want to be the cause of any such action against us or the league as a whole.

Not all clubs shared our by-the-book approach. Three weeks before the strike, Bob Ferguson, our director of player personnel and the man in charge of finding replacement players for us, came to me and say, "Listen, there's a team that has a full squad practicing at an off-site location...there's another team that's signing up everybody that's been in training camp with them; they're signing guys to future contracts after they cut them to get to the final 53. We need to do something to try to keep up with them."

"No, we're not going to do it," I said. I knew I was making his life miserable, but we were going to play by the rules. Period.

It was the "real" Bills team that was important, not the replacement team, which was dubbed by the media as the "Counterfeit Bills."

So when the strike began, we had no players under contract. The guys that we had wanted to bring in had been signed elsewhere, because other NFL teams weren't playing by the rules. They were giving out guaranteed contracts left and right. That forced us to go back to a list of guys that were cut really early in training camp, or who had been cut from the Canadian Football League, or had not been in any professional league at all.

We signed graduate students, undergraduate students, and guys working various jobs ranging from bartenders to policemen to truck drivers. It really was a very, very low level of talent compared to the National Football League and when I look back on it now, how you could promulgate these rules and expect to put a product on the field that fans would accept as legitimate is beyond me. Nevertheless, we went out and played.

Before our first strike game, against the Indianapolis Colts, we were given instructions by the NFL Management Council to make sure that there would be a heavy police presence around the bus, and that the teams not stay in hotels in Buffalo because of the presumption that Buffalo was such a strong union town and that there might be backlash from other unions. We spent a lot of time developing strategies and security practices to make sure that both teams were safe. As a matter of fact, we took our team to a hotel about 30 miles away, something we would never do under normal circumstances.

Our varsity did a little egg-throwing and cat-calling at a bus carrying the replacement players, but that was the worst of it. There were other places around the league where it was more virulent and violent. There were questions as to whether ushers, concession workers, or other unionized employees, including those who worked for the television networks, would cross the picket line. Most did, so the games went on without major disruption, but they were artistically awful. That was true even for the best teams, such as San Francisco and Washington. As a matter of fact, the 49ers ran the Wishbone offense, a great move by Bill Walsh.

But the atmosphere around the stadiums was toxic and the games were not well attended. Attendance for the Colts game was 9,860 in 80,000-seat Rich Stadium. It was the second-smallest crowd in franchise history. Veteran quarterback Gary Hogeboom decided to cross the picket line, and he threw two touchdown passes to another regular player, Walter Murray, on the way to a 47–6 Indianapolis victory. We lost our second game, too, at New England.

Our third game with replacement players was at home against the New York Giants. Although the late Gene Upshaw, the head of the NFL Players Association, called off the strike before the game, the regular players would be locked out because they didn't report before a 1:00 PM deadline on the Wednesday before the slate of games.

Talk was circulating that the real Giants were planning to come in as a team so I called someone at the NFL Management Council in New York and said, "You need to let me know if the Giants are coming in as a team because if they are, then our guys will come in. If they don't come in as a team, then our guys won't come in. But our guys aren't going to let the Giants come in as a team and beat up on our replacement players. Have they come in? Have they come in?"

The guy at the other end of the phone said, "How the hell do I know? I'm on Park Avenue."

As it turned out, only one of the real Giants came in. But he was a pretty significant one: Lawrence Taylor, their future Hall of Fame linebacker. Mr. Wilson then called me and said, "Oh my God, how are we going to block Lawrence Taylor?"

"I don't know," I said, laughing.

"He'll kill someone! We've got to do something."

We were kind of laughing and crying at the same time. We talked about it, and I think that it was Fergy who came up with the idea of bringing back Will Grant—a scrappy veteran center we had released in 1985 and who subsequently joined the Seattle Seahawks in 1986— for one game. The plan would be to move Will to tackle and have him hold Taylor on every play. There would be a catch, though. Will insisted on a guaranteed contract for the entire year. I called Mr. Wilson to see if he approved.

"Do we have to keep him on the team for the whole season?" Mr. Wilson asked.

"No, we can put him on injured reserve, but you're going to have to pay him while he's here."

"Okay, do it. It's preferable to Lawrence Taylor maiming someone."

We signed Will and told him, "Whatever you've got to do, hold Lawrence Taylor every play. Whatever you've got to do! If you get a penalty every play, forget about it; we don't care."

The game sold out well in advance, but that was largely the result of Giants fans from upstate New York, unable to get a seat at Giants Stadium, buying up a lot of tickets. The Giants were coming off of a Super Bowl victory against Denver...but those weren't the Giants who would be coming to Rich Stadium, because George Young took the same approach we did. Consequently, all but 15,737 of those 80,000 sold seats were empty.

It didn't take long for the game to deteriorate into a comedy of errors. The teams combined for nine fumbles (we lost four), five interceptions, five missed field goals, 42 incomplete passes, and 26 penalties for 258 yards. It was just awful.

Many of those yellow flags were holding calls on Will, who did exactly as we instructed. He was just tackling Lawrence, who played tight end as well as linebacker, and because he wasn't in top condition, he was worn out by the third quarter. Will was grabbing his jersey, grabbing his pants, doing everything he could to keep him off of our quarterback, Willie Totten, whose claim to fame was that he threw passes to Jerry Rice at Mississippi Valley State. And somehow we were surviving.

With 16 seconds left in regulation, the Giants had a chance to win the game with a chip-shot field goal, but their kicker missed it, sending the game to overtime. We got the ball, and our guy kicked the winning field goal.

I got onto the elevator after the game with George Young, the Giants' general manager, and Wellington Mara, their owner, who was just ashen.

"Look at it this way," I said to Mr. Mara, "you were part of the greatest game ever played between the Colts and the Giants in 1958 and now you have been in the worst game ever played."

George and Wellington just laughed.

I walked through the locker room to thank the players. I did more thanking than congratulating, because this was the end of the line for most of them. The vast majority of the replacements throughout the NFL wouldn't play another down of professional football, so this was an experience that they would hang on to for the rest of their lives.

One player actually asked me, "Do we get to keep our jerseys?"

"Yes, you do," I said. "Absolutely you do."

Our first game with regular players was a dramatic 34–31 overtime victory at Miami. That did plenty to help put the strike behind us. But what really helped turn things around was when Bob Ferguson walked into my office the Thursday before our next game. Bob said he was hearing that outside linebacker Cornelius Bennett, whom the Colts had made the second-overall pick of the '87 draft but were unable to sign, was available in a trade.

"Wow!" I said.

I had scouted Cornelius at Alabama and I was head-over-heels in love with his talent. I think that he is one of the most dynamic college players that I have ever seen. He was compared, and I think rightly so, to Lawrence Taylor in terms of his impact on the game as a 3-4 outside linebacker. We had Bruce Smith on one side and no real game-changing rusher on the other. If you have two rushers who can win one-on-one against anybody, then you really have a chance to be great, so we were trying to find one. We'd had the third-overall choice that year, and we didn't think we would have a shot at him. And we didn't, because after the Buccaneers selected quarterback Vinny Testaverde at No. 1, the Colts grabbed Cornelius with the next pick. We then traded down to No. 8, where we grabbed the best inside linebacker of the draft in Shane Conlan.

"Do you think it's a good source?" I asked Fergy of his information about the Colts' desire to trade Bennett. "Well," Fergy said, "there's only one way to find out: call Jim Irsay."

Jim was the vice president and general manager of the Colts, who were owned by his father, Bob. I called Jim and asked if the rumor was true.

"Yeah, that's true," he said. "You want in?"

"What's the asking price?"

"Two ones, for an opener."

"Okay, let me get back to you."

I called Mr. Wilson, who told me to run it past Marv Levy and if Marv was okay with it, we could begin negotiations. When I informed Marv of the Colts' asking price, he was a little taken aback but gave me his blessing to proceed.

I called back Jim and he asked what else we could offer besides the two first-round picks. Without hesitation, I said, "Greg Bell."

"That's interesting," Jim said. "What's the problem there?"

"Marv has sort of lost faith in him and it's just not the right fit. He's still a good player, by and large a decent guy, but he's just not happy here and it's the wrong fit."

It was then that Jim told me that he had a deal working with the Los Angeles Rams and that we might be the "ideal third party." He went back to the Rams and told them we were willing to move Greg to Indianapolis and then asked if they were interested in trading their excellent running back, Eric Dickerson, to the Colts in return for Bell and a combination of draft choices from Indianapolis and Buffalo. They said they were, setting in motion a blockbuster deal for the ages.

Soon thereafter, John Shaw, the Rams' de facto president (before he officially assumed that title in 1994), called me and talked at some length about Bell. I told him, "He still can play, he's a talent. A change of scenery is probably a good thing for him."

The negotiations continued through the next day and night. The Minnesota Vikings had tried to get into the mix, but they never could get enough traction to really be a player. Their general manager, Mike Lynn, subsequently told me that he had gone to the movies and was never able to make his best offer. I also found out later that the Vikings' failure to get involved in our deal was the impetus for their acquiring Herschel Walker from the Dallas Cowboys two years later for five players and six draft picks (that became running back Emmitt Smith, defensive tackle Russell Maryland, cornerback Kevin Smith, and safety Darren Woodson) that sparked the Cowboys' winning three Super Bowls in the 1990s.

We negotiated late into Friday night, and after going back and forth, the asking price for Cornelius was Greg Bell, our first-round pick in 1988, our first-round pick in 1989, and our second-rounder in '89. The Colts then planned to ship Bell, the three draft choices, running back Owen Gill, their own first- and second-round picks in '88, and their second-round selection in '89 to the Rams for Dickerson. I initially balked at us having to give up our second-pick in '89, but Jim told me the Rams wouldn't do the deal without it.

"Okay, let me run it by Marv and Mr. Wilson and I'll call you back," I said.

Marv thought the price was too steep.

"But, Marv, it's for Cornelius Bennett," I said.

"No!"

"Look, do you want to win the trade or do you want to win the Super Bowl? Because that's what this is about. It's important to make a good trade, but it's also important that we get a player that we believe is a total, complete difference maker for us."

"But don't you think it's too much?"

"No, I really don't. I respectfully disagree with you. I think that this is as far as we go, but you've got to pay what you've got to pay. This is maybe a once-in-a-lifetime opportunity. This is a great, great player."

"Well, alright, but no more dickering. Call Irsay back and tell him that if that isn't good enough, then we are out. No more dickering!"

I then filled in Mr. Wilson, and he wanted to know what it was going to cost to sign Bennett, who had already refused to come to terms with one team. I told him it would be a king's ransom. Mr. Wilson also wanted to know if there would be ramifications with the contracts of Jim Kelly and Bruce Smith, and I said there wouldn't.

"But it's going to be in that market," I said. "And, by the way, he's that good a player."

You need difference makers. That's the coin of the realm. If you don't have difference makers, there is very little likelihood that you are ever going to be a championship team. Difference makers come along very rarely. Think about it: how many pass-rushing outside linebackers have come along since Cornelius Bennett who really could be called difference makers? Clay Matthews immediately comes to mind. Willie McGinest, Kevin Greene, Derrick Thomas, Aldon Smith? So there is always a premium for difference makers, whether it's draft choices or the cash you spend in free agency. Sometimes they don't work out, but they're obvious to the naked eye. That's why they carry a heavy price.

And to Ralph Wilson's everlasting credit, he recognized that. He would get far more upset about the contract demands of a lesser player than he would for a difference maker. He recognized—all the way back to O.J. Simpson, I guess—that there is a premium that you pay for difference makers and they do change the game in every respect.

I called Jim Irsay back and told him we were willing to go with the two, but no further. I also told him we had to be able to talk with

Cornelius and his agent, Eugene Parker, to be sure that we could meet his demands—that they hadn't decided that they wanted 20 percent more than what they were seeking from the Colts because we were willing to give up so much for his rights.

I spoke with Eugene, who let me know that the salary range was about $1 million, which was exactly what we expected based on his unsuccessful negotiations with Indianapolis. After getting the approval of Mr. Wilson, I negotiated with Eugene late into the night and we finalized the deal the next morning, which was the day before we would face the Redskins. Having not played for more than a year, Cornelius would be a spectator for the game.

The whole process covered three days, each lasting between 18 to 20 hours, because every phone call of negotiation would be followed by two to three hours of game planning. It's not just the negotiating. It's the preparation, the marshaling of facts and figures, and the logistics. What made the trade work were Jim Irsay's integrity and the fact that Jim, John, and I were colleagues and friends. No one could have conducted themselves with more honor and integrity in that deal than Jim, who had the most difficult role as the middle man. Never did I think that there was any skulduggery going on. I would describe it as a win/win/win. And, by the way, Bob Ferguson deserves a large measure of credit for this and many other key acquisitions he helped put together.

Ironically enough, in Indianapolis, it's referred to as "The Eric Dickerson Trade," but in Buffalo it's "The Cornelius Bennett Trade." And this was the move that would propel us from pretender to contender. If signing Jim Kelly lifted the dark cloud from over Buffalo, the Cornelius Bennett trade brought the sun out. The whole psychological tenor of the fans in Buffalo changed when Cornelius— the "Biscuit" as he was known since childhood—came on board. There was a feeling of, "Wow, these guys know what they're doing. Boy, look at this team...we are ready to go!"

Cornelius Bennett's first game with us would be at home against Denver. Marv came into my office the previous Monday and said, "I don't know if we can get Cornelius ready to play. Maybe we can get him in on some nickel situations, but I don't think he knows enough. I want to be really sure that we don't overtax him physically. You know, he hasn't played football in more than a year, and I want to make sure that he's ready."

"You're absolutely right," I said. "Don't give it a second thought; he plays when you think he's ready to play, when [strength and conditioning coach] Rusty Jones thinks he's ready to play, when Abe [trainer Ed Abramoski] thinks he's ready to play."

Two days later, as I was in my office making sure that all of the i's were dotted and t's were crossed on the official papers for the Bennett trade, Fergy called and said, "Get down to the field right now. You have got to see this."

"See what?"

"Bennett."

I went down to the field and Biscuit was running around like he was shot from a cannon. He was rushing the quarterback. He was beating Bruce Smith to the passer. At one point, he jumped over a blocker, and the entire defense was jacked up. They were hooting and hollering. It was amazing.

I went back upstairs to my office, and got a call from a friend of mine from Buffalo who happened to be a Yankee fan, and he asked, "How does Bennett look?"

"I just saw Mickey Mantle in football cleats," I said.

"That good?"

"That good!"

After practice, Marv told reporters that Cornelius was a long way from being ready to play in a game. Afterward, he told me that Walt Corey, our defensive coordinator, didn't think he could get Cornelius ready, even for nickel situations.

"I hate to put him out there if he's not ready," Marv said.

I told him not to worry about it.

The next day, Cornelius destroyed practice again. Marv told reporters that Biscuit's conditioning looked good and that there "may be some small window" to get him on the field in nickel situations.

Meanwhile, the coaches are coming to me and saying, "Where did you get this guy from? Mars? He's unbelievable!"

During the game, which we won 21–14, Cornelius only played in obvious passing situations. On his first play, he pressured John Elway into an incompletion. Later, with the Broncos backed up against their own goal line, Cornelius sacked Elway and almost got a safety. Elway got up and looked around as if to say, "Where did this guy come from? Who the hell is this guy?"

The next play, Elway stepped up before the snap and he pointed at Cornelius and he said to the tackle on that side, "Get this guy!" I think Elway moved a back onto Cornelius, too, but Biscuit came flying off the line again. Elway barely got the ball off and just avoided being decapitated.

Finally, on third down, Elway came up to the line looking for Cornelius and he was on the side of the defense opposite where he had been previously. Elway looked over, saw him and yelled, "Timeout!" He walked over to the bench and got in the face of the Broncos' coach, Dan Reeves. You could read his lips as he said, "You gotta block that guy! I don't give a damn what you gotta do, you gotta block him!"

Biscuit would be the cause of similar unpleasant conversations for our opponents through the rest of his rookie season...and for most of the balance of his career.

8

Hold the Sugar

"In the end, all you have is your word. Always keep your word, no matter what it costs." —Ralph Wilson Jr.

WE ENTERED THE 1988 DRAFT in need of an every-down running back. Ronnie Harmon, our first-round draft pick from Iowa in 1986, had not worked out in that role the way we thought he would, so we needed to find someone else who could get the job done. The catch was that we didn't have a first-round choice, because of the Cornelius Bennett trade. That meant we would have to hope that we could find the answer in the second round, with the fortieth-overall pick.

We went through film of any number of college running backs. In mid-March, John Butler, our personnel director, and I were in a conference room watching film of Thurman Thomas from Oklahoma State. We called Marv Levy into the room to watch the film with us, reminding him that a couple of months earlier Thurman was the MVP of the Senior Bowl after rushing for 104 yards for the North squad.

We also explained that Thurman had a knee problem, the result of a torn anterior cruciate ligament he had suffered in his left knee during a pickup basketball game before his junior season. The knee was repaired via an arthroscopic procedure rather than the major surgery commonly done on ACLs. The doctor then prescribed several weeks of rest and fitted Thurman with a sophisticated knee brace, which he wore while rushing for 741 yards as a junior and 1,613 yards as a senior.

"So we might have a chance at him with our second-round pick," I said, figuring there were going to be teams that saw him as too big a risk to be taken in the first round.

We put the film on, and it happened to be Oklahoma State's game against Wyoming in the Holiday Bowl in San Diego. We saw Thurman enter the game and perform as well as he did in other games. But then we saw another running back come into the game, and he started to do miraculous things. And with each amazing run and ankle-breaking move that he would put on another defender, Marv, John, and I started yelling, "Holy cow! Wow!"

The next thing we knew, a crowd began to form in the conference room as offensive coaches and even some defensive coaches who heard us became curious about what we were watching. And all you could hear was, "Whoa! Run that back! Holy crap! Run that back! Oh, my God! Run that back!"

Finally, John blurted out, "Dammit, guys! That's Barry Sanders, and he's a junior. He's not coming out! We're looking at Thurman Thomas!"

You couldn't blame us, of course. Barry put on the sort of show that defined his Hall of Fame career on the way to rushing for 222 yards and a Holiday Bowl–record five touchdowns in Oklahoma State's 62–14 victory. Thurman obviously came out second-best in that comparison, but so would any other back in football history.

Nevertheless, we decided we were interested in Thurman and we went through all of the medical protocols, which is the last part of the pre-draft process. The reason it is the last part is because there is something called "Indy 2," which takes place about three weeks before the draft. This is when prospects who have undergone operations or dealt with some sort of physical ailment and didn't have complete physicals during the Combine return to Indianapolis for a complete physical.

Dr. Richard Weiss, our orthopedic surgeon, failed Thurman Thomas on the physical. He told us that Thurman's medial collateral ligament was frayed. I informed Dr. Weiss that Thurman had undergone surgery before playing his final two seasons in college, and I suggested that he take a look at the videotape of the operation, which he did.

Afterward, Dr. Weiss said, "Well, this could go either way. He could come in and be fine or he could come in and blow it out, in which case I could reconstruct it. So he's not a total washout. I can pass him. And we're talking about him as a second-round pick anyway. You're not thinking about trading up to get him in the first round, are you?"

"No, we're not," I said.

"Then I would pass him under those circumstances."

In one respect, we were ecstatic to know that the knee wasn't going to be in issue. But in another, we were discouraged about our chances of actually getting Thurman at No. 40. In fact, I told Marv, "I don't think he's going to be there. He's too good a player. Other people know what we know."

We took our seats in the draft room, assuming our very uncomfortable roles as spectators for the first round. In front of us were the names, listed vertically according to how we ranked them, of 360-plus college players on 12" x 6" laminated cards magnetically affixed to a big white wall. Besides the name, each card contained the player's height, weight, 40-yard dash time, school, and position. Thurman's name was right where we hoped to take him, at 40.

A table facing the board had seats for Mr. Wilson, whomever he designated from his Detroit staff, Marv, myself, John, and Norm. In rows behind us were seated the scouts and assistant coaches, Dr. Weiss, and our trainer, Eddie Abramoski. That way, if you had any last-minute questions before making a pick or a trade, the answers were readily available. There would be Steve Champlin, whom we designated to speak with the people we assigned to our table in New York to submit the card with our choices. There would be two secretaries, one whose job was to answer incoming calls and the other whose job was to get the player on the phone before we actually put the card in to make sure he didn't have an injury or some untoward situation. Mr. Wilson wasn't in the room for the start of the draft. As with most owners with whom I've worked, he would be in his office and only enter the draft room when our top pick was 30 minutes or so away, and he'd leave until our next pick.

Sure enough, we watched the entire first round go by without Thurman being picked. ESPN had a camera at his apartment, the forerunner of the "green room" cameras that capture the looks of anxiety, elation, and despair on the faces of the prospects invited to New York for the draft. It was easy to tell that Thurman was clearly annoyed that he was still on the board for the start of the second round.

We started talking among ourselves and came to the conclusion that we had better trade for a higher pick in the second to get him before somebody else did. So we began making trade offer after trade offer, but to no avail. As Thurman continued to fall, Marv said, "Maybe this elevator's going all the way to the bottom and we'll get him."

"You might be right," I said. "I hope you are."

After that, we decided to have a meeting with Mr. Wilson to inform him of what was going on. The tricky part of that for a pair of highly superstitious people like John and me is that it would cause us to violate a rule that we both held sacred: you never mention the name of the pick you're hoping will fall to you out loud, because when you do, more often than not he'll be chosen by someone in front of you. And if you touch the card bearing his name on your draft board, it's for certain that he goes before your pick. No one was allowed to touch the card until our pick was made.

But we knew we didn't have a choice. Mr. Wilson had to be briefed, which meant we were going to have to break our rule and mention Thurman's name. No sooner did we walk in than Mr. Wilson asked us, "Who's this guy Thurman?"

I gave him the thumbnail sketch of what Thurman had done, saying, "This guy's a difference maker. He was the MVP of the Senior Bowl. He can make people miss. He can run inside, he can block, he can catch the ball. He's not quite as electric as Joe Cribbs, but he's better because he's stouter."

Dr. Weiss gave him the rundown on Thurman's knee situation. And then someone, although I don't recall who it was, raised a question about Thurman missing practice a lot of time because the knee would periodically swell, and we said that wasn't the case.

"Are you sure?" Mr. Wilson asked.

With that, Marv told me to get Pat Jones, the Oklahoma State coach, on the phone. Pat verified our information, noting that Thurman was only rested on Thursdays so that he would be ready to play on Saturday.

"Look, this is a gamble," I said to Mr. Wilson. "It's your money; you've got to make this decision. You've got to sign off on it."

"Is this guy a good player?" Mr. Wilson asked.

"Yes, he's absolutely a good player. He's a first-round pick if he's healthy. But I can't sit here and tell you this is not a gamble. It is. If we win, we win big. If we lose, it could be that we've blown the pick."

"Ah, everything in life's a gamble. Go ahead!"

We went back into the draft room and started praying: "Let him come to us!"

As more picks were made in the second round without Thurman hearing his name—including running backs Ickey Woods, from UNLV, to Cincinnati at No. 31 and Tony Jeffery, from TCU, to Phoenix at No. 38—he actually (and because of that ESPN camera, *famously*) fell asleep. And when he fell to us, we woke him up with our call to inform him he would be our pick.

The rest is Hall of Fame history, as Thurman would prove to be one of the greatest all-around backs the game has ever seen. My distinct memory of him above all others is that he had an extra gear in big games. When the division championship was on the line, in the playoffs, in the Super Bowl, he came out flying. For a big game at Rich Stadium, we'd give it to him two or three times right off the bat and he'd rip off six or eight yards, he'd rip off 10, he'd rip off another 10, and before you knew it, the other team was on their heels and the stadium was rocking. And, then, boom, we'd throw a touchdown pass off play-action.

The 1988 season was magical, because we ended up winning the AFC East for the first time since 1980. And we won it in dramatic fashion, beating the New York Jets 9–6 in overtime. Freddy Smerlas, our big nose tackle whose vertical jump could barely be measured with a popsicle stick, somehow managed to get far enough off the ground to block a would-be winning game-winning field-goal attempt by Pat Leahy to force OT.

The fans celebrated the victory by overrunning the field and tearing down the goalposts. Van Miller, our legendary play-by-play radio voice, described the unforgettable scene as "Fan-Demonium!"

Many people around the league made a big deal about our fans rushing the field after a division-clinching win, but I thought it was just typical Buffalo. Why wouldn't they? It's what they deserved after a long time in the wilderness.

I don't think that anyone thought that we would go to the top that quickly, but I, for one, wasn't the least bit surprised. I felt we had virtually all of the right pieces in place to be a contender. I knew we had the right players. I knew we had the right head coach. I knew we had everything aligned in a way that would allow us to have success.

The overarching rubric is you get good people and you let them do their jobs. Marv Levy brought in assistant coaches who were familiar with each other, familiar with Marv, and with whom I was familiar. We had a universal philosophy of how we would do things, and it sort of bled down from Marv to the coaching staff, into the training room, into the equipment room, so the organization really was, in one fell swoop, together almost from Day One.

We would beat the Houston Oilers in the divisional round to advance to the AFC Championship Game at Cincinnati. That game—or at least the days leading up to it—proved to be a wild experience. In their divisional-round game against the Bengals a week earlier, the Seattle Seahawks, coached by former Bills coach Chuck Knox, had their players, by all accounts, feign injury on virtually every other play in order to slow down the Bengals' "Sugar Huddle" offense.

Sam Wyche, the Bengals' coach, would huddle with 13 or 14 guys on the sideline and then run 11 guys onto the field at the last minute. Of course, you couldn't identify who those 11 were until they were lined up and ready to snap the ball, so it made it almost impossible to properly match up your defensive personnel with their offensive personnel. That was contrary to both the spirit and the letter of the rule, and many teams were thinking about how to deal with it. Seattle chose to fight fire with fire by feigning injury, which also was against the rules.

The Monday before the game I got a call from the late Pete Rozelle, commissioner of the NFL. I had met him previously at league meetings and other business settings, but Bill Polian and Pete Rozelle weren't exactly bosom buddies, to say the least. And it's not often that I would get a call from the commissioner, at least not in my tenure as a general manager, so I was scared to death, to put it mildly.

"Bill, we have a problem here," Commissioner Rozelle said.

"What is it, Commissioner?"

"We can't have people feigning injury."

"Well, I understand that, Commissioner."

"Let me propose something to you." (As if I was going to make a counter proposal to the next-highest person to God in the football world.) "If I assure you that Sam is not going to 'sugar huddle' you and put you in a position where you can't match up, will you assure me that you won't feign injury?"

"Yes, sir, no question about it."

"I'm counting on you."

"We're on board, Commissioner. Don't worry about it. As long as we can match up, then we are fine."

Off we went to Cincinnati, arriving the Friday before the game, which would be played on a Sunday. The NFL required the visiting team to be on site two days in advance for press conferences with the head coach and selected players from each team.

Sam went first.

"Oh, yeah, nothing's changing, we're going to use the 'Sugar Huddle,'" he told reporters. "We've not been told anything contrary. We're going to continue to do it. It's the way we play. It's not illegal."

Marv was sitting in the wings fuming. He then went on the stage, and when he was asked about how he would deal with the "Sugar Huddle," he said, "I'm not taking anything off the table. I'm not giving away anything. We're doing everything at our disposal to try and win the game."

We got back to our hotel and it seemed like I was in my room for all of about five minutes when the phone rang.

"Bill?" I heard the instantly recognizable, gravelly voice of the commissioner at the other end say. "Pete Rozelle."

"Yes, Commissioner Rozelle."

"I thought we had a deal."

"We do, Commissioner, but Sam apparently hasn't gotten the word."

I then explained what happened at the press conference.

"Okay, do we still have a deal?" the commissioner said.

"Yes, sir, we still have a deal and I give you our word. We won't do anything that's against the rules as long as we can match up."

Don Weiss, who was then the executive director of the league and Pete Rozelle's right-hand man, was in Cincinnati to supervise the game. After our Saturday practice at Riverfront Stadium, he met with Marv and me at our hotel and informed us that whenever they ran their offense in from the sideline, the umpire would stand over the ball and give us an opportunity to match up on defense. Don also informed us that the Bengals and the game officials had been told the same thing.

"That's perfectly fine," Marv said. "Thank you very much."

The next afternoon, during pregame warm-ups, Sam Wyche came storming down the tunnel. Bob Trumpy, the former Bengals tight end who was doing the broadcast for NBC, was walking next to him. Sam was gesticulating and you could just tell that he was all fired up. Trumpy came walking over to us and said, "Sam just told me he just found out from a league guy that the officials would prevent them from doing the 'Sugar Huddle,' and you're in on it."

"We didn't negotiate with the league," I said. "We were told by the league yesterday how they were going to handle it. We were also told that the Bengals and the officials were informed yesterday as well."

Sam was furious, but the officials came out and ran the game just the way they said they would. Not that it helped us. We wound up losing 21–10.

As it turned out, Sam came up with another tactic that was totally legal to help the Bengals win the game. Realizing that one of our cornerbacks, Derrick Burroughs (who was a very good player), had a short fuse, Sam had his receivers continuously go after his legs with cut blocks in the red zone. At one point, Derrick threw a punch at receiver Tim McGee late in the third quarter and received a personal-foul penalty. That gave the Bengals a first down at our 4-yard line, setting up their clinching touchdown. Derrick also was ejected from the game for arguing the call.

It would stand to reason that the only thing worse than losing a conference championship game is losing a Super Bowl. I've come to believe that actually losing in the championship game is even worse, because at least when you go to the Super Bowl you have all of the good memories of having won the conference championship to fall back on. When you lose in the championship game, you've had a great year…but it doesn't feel that way.

We went back to work convinced that we were a good team and that we were on the verge of taking the next step. The next season, we reached the divisional game in Cleveland. Scott Norwood suffered a pulled hamstring, and he couldn't get any power into his kickoffs. So we would go down the field and score, Scott would kick off, Eric Metcalf—one of the best return men in the game—would run it back to about midfield and the Browns would go in and score.

It was late in the second quarter when Ted Marchibroda, our offensive coordinator, said to Marv, "There's nothing we can do about this because Scotty can't kick off. Let's go no-huddle the whole time and that way we just keep up with them and have a shootout." And so we did.

We ended up losing the game 34–30, with Clay Matthews intercepting Jim Kelly at the goal line to seal the win for the Browns, but that was moot. On the previous play, Ronnie Harmon was wide open in the end zone and dropped a pass that would have won the game. Just as in baseball, when somebody makes an error, the next guy up gets a hit. In football, when you drop a touchdown pass, the next play is bad. It's going to be a fumble, an interception, or a sack. Don't ask me why. That's just the way it is. I must have seen it happen a hundred times.

During the off-season, Marv and Ted spoke with the offensive staff and the defensive staff. They said, "Running the two-minute drill for half of the playoff game was so good and it fit Jim so well and we were so efficient with it, why don't we try this full time?"

We took on an offensive identity that was brand new. It was different than what Sam Wyche had done because we didn't really substitute; we would start and finish each series with the same group. We didn't have to find players who were specific fits for the system, because those were the kind of players we already had.

The system came about because of the smart, athletic people that we already had in place. It was the most efficient and revolutionary use of the people we had in place. That's a classic example of why Marv always said, "It's not about systems. It's about people and preparation."

Marv had a rule that basically said you always take a chance on a failed first-round draft pick because somebody saw something in him. And that was exactly what we did midway through the '89 season when we acquired James Lofton, a former Stanford star who was a highly publicized first-round choice of the Green Bay Packers in 1978. James had some off-the-field difficulties that led to his release from the Packers in 1986. In 1987, he signed with the Oakland Raiders, but in the 1989 preseason, Bob Ferguson informed me that he had caught wind they were getting ready to cut him.

"Man, he's old, isn't he?" I said.

"He's 33," Fergy said. "You want to take a chance on him?"

"What about those off-the-field problems?"

"I've looked into all of it; it's not as bad as you think. I'm sure we can overcome it. He's a heck of a guy, and you're really going to like him and he will be a good addition to our team."

We talked with Marv and Ted about it. Teddy was enthusiastic. Marv said, "Are you sure?" One of Marv's axioms was, "Don't shake up the Pepsi bottle in season; it might overflow."

"I know we're shaking up the Pepsi bottle here," I said. "But Fergy really believes that this will be a good addition for us."

We signed him. And although James was at the end of his career, he gave us the speed threat on the other side with the deep route and the comeback route that we had previously lacked, to say nothing of the professionalism and camaraderie and team spirit he brought to the locker room. Not only did he fit right in, but he became a leader right away.

Fergy also was instrumental in our picking up another former Packer, running back Kenny Davis. The Packers had cut Davis three seasons after making him a second-round choice from TCU, and I recall Fergy telling me he had seen his name on the waiver wire and my responding that I was about to tell him the same. We both ran down into Marv's office and said, "We have to claim Kenny Davis!" And Marv, being Marv, said, "Why are they letting him go?"

"He doesn't fit their passing game," Fergy said. "He's a one-speed, one-direction guy, a north-south guy. He doesn't have any wiggle. But he's a better receiver than they give him credit for."

I echoed all of this and then I said to Marv, "Look, he's not going to challenge Thurman, but he's going to be in our running game. He has the acceleration in the hole to be exactly the kind of guy we want to back up Thurman and to give Thurman a blow during the game."

"Well, okay. You guys feel that strongly about it, then do it," Marv said.

Kenny proved to be another tremendously valuable piece. He was every bit the explosive runner we thought he would be in relief of Thurman and he was an exceptionally talented receiver.

Were the Football Gods smiling on us? Sure, but we knew what we wanted, we knew what fit, and strangely everybody in the organization—without ever annunciating it—had a feel for who would mesh well with the new offense. Pete Metzelaars was the blocking tight end and we drafted Keith McKeller to become the receiving tight end long before it was standard procedure.

James really was one of the final additions to allow us to come out of the blocks flying in '90 with the ability to play an up-tempo, no-huddle offense that allowed us to score quickly and frequently—while taking advantage of the defense's inability to substitute—and help the Bills get to four Super Bowls. Of course, it became famously known as "K-Gun," which had nothing to do with anything other than McKeller's nickname, which was "Killer," and the fact he was on the field a lot of the times when we went up-tempo. Pete would come in on goal-line, short-yardage, and other situations when we were slowing down or whenever we wanted to go with two tight ends.

The no-huddle gave us something that nobody had ever had before—the ability to play a fast-paced offense for an entire game. The overriding quality of the people executing it was that they were all smart football players. Now, did Marv's coaching help make them that way? It certainly had a lot to do with it, but there was a lot of wherewithal to begin with. As Marv always said, smart players get better and those who are not so smart don't.

One of the first things that Marv did when he arrived in Buffalo was focus on the two-minute drill, both offensively and defensively, so we did a lot of practicing of two-minute situations. Ted Marchibroda constructed a system whereby we had only a few plays, making it easy to learn and to put the terminology into shorthand. For instance, we would simply call a play "Gun Right 98" or "Gun Left 98." That meant the tight end would be on the right or left, while Andre Reed would be on the opposite side, and 98 explained the route combination, the backfield action, and the protection. It was difficult to design, but easy for everyone to understand and execute, especially with smart players who were able to assimilate a rather verbose play and remember that it was 98.

Doing that gave you an advantage because you never let the defense get set. As soon as the whistle blew, we were up and ready to go again. You could, by formation, dictate what the defense did, so if we had three wide receivers in the game, the defense had to put in nickel personnel and in those days the nickel backs had very little coverage ability. Therefore, you would have the nickel back, who is the weakest coverage guy for the opposition, on Andre Reed. Good luck!

Because we ran a spread offense, the opposing defense had to basically declare its coverage. You got a pretty good pre-snap read and you got a post-snap read that was immediately correct because the defense had to show you what it was doing. Later on, we would put Andre in motion, which would tell us if the coverage was man-to-man or zone, something that now is quite common in all of football.

Jim Kelly was able to operate this well, because the up-tempo approach was right up his alley. He couldn't wait to get the ball snapped and go again. We dictated tempo, we dictated when the ball was snapped, and we basically dictated coverage. We were in charge.

Jim also had his alter ego on the sideline in Frank Reich, who was equally terrific at deciphering coverages.

In addition, we had, in large measure, very athletic offensive linemen. We had an undersized center in Kent Hull, and an undersized guard in Jim Ritcher. Our tackles, Will Wolford and

Howard Ballard, were far from undersized, but they were athletic. And our other guard, John Davis, was a big, powerful bulldozer that you could run behind in short-yardage and goal-line situations.

Rusty Jones, our strength and conditioning coach, invented a whole new way of conditioning the offensive linemen. He never had them run the conventional, post-practice gassers. Instead, he had them on the treadmill because it relieved their knees, took pressure off their backs, and gave them the stamina to operate an up-tempo offense.

Long before we ever introduced the K-Gun, the question was constantly asked, "Why don't you run two-minute all of the time?" The answer was that you couldn't, because you couldn't possibly have the offensive linemen in the kind of aerobic shape necessary to do it. That was why it was only done in the final two minutes of the half or the game. But between prescribing a diet that promoted consumption of food far lower in fat than what players were normally encouraged to eat at the time, a new form of weight-lifting that called for lower weights to be lifted with higher frequency, and conditioning on the treadmill, Rusty found a way to get them to the point where they could do it for an entire game.

Another factor was that, in accordance with Marv's philosophy, we practiced so quickly. We were on and off the field in an hour and 20 minutes most of the time, so our guys were never burdened by fatigue. They didn't have to fight through fatigue as we got toward the end of the season. I can remember many times during that Super Bowl run where we would get to the playoffs and Tom Bresnahan, our offensive line coach and later our offensive coordinator, would plead for a nine-on-seven drill. Marv would say, "Okay, we will do it once a week. And after 12 plays, we take the pads off."

Now, that is the way it's done all around the league, but we were one of the few teams doing it then. We were a fresh team every week and that might be the most hidden aspect of how we went to the four Super Bowls. We were never worn down or beaten down physically because of the way Marv prepared the team in minicamp, training camp, and all the way through the regular season.

Our first Super Bowl was the one that is the most vivid in my memory, both because it was the first one and so important to the people of Buffalo, and because it was so out of character because it was one week, not two. Then there was the backdrop of the Gulf War and the stirring national anthem. To this day, whenever people in my family—or even in the Bills family—hear the Whitney Houston rendition of "The Star-Spangled Banner," they refer to it as "our national anthem." That one is the most vivid in my memory.

After Scott Norwood's field-goal attempt sailed wide right in the final seconds of our 20–19 loss to the Giants and we all returned to the hotel, I told every player, coach, and front-office staffer I met: "Hey, hold your head up high. We did the best we could. It's a bad break, we didn't make it. Scotty got us here. There's nothing to worry about. Yeah, we're going to shed some tears. It's an Irish wake. We didn't win, but there's nothing to be ashamed of. And we'll be back."

I went around to each table and delivered that message, and so did Marv.

The scene was quite different after our 52–17 loss to the Dallas Cowboys in Super Bowl XXVII, my last with the Bills. I returned to my hotel room, sat on the bed, buried my face in my hands, and choked up.

Then I gathered all of the gear I had received bearing the Super Bowl XXVII logo—all of the shirts and the jackets and the duffel bags—and tossed it into trash. Whatever wouldn't fit, I piled up next to the pail.

All I could think was, "This is over now, and we didn't get to where we wanted to go."

I've never taken the Super Bowl losses personally. It's never been about me or about my legacy. It was about all of the other people that are part of this that you have responsibility for—players, coaches, trainers, equipment people, doctors, and front-office staff. That's your football family. Those are people you spend so much time with. You spend more time with them in a given year than you do with your own family. You badly want them to go out on a high note, and it didn't happen.

After that, I went downstairs to another Irish wake. As much as possible, I wanted to just make sure that I thanked everybody. The coaches kind of had an inkling that it was my last game with the Bills. And there was a lot of emotion that wouldn't otherwise be there. But what helped me get through it was an old Paterno-ism that I often heard from George and Joe: "Success is never final and failure is never fatal."

As we were practicing before our first Super Bowl, Ted Marchibroda said to me, "It will never be quite the same again."

"What makes you say that?" I said.

"The first time everybody is just thrilled to be here. In the future, there will be more contract issues, there will be more extraneous issues. It just comes with the territory. Believe me, it will never be better than it is now."

He was right. Vince Lombardi was, too, when he said it's much harder to stay on top than it is to get there. For one thing, you have all of those individual competing desires, which are natural. That's human nature. Everybody wants a bigger piece of the pie.

I've said this to virtually every agent with whom I have ever spoken: "If your player performs, we will reward him. Now you and I may disagree as to the size of that reward, but we won't argue about the fact that he deserves to be paid." That was the approach we always took.

And it was the approach we took when two of our offensive linemen, Will Wolford and Kent Hull, were simultaneously seeking a pay increase as the team was rounding into a contender. Ralph

Cindrich, the agent representing both players, visited me almost two months before training camp and we had a pretty testy meeting. Afterward, I mentioned to Ralph Wilson that he should prepare for them to hold out from camp as a tandem.

"Well, they're not Drysdale and Koufax," Mr. Wilson said, referring to when former Dodgers pitching aces Don Drysdale and Sandy Koufax held out from spring training as a duo in 1966.

Mr. Wilson then pointed out, "You can only pay so many people before the money runs out, and you have to build your team based on economics." What he was essentially saying, long before its time, was that there was an internal salary cap that you couldn't ignore.

I told Marv to plan accordingly. Marv was tremendous on such matters. He would never, ever pressure me to get someone signed. In fact, it was rare when he would come and ask about the status of a particular negotiation. I would usually have to go to him to bring him up to date, which I did on a regular basis. But he never put any pressure on me.

I then went to our offensive line coach, Jim Ringo, and informed him of the impending holdout.

"Oh, that's good news," Jim said.

"Why?"

"They don't need training camp anyway. They played enough long seasons. Let them hold out. I'll tell you when we need them."

Jim knew that they would never be out of shape. Besides, he wanted to work with the younger players. Jim also understood the dynamics of a holdout and how Mr. Wilson looked at it because Jim had previously been an interim head coach.

On the bus ride back from a rookie scrimmage we had against the Cleveland Browns in Edinboro, Pennsylvania, Jim said, "It's time to let the boss know that he should start thinking about signing Will and Kent." I did, and Mr. Wilson seemed to come around.

After our first preseason game, Jim advised me to give Ralph Cindrich "a little hope." And as we reached the end of training camp, Jim came up to me and said, "Time to bring them in."

I got with Ralph Cindrich and it took about two days for us to iron everything out. Mr. Wilson, in his infinite wisdom, knew when the time was right, too; he was a tremendously canny negotiator. When I came back to him with the final deal on which Ralph Cindrich and I had agreed, Mr. Wilson said, "Well, it's more than I wanted to spend, but go ahead."

Yes, economics play a major role, but you have to recognize that ultimately this is a talent business. As a general manager, you have to find a way to balance the economic needs of the business against the idea that talent is ultimately what drives success.

Among the other extraneous forces coming in was that it seemed like everybody on the team had a radio show in Buffalo. Many of the players had shows, including our long-snapper, Adam Lingner. Marv had a show. Even I had a show.

One day, a veteran player walked up to me and said, "Why don't I have a radio show?"

I laughed out loud and said, with a smile, "Do I look like your agent? I don't know why you don't have a radio show. I don't do radio shows. That's your agent's job."

There were other humorous episodes that surfaced as the team grew older and more savvied. One day we were practicing outdoors in November and December, as Marv always did regardless of the weather, and several defensive players came to me and said, "You have to have Marv get us a heated bench because when we're not in our drills, we're freezing."

"I don't know if I'll have any success," I said. "But I'll give it a try."

At first, Marv declined the request. The players urged me to go back, and I did. This time I pointed out that the players were serious about it and that Rusty Jones felt if the players were off their feet and warm, it would retard injury.

"Okay, I'll do it because you are asking me," Marv said. "But I don't want them fooling around one iota. If I see that, I'm taking it away."

The players held up their end of the bargain and the heated bench stayed.

9

You Never Roam Too Far From Buffalo

"Every time you compete, you must take something positive from it, regardless of the score." —Don Shula

"More games are lost than won." —Joe Paterno

There's a saying for coaches and general managers in the National Football League that 10 years is about the limit any of us should expect to remain with one team.

I read a quote to that effect attributed to Al Davis, who hired and fired more than his share of GMs and coaches when he was managing general partner of the Oakland Raiders. Bill Walsh, another legendary figure who coached the San Francisco 49ers to three Super Bowl victories, told me the same thing.

When you spend 10 years in a decision-making position, you are going to have to make a lot of decisions that are going to make a great many people unhappy. It's just the nature of the job. It can be mundane things like who gets to eat in the cafeteria at what time versus huge things like whether or not you keep or release Peyton Manning. It runs the gamut.

You are also a public figure, whether you like it or not. In spite of the fact that I've made a decent transition to television, I did not enjoy that aspect of the job. It just becomes very, very wearing. It's a little like two pieces of wood rubbing up against one another. Pretty soon, they're worn down to the nub, and I think that's the way it is in the NFL.

In addition, you can't win every year. You can't win the Super Bowl every year. You can't even make the playoffs every year, although we did for a long time in Buffalo and for a very long time in Indianapolis. As a result, the expectations wear on you as well. Not in any given year or even in a four- or five-year span, but over a period of about 10 years, if you're fortunate to last that long with the same organization. The criticism, the expectations, the what-have-you-done-for-me-lately mentality that permeates throughout the game wear on you over time. I'm not complaining about it, but it is a harsh reality of this business and why I think 10 years in one spot is about enough.

In the spring of 1992, after our second consecutive Super Bowl appearance, I was approaching my 10th season with the Bills, eighth as general manager. My contract was coming up and there was a transition at our corporate headquarters in Detroit. Dave Olsen, who had become executive vice president and chief financial officer for Ralph Wilson Enterprises, left and was replaced by Jeff Litmann, who had also worked on the financial end of the organization. I had no relationship with Jeff, and that was my own fault because I didn't cultivate one.

Jeff didn't have Dave's ability to deal with creative kind of people. Dave had been a high-level collegiate athlete as a basketball player at Utah State; he understood athletics as well as the business side of the game. Jeff understood the law and finances. We simply didn't get along, and that caused Ralph to be upset with me.

On top of that, the league was head and shoulders into Plan B free agency, which, beginning in 1989 had permitted all NFL teams to preserve limited negotiating rights to no more than 37 total players in a season. If a player was a protected Plan B free agent, he couldn't sign with another team without providing his previous club the first chance to re-sign him. The rest of the players on the roster were left unprotected, and therefore free to sign with any team of their choosing. Eight players had successfully sued the league in U.S. federal court, saying Plan B was an unlawful restraint of trade, and a jury awarded damages to those players in '92.

Working with the NFL Management Council, I was focused on trying to find an alternative to Plan B as a free-agency system, and obviously we had a lot of decisions to make as a league. Right around that time, there was a lot of contention in terms of what decisions the Bills would make as a team. I guess Ralph felt that Jeff was entitled to have a say and I sort of resisted that. Frankly, in hindsight, I didn't handle it nearly as well as I could have, but the damage was done.

The day after our final preseason game of '92, Mr. Wilson called me over to Detroit.

"This is not working," he said. "I can't have this kind of contention in the organization. I appreciate everything that you have done, but it's just not working. I have to make a change."

It took a moment for Mr. Wilson's words to sink in, but the fact was that seven months after our second consecutive AFC championship, I was out as general manager of the Bills. I can't say I was shocked out of my shoes, although the timing of it was a little bit unsettling. After all, we were a week away from the start of the regular season.

"Fine, that's your prerogative and I appreciate that," I told Mr. Wilson. "I can't ever thank you enough for the opportunity you have given me."

It was not a contentious discussion whatsoever. I made no attempt to try to get Mr. Wilson to change his mind, because I knew we were beyond that. I did ask him, however, if, for the sake of the team, he would at least consider delaying my firing until the end of the season.

"Look, we have a chance to go to the Super Bowl again," I said. "We have a great team here and if you fire me tomorrow, it will be a public issue. It will be a distraction to Marv and it's not something that's going to bode well for the football team. You've made the decision, I respect it, and out I'll go after the season. But we have a chance together to finish the job we started—to win a Super Bowl."

"Well, there's some merit to that," Mr. Wilson said. "Let me give it some thought. But remember, we have reached a decision."

"I absolutely understand that. I also feel bad about it."

"Well, I do, too."

"You have my eternal gratitude for the chance you have given me and the support you have given me. But let's go finish the job."

Mr. Wilson then said he would drive me to the airport for my flight back to Buffalo. As we reached the access road leading to the main terminal, I looked at his gas gauge and it was on empty.

"You know, you'd better get some gas before you drop me off," I said.

Mr. Wilson then dug around in his pocket and he couldn't find his wallet.

"You have 10 bucks on you?" he asked.

"Yeah, sure," I said, and I handed him a $10 bill.

He put $10 of gas in the car and dropped me off at the terminal. Both of us were roaring with laughter about the awkwardness of the situation.

"This is a hell of a deal," I said. "You just fired me and I loan you 10 bucks."

"Well, that's life, huh?" Mr. Wilson said.

The next morning I went into the office. A Federal Express envelope arrived from Mr. Wilson with a letter from him that said, in effect, "I'm good with what we talked about; let's finish the job!" And folded up in the letter was a $10 bill.

We didn't need anything more than that note, because that was the kind of relationship we had. He trusted me and I trusted him. If Mr. Wilson gave you his word on something, that was that. I like to think he felt that way about me as well.

I told my wife, Eileen, about what had transpired, and she was upset. But at those times, she really wants to be a helpmate. She was more concerned about me than anything else, and I assured her that everything would be fine. "We've got a year to go, so there's no need to go looking for a job immediately," I said. We agreed not to tell the children and not to put the house up for sale, so as to not cause people to start jumping to conclusions. I was somewhat vague with Marv, telling him, "The meeting didn't go well, it's not looking terrific, but we are definitely going through this season, so let's go finish the job." I'm sure he got the drift.

My focus from that point forward was on us winning another championship. My day-to-day dealings with Ralph were the same as always. The topic of my impending dismissal never came up. As far as every player was concerned, every member of the coaching staff was concerned, every member of the front-office staff was concerned, it was business as usual. I was so focused on what we had to do as a ballclub and on my work with the NFL Management Council that there really wasn't time to think about anything else.

Years later, Tony Dungy would tell our Colts team the parable of the guy whose job it was to break this giant boulder. Every day he took this giant sledgehammer and pounded away. He did this for years and years, but nothing happened, not even the slightest fissure. So he gave up. He put the hammer down and walked away. Then, a little five-year-old boy came along with a very small hammer in his hand. Out of curiosity, he just tapped rock the and the thing broke into a million pieces.

The moral of the story: you never know which blow it is that will finally break the rock, so keep on pounding. That gave voice to exactly what I told Eileen and Ralph I was going to do—just keep on pounding, just keep focused, just keep doing the job I was being paid to do.

Marv used to always tell the story of receiving letters from coaches at the high school and small-college levels, asking, "How can I be an assistant coach in the NFL?" Marv's reply was always the same: "Be the best assistant coach you can be at your current level and someone will notice." That was my approach, too. I was going to be the best general manager that I could be until I wasn't the general manager anymore.

Once the season began, the only time I truly gave thought to my fate—other than the late-night pondering of mundane things such as sending out résumés, and deciding where we would want to move—was while we were trailing 28–3 at halftime of our wild-card playoff game against the Oilers. I said to myself, *Gosh, what a way to end my tenure here.*

The Football Gods were on our side that day, however, because although injuries had cost us the services of Jim Kelly, Cornelius Bennett, and Thurman Thomas, we rallied from a 32-point deficit in the third quarter to win 41–38 in overtime. With Frank Reich at quarterback, we staged the greatest comeback in NFL history. That victory reflected the courage, resiliency, and never-say-die attitude of everyone on the team. We believed, to a man, that because of who we were, the whole was always greater than the sum of the parts. The "Greatest Comeback" epitomized what we were.

Frank did a marvelous job in the next game, too, a 24–3 divisional-round victory at Pittsburgh. Now, with Jim recovered from a knee injury, we were headed to Miami for the AFC Championship Game, and the big debate in the media was who should start: Jim or Frank? Of course, Marv and I were front and center saying Jim Kelly was the starting quarterback and that was the way it was going to be. But thank God Frank was Frank. He was a great team guy who accepted his backup role and valued his close friendship with Jim too much to even think about rocking the boat. Otherwise, it really could have been a bad problem.

It also helped that, with Jim back, we went on to to beat the Dolphins 29–10.

Super Bowl XXVII in Pasadena, California, was a disaster. Everything that could possibly go wrong did. We turned the ball over nine times on the way to a 52–17 loss. I look back on it now and say we made a lot of mistakes in preparation and logistics that we never should have made. The Friday before the game, we decided to move out of the hotel in downtown Los Angeles, which was in a bad locale; it wasn't terribly safe. We went up to Pasadena, thinking it would be a better spot for the players to get away from all of the pregame nonsense and just focus on the task at hand, and it turned out to be the wrong thing because the many veteran players on the roster felt sequestered and were edgy.

We also never anticipated the impact from the constant negative reinforcement that came via the media sessions that week. *What if you lose a third Super Bowl in a row? Will you be the greatest losers of all time?* That was repeated, over and over and over and over, and consequently we were very uptight, which was not like us at all.

I'll never forget, on the bus going back to the hotel after the game, I said disgustedly to Marv, friend to friend, "You know all the stuff we worried about? All the stuff we agonized about? All the details we worried about? To hell with them! Just win the football game. Show up five minutes before kickoff and just win the football game. Everything else is irrelevant."

We get a kick out of remembering that conversation now, but it was a tough pill to swallow and it was a tough way to end my career with the Bills.

When we got back to the hotel, we had what amounted to our third Irish wake in a row. Just as with the previous two, I went around to virtually every table, to every player and coach and their family members, and thanked them for all that they had done. "We will live to fight another day," I said.

I told Don Beebe how particularly proud I was of the effort that he made when, with the Dallas holding a 52–17 lead, he gave chase as Cowboys defensive tackle Leon Lett was running toward the end zone after a fumble recovery. Don called upon every ounce of his incredible speed to prevent Lett from reaching the end zone. Confident that he was going to score, Lett began celebrating by holding the ball out to his right side. Don caught up to him, knocked the ball out of Lett's hands just before the goal line, and it rolled through the end zone out of bounds for a touchback to prevent the Cowboys from scoring what would have been a Super Bowl–record 58 points.

In a terrible loss, as Don Shula said, that was the one positive thing that we could all take away—that we fought until the end when there was nothing left to fight for.

Afterward, I was kind of sitting off to the side with my family and by that time, coaches and some of the players had gotten wind of the fact that something was going on. One by one, they came over and said, "Hey, if this is the end, we want you to know how much we appreciate what you did."

I later found out from Marv that the morning after the Super Bowl, he reached out to Mr. Wilson to try to talk him out of firing me. I'm too embarrassed to share some of the incredibly nice things that he said on my behalf, but suffice it to say that I couldn't have had a better advocate.

Of course, it didn't matter. Mr. Wilson told Marv that he made his decision, and that was that.

The Tuesday after the Super Bowl, I held a news conference. I realized that losing in the Super Bowl for the third year in a row was bitterly disappointing, but I wanted fans to know the reason it had been my honor and pleasure to witness this team from close range: "They're a very special group of men. Cherish them. You will not see their like again."

My relationship with Ralph Wilson never soured. We remained friends and became even better friends as the years went on. Eileen and I would hear from him on our anniversary every year. We would hear from him at Christmas every year. When he was still going to league meetings, we would stop and talk and he would have a joke for me or I would have a joke for him. It was a great relationship.

Even though I would go on to do other things, there was a very big part of me that never left Buffalo. I never really stopped being a Bill. I always think back to when I first arrived in Buffalo and I ran into Jerry Glanville, who had been a defensive backs coach for the Bills a couple of years before I joined them.

"Let me tell you something about Buffalo," Jerry said. "If you stay there for more than one season, you will be a Buffalo Bill for life." And he was absolutely right, which is a testament to the way people in western New York make you feel. Whenever I go back there—whether it's to play in Jim Kelly's annual golf tournament or when one of the teams I worked for played against the Bills—someone, without fail, comes up to me and says, "Welcome home!"

To bring the story of my time in Buffalo full circle, I got off a flight to San Francisco in May of 2012 and saw that I had three messages on my cell phone from Scott Berchtold, senior vice president of communications for the Bills and an old friend from our time together with the team. I returned the call and Scott said, with great urgency in his voice, "You need to call Mr. Wilson in Detroit immediately! Here's the number."

I was shocked and concerned. After all, Mr. Wilson was approaching 92 years of age. Was something wrong? Had there been an emergency of some kind? Mr. Wilson's assistant answered the call, and put the call through to him right away.

"Bill," he said, in his soft and distinctive voice, "I wanted to be the first to tell you that you have been selected to the Bills Wall of Fame, and you will be inducted this year. It's well deserved and I'm happy to be able to give you this news."

I was speechless. I stammered, and then said, "Wow! Thank you!"

Mr. Wilson went on to say that it was getting harder and harder for him to travel, but he hoped very much to be present for the ceremony and, particularly, to meet all of our grandchildren. I thanked him again and told him it was the greatest professional honor of my career. I also said that I couldn't find words adequate to express my gratitude, but would write to him at length very soon.

The ceremony was held in conjunction with the Bills-Tennessee game that fall. My youngest son, Dennis, who was on the Titans' coaching staff, was able to attend, as did Chris, then with the Falcons, and Brian, then on the Texas A&M coaching staff. My daughter, Lynn, and daughters-in-law Debbie and Laura shepherded all seven grandchildren. They joined lots of extended family, my closest friends from grade school, and Marv, Jim Kelly, Bruce Smith, Thurman Thomas, Andre Reed, Leonard Smith, and many staff members from our Bills years for a great reunion.

Most importantly, our grandchildren got to see "Grammy" and "Poppa" honored in a place they had only heard about or seen in brief NFL Films clips. Our grandsons, Will and Jack, described it perfectly when they said, "Poppa, this is a really big deal."

Welcome home, indeed!

After about six weeks, the NFL Management Council hired me as a consultant to help put the finishing touches on a new collective bargaining agreement, which had been four years in the making. We finally put together a deal that worked—one that would grow the game, that would be fair to the players, that would be fair to the clubs. And it ultimately happened because NFL Commissioner Paul Tagliabue was able to sell the NFL Players Association executive director, Gene Upshaw, on the idea that a salary cap, coupled with free agency after four seasons, would create competitive balance throughout the league and therefore every team would prosper. And if every team prospered, then the pot for the players would grow exponentially. It was better than what we had at the time and it would create, in essence, a larger pie for the players. But it took incredible salesmanship on Paul's part to get Gene to go along with that. It took incredible courage on Gene's part to accept that, but when it was all said and done, they were both statesmen.

Once the players ratified the CBA, Commissioner Tagliabue hired me as the league's vice president of football operations, also known as the "Dean of Discipline." In accepting the position, I told the commissioner my preference was to go back to being a GM and that I would continue to seek such an opportunity. He understood my point of view and encouraged me to take the job and get the position started and look at other opportunities down the road.

My job was to levy fines and/or suspensions for players who violated league rules. I got the greatest management training you could ever have working for Paul Tagliabue. One of the best examples came after we enacted rules to protect the defenseless receiver. We hadn't spelled out that a defender launching himself to make contact was illegal, but we did have rules that you could not lead with the crown of the helmet and hit anywhere on the body. The late Jerry Seeman, who at the time was the NFL's senior director of officiating, wanted to enforce the rules literally. But there was a disparity in the league in how coaches taught a defender to separate the receiver from the ball, and when I explained this to the commissioner, he said, "Why don't you bring in some coaches who really teach these techniques properly and we will get all of the officiating people and a very small group of football people together and have them discuss the techniques they use? It will be very instructional and educational."

We brought in Pete Carroll, who was the defensive coordinator of the New York Jets at the time and who was great at teaching one of the techniques being used by defensive backs in the league. He explained that if the deep safety in a "Cover Two" zone couldn't get to the ball, he was taught to hit the receiver in the chest with his helmet, causing his arms to separate and the ball to come out. The directive was, "Get your hat on the ball."

We also had Rod Rust, a longtime defensive coordinator in the league and a former colleague at Kansas City who was out of football at the time, come in to explain a totally different technique. Rather than having the defender put his hat on the ball, he instructed him to drive his hands up through the receiver to knock him backward while lifting him off the ground. That would cause the receiver's arms to separate and the ball to come out.

"When it's all said and done," the commissioner said, "it's pretty clear that you can get the job done without launching and without hitting people with the crown of your helmet." That was the genesis of all of the rules that have since been put in place.

Another example of Commissioner Tagliabue's exceptional management skills was the "Chuck Cecil Case." Chuck, a safety for the Phoenix Cardinals at the time, was launching, he was leading with the crown of the helmet, he was doing all of the things to defenseless receivers that have made so many headlines in recent years. After a preseason hit, Jerry Seeman wanted Chuck suspended. Jay Moyer, the league's general counsel, whose job it was to make sure that these decisions comported with the CBA and were unchallengeable in court, agreed that Chuck should be suspended. I thought that was the right thing to do as well, because Chuck had been warned and the final straw was the hit in the preseason game.

I sent a memo to that effect to the commissioner, who had final say on all disciplinary matters. The commissioner then called me into his office and said, "I understand why you're doing this, but here's what I'm going to do. I'm not going to suspend him, I'm going to fine him. We are also going to bring him here for a meeting and put him on notice and if he does it again, he'll know what his penalty is. I'll tell him when we meet and you'll be in that meeting."

We had the meeting, and the commissioner said, "Polian wants to suspend you, but I think that I'm going to give you the benefit of the doubt because I think you're a good guy. But what you're doing is unacceptable, so I am going to give you a chance to straighten out. If it happens again, it's going to be a suspension, and I don't care how much you appeal or don't appeal, it's a suspension. Do you understand where we are coming from, Chuck?"

"Yes, Commissioner, I do," Chuck said. He really didn't have any other response.

Paul's feeling was always to give people an opportunity to change their ways before bringing down the ultimate hammer. And Chuck did just that. He never was involved in another situation like that throughout the rest of his career. He was, however, upset with me for quite some time. We finally "got it straight" when Chuck was on the Tennessee coaching staff and I was in Indianapolis.

Another example of Commissioner Tagliabue's win-win philosophy was the resolution of a long-standing feud between a significant number of college head coaches and pro football. I say pro football because the dispute had its genesis in the signing of Herschel Walker by the USFL before his eligibility had expired at the University of Georgia. For some reason, the college coaches decided to ban scouts from both the USFL and NFL from their campuses. Although the USFL went out of business in 1987, the ban took on a life of its own and became a real problem for the NFL.

In the early '90s, Commissioner Tagliabue asked George Young and me to accompany him to a meeting that we arranged with the American Football Coaches Association (AFCA) board of directors. To say the meeting was contentious would be an understatement. The board let the commissioner have it with both barrels. Gene Stallings, then at Alabama but previously let go by the Phoenix Cardinals, was particularly harsh. Commissioner Tagliabue took the criticism with great forbearance and let the storm blow itself out. Jim Sweeney of Washington State then allowed that we should try to get a positive result from the meeting.

Commissioner Tagliabue readily agreed and explained that the NFL was instituting a "three years from high school" eligibility rule which he, as a preeminent anti-trust lawyer in a previous career, believed would withstand legal challenge. He further pledged that if the colleges would open their campuses to NFL scouts, the league would, at its expense, fight any legal challenge to the eligibility rule "all the way to the Supreme Court." The commissioner's forbearance, integrity, and sincerity broke the fever and the AFCA agreed to open the campuses. Commissioner Tagliabue was, of course, as good as his word. Years later, Maurice Clarett of Ohio State challenged the rule "all the way to the Supreme Court," and lost.

George Young and the late Dick Steinberg of the New York Jets came up with the idea for the NFL College Advisory Committee to help evaluate and advise underclassmen thinking about declaring for the NFL Draft. With great help from Grant Teaff, executive director of the AFCA, and Joel Bussert, NFL vice president of personnel, I implemented the College Advisory Committee in 1993 when working in the league office. It functions well to this day and relations between the colleges and the NFL have never been better, all because

Paul Tagliabue devised and sold a "win-win" with "respect for the other guy." It is a lesson I have never forgotten.

Upon his retirement, Commissioner Tagliabue was given the Tuss McLaughry Award for long and distinguished service to college football by the AFCA. No one deserved it more. Hopefully, the Pro Football Hall of Fame electors will soon see their way clear to honoring Paul for the incredible success and prosperity his efforts brought to the NFL. The Pro Football Hall of Fame in Canton, Ohio, is incomplete without him.

The commissioner had appointed me to the NFL's competition committee in 1989. The committee studies, develops and recommends rules and changes to rules for both on- and off-the-field facets of the game. It functions much like a congressional committee in that a proposal must receive majority approval from the committee to be given serious consideration by full league membership. The committee's proposals are placed on the agenda of the league's annual meeting in March and voted upon by owners or representatives of all 32 clubs.

Unlike congressional committees, the competition committee's members are not elected. They are appointed by the commissioner after consultation with the committee chairman and staff. It originally consisted of five members, but over time has expanded to eight. Some of the original members when the committee was formed in the early '70s were Wellington Mara, Paul Brown, Tex Schramm, and Vince Lombardi. More recent illustrious alumni include Bill Walsh, Chuck Noll, and Al Davis.

The NFL director of officiating and a senior league executive are ex-officio members, although they do not vote. Some legendary figures who have served on the committee are directors of officiating Art McNally, Jerry Seeman, and Mike Pereira, and senior executives Don Weiss, Joel Bussert, Peter Hadhazy and Gene Washington. The membership has evolved over the years to include at times owner representatives such as Jerry and Stephen Jones of the Cowboys, Mike Brown of the Bengals, John Mara of the Giants, and Mark Richardson of the Panthers. Jerry and Stephen brought a great, new business focus to the deliberations, while Mike and John—sons of founding members of the NFL—brought incomparable historic knowledge as well as modern CEO experience.

Among the coaching fraternity that has been well represented on the committee are Marvin Lewis, Jeff Fisher, Mike Holmgren, Bill Cowher, Mike Martz, Jack Del Rio, Ken Whisenhunt, Dennis Green, and Tony Dungy, who I got to know on the committee before we would become colleagues in Indianapolis. Among some very competent GMs who have been on the committee are Ozzie Newsome, Harry Gamble, Bob Ferguson, Matt Millen, Rick Smith, Mark Murphy, Charley Casserly, and Bill Tobin.

Jim Finks, who was general manager of the New Orleans Saints at the time, had just taken over as chairman. He was a mentor to me, always available for advice and counsel. Paul Brown, the father of modern-day football, was on the committee then. So, too, were Don Shula, George Young, Tom Flores, and Marty Schottenheimer.

Before free agency, the meetings were in Maui, Hawaii, but now are held twice per year—in Indianapolis, just before the Combine, and in Naples, Florida, just prior to the NFL's annual meeting. The setting may be nice, but the work is hard.

The first meeting I attended was in Maui, and there I was sitting with these icons of football in America. I would sometimes say to myself, *What am I doing here?* Tom Flores would later tell me that the greatest honor you can have in professional football—other than being in the Hall of Fame—is to be a member of the competition committee. And he was absolutely right.

While I made great friends and got wonderful advice from everyone on the committee, Don Shula became a special friend. Think about this: here was the winngest coach in the history of the game jogging, dining, golfing and sharing football thoughts and philosophy with the general manager of his principal divisional rival. Don even gave me my first formal golf lessons. Sadly, though he remained a great coach, I was not a great pupil.

I would ask Paul Brown questions about how to run a team, how to handle contract disputes, and he would tell me about the founding of the Browns, the founding of the Bengals, and how he dealt with different contract disputes, how the draw play came to be, and what it was like coaching Massillon High School in Ohio. I also sought his advice about how to avoid a quarterback controversy, which became a possibility after Jim Kelly had been hurt and Frank Reich led us to victory in a winner-take-all game against Miami for the AFC East title. He looked at me with that piercing Paul Brown stare and said, "Don't have one."

Jim Finks had a rule that no competition-committee meeting could start until Paul, whom Jim nicknamed "The Wily Mentor," told a joke. Paul would always recite something from Henny Youngman, and no matter how old and corny it was, everybody would laugh. That was Jim's way of setting a friendly tone because he knew that these meetings could get very contentious at times. We would get into it about things that would affect one team or another, particularly the Dolphins and Bills because that was the big rivalry at the time. But everybody recognized that what you were there to do was make the game better. You checked your club credentials at the door.

In many cases a person would start out on one side of an issue and end up on the other because we had so much respect for one another. The discussions were so good and so in-depth, and the camaraderie was so good that oftentimes when it came down to a specific issue, a guy who had a strong objection might go along just to make it unanimous.

I remember a time where Jim Finks was decidedly opposed to some issue and the vote was going to be seven-to-one, with Jim as the one. I then said, "Listen, you're the chairman and without your vote, this is not really legitimate."

Jim, who had an incredible sense of humor, said, "Alright, you've got my vote...but it's under protest!"

Over the years, the committee has dealt with many controversial subjects. In 1986, the NFL instituted instant replay as an officiating tool. It faced an uphill battle to remain in the league, and during my early years on the competition committee, instant replay brought about the most emotional and contentious discussion on a subject I can ever remember. People who were anti-replay believed very firmly that the game ought to be coached, played, and officiated on the field without the aid of any technological means whatsoever. They also believed that replay would not solve all of the problems that the proponents of replay believed they would solve and that it would lengthen the game to the point of being unwatchable.

I have never seen sides taken so passionately. Friendships ended because of replay. Fortunately, that wasn't the case on the committee, although Paul Brown and George Young were fervently anti-replay. George said famously, "All you are doing is substituting one person's bad judgment for another's." NFL people still quote him on that to this day. Don Shula was the most fervent and eloquent proponent of replay, feeling that we should strive for perfection in every facet of the game.

I was for replay, because I felt it could improve the game. As long as we did it in a way that was functional, we could fix officiating errors made on the big, game-changing calls. No one should lose his job over a bad call. No one should lose an opportunity to be in the playoffs because of a bad call. No one should lose a playoff game or, God forbid, the Super Bowl because of a bad call that can be rectified. I felt we had the technology to do it and that it wouldn't be intrusive. Don't bother with the little, niggling stuff, such as, was the ball spotted a half inch closer to the line than it should have been? That's immaterial.

Mr. Wilson was anti-replay and would always vote against it. Each year, I would tell the rest of the committee members, "I'm voting yes as a member of the committee, but you know that my boss is going to vote no when it goes before all of the owners." And everybody would say, "Yes, we understand." I asked Mr. Wilson if, because I planned to vote in favor of replay on the committee, he wanted me to recuse myself and he said, "No, they put you on the committee for a reason. Vote your conscience."

When owners voted to do away with replay in 1992, it was because that system did exactly what the opponents believed it would—it slowed the game down. It had mistakes galore and replay officials upstairs intruded on the game when they had no business doing so. But then came a controversial play in 1998 that served as a classic example of why officiating couldn't be left entirely to the human eye. Vinny Testaverde of the New York Jets clearly fumbled the ball before crossing the goal line on a quarterback sneak, yet was awarded the decisive touchdown in a 32–31 Jets victory over Seattle. Dennis Erickson, the Seahawks' coach, effectively lost his job because of that call.

When the committee got together after that season, Commissioner Tagliabue said, "We have to do something. We have to create a system that rectifies those calls." So, under the leadership of Rich McKay and Mike Holmgren, what what we came up with was the philosophy that we were going to correct only the big, game-changing plays such as touchdown/no touchdown, catch/no catch. We would leave the decisions to the referee, an on-field official, who knows exactly what he is doing. The replay official would only be there to facilitate the process. We also added a limited coach's challenge, which allowed coaches to request that officials review specific plays in order to speed up the game. That was enough to convince the owners to restore replay in 1999.

Even with the decision in 2014 to involve extra sets of eyes in the officiating process from a command center at league headquarters in New York, I still think the NFL has the best replay system in sports. Just look at baseball, which has followed our lead with the challenge system.

Now there are people who still say, "Correct every call, right every wrong." We have the technology to do it, but we know from our previous experience that you cannot do that. It just slows the game down to a snail's pace. It makes the game non-functional, because it takes it out of the hands of the athletes and coaches and puts it into the hands of machines or people in a booth somewhere.

The people who criticize the NFL for not reviewing every call either do not understand the history of replay...or they want to have four-hour games.

More recently, injuries, particularly concussions, have become the most talked about (and litigated) subject in the game. All the legislation from the "defenseless-player rules" in 1994, spearheaded by Commissioner Tagliabue, to the most recent "head-to-head collision" rules, championed by Commissioner Goodell, have been developed by the Competition Committee. The first subject on the agenda for the past 10 years has been injuries. The committee views tape of every significant injury of the previous season and is given updated statistics on injury trends, which are broken down minutely year after year. Club and outside physicians, as well as experts in medical statistics and bio mechanics, make presentations to the group.

I think it is fair to say there is no more well-informed group of people in the football world regarding injuries than the members of the Competition Committee. I am baffled when I see so many "experts" appearing in the media, many of whom are lawyers, while rarely is a member of the Competition Committee called upon for expertise. I volunteered at ESPN to appear opposite a critic who alleged that Commissioner Tagliabue and others did nothing to stem the tide of concussions in the league. To their everlasting credit, my ESPN supervisors said, "… by all means, go on the show." They gave me a chance to refute, with facts and first-hand knowledge, what I considered to be a very unfair assertion.

Let me state unequivocally that the NFL cares very much about player health and safety and no group in the league cares more than the Competition Committee. Paul Brown once called the committee "The Guardians of the Game."

As a 19-year member of the committee, I know every member takes that obligation to heart.

10

With Expansion Comes a Lot of Contractions

"Everyone wants to be a football man." —GEORGE ALLEN

AFTER ABOUT A YEAR AT THE LEAGUE OFFICE, I began getting feelers about opportunities to become a general manager again. I spoke with a few teams, including the Carolina Panthers, who, along with the Jacksonville Jaguars, would begin play in 1995 as expansion franchises.

It came down to a choice between an existing club and the Panthers. I chose the Panthers because I felt they presented a unique opportunity and I thought it would be fun to be on the ground floor with a new franchise. Jerry Richardson, who had briefly been a flanker/halfback for the Baltimore Colts, was the owner. He had already hired the late Mike McCormack—a Hall of Fame offensive tackle for the Cleveland Browns and former head coach of the

Eagles, Colts, and Seahawks and a man I admired greatly—as team president.

There was a lot to like about my experience with the Panthers. Eileen and I made many great friendships there and it's the place that we still call home. But it was not what I anticipated. I thought it would be similar to my time with the Bills—all football and just putting the roster together. I assumed all of the other things were in place. I assumed incorrectly.

Consequently, along with Mike, I wound up dealing with a lot of issues on sort of an ad hoc basis. That was counterintuitive to how I had done things through my career up to that point. I always tried to anticipate what the challenges would be down the road.

Among the unfamiliar items on the to-do list was refining the uniforms that had been designed by NFL Properties. We found out that the colors and the accents on the white uniforms had to be changed because they didn't show up quite as well in the sun as they had perhaps looked in the design studio. We discovered that after conducting a test on a sunny day that involved members of our equipment, training, and scouting staffs wearing the uniforms, with pads and helmets, running around on the field of Charlotte's Memorial Stadium while several of us sat in the upper deck.

Other items on that list were choosing a radio station to broadcast our games, a television station to broadcast our preseason games, as well as the talent for both broadcasts, and a hospital and doctors to provide medical care to our players and staff. The hospital choice proved to be one of the more challenging duties of them all. I didn't realize that there was what amounted to a civic battle and all the leaders in the community between the two entities vying for the designation as the Panthers' hospital: Presbyterian Hospital and Carolina's Medical Center.

Unbeknownst to me Carolina's Medical Center had grown and expanded and was now challenging for preeminence over

Presbyterian Hospital, which had been a long-standing medical leader in the community. People who were associated with one didn't think well of the people who were associated with the other. I would literally be out to dinner and someone would come up and say, "You can't choose that hospital, you have to choose this hospital...That hospital is no good, you have to go with the other one." I have never seen anything like it in my life. We settled on CMC, knowing we were in a no-win situation.

Either way we decided, we knew we would upset a fair amount of people, but the goal was to put together the best medical team we could for our players. The Richardsons shared that goal and supported us, although I'm sure they heard more feedback than the rest of us.

Our games would be played in what was then known as Ericsson Stadium (now Bank of America Stadium), which was being built in downtown Charlotte. The stadium was privately funded and all that the local government committed was infrastructure costs. I don't want to pooh-pooh that because they were considerable.

The stadium essentially would be funded by personal seat licenses (PSLs), which was the brainchild of a brilliant man named Max Muhleman, a Charlotte sports-marketing expert. He adapted it from what had gone on at the colleges in the Atlantic Coast Conference and the Southeastern Conference, among others, where donations at a certain level were required before you could purchase a season ticket in an advantageous location in the stadium. It proved to be a success at the professional level and provided funding for many stadiums—most notably Met Life Stadium in East Rutherford, New Jersey—where municipalities are unwilling or unable, or both, to fund the building of modern stadiums.

When we arrived, we had roughly 20,000 PSLs sold in a stadium that was going to seat 70,000 or so. The construction had begun, but it was nowhere near complete. As a result, we did not have a training facility, nor a firm place to play our home games. The Richardson family was negotiating between the University of South Carolina in Columbia, which would have been about an hour and a half away, and North Carolina State University in Raleigh, which would have been about two and a half hours away, but readily accessible by train. Neither proved workable.

Ultimately, ownership decided we would play at Clemson University, which was the alma mater of then-Panthers executive vice president Mark Richardson, one of Jerry Richardson's sons. Clemson had the largest capacity of the three schools and was roughly three-and-a-half to four hours away. That meant people in Charlotte were going to have to make a major commitment to travel to our games.

Nonetheless, Clemson was a great landlord and terrific to us. We also were going to make our permanent home office and training facilities at the new stadium in Charlotte, so we had to find a temporary training facility. Thankfully, we found one at Winthrop College in Rock Hill, South Carolina, which was also somewhat removed. We held training camp at Mr. Richardson's alma mater, which was at Wofford College, in Spartanburg, South Carolina, halfway between Clemson and Charlotte. We were in a position where we had to immediately put a team on the field that was going to excite people because we had to sell PSLs, we had to sell season tickets, we had to get the stadium built, and we weren't going to be in a vicinity where people from Charlotte could travel 25 or 30 miles and see the games.

We hired Dom Capers as our coach because he was an outstanding defensive mind and we felt that the best way to get good fast was to have a good defense. The media had clamored for us to hire Joe Gibbs, who had been retired since winning three Super Bowls as coach of the Washington Redskins and would have been an ideal choice. But Joe had made it clear that he did not want to coach the Panthers. He was retired and intended to stay retired (although he would return to coach the Redskins in 2004). Nevertheless, Joe and I struck up a friendship and he came down and talked with us and gave us some ideas on building a championship team.

In Dom Capers, we had a guy who we were very confident could take care of the defensive side of the ball. He had the other side well covered with a staff headed by offensive coordinator Joe Pendry, so we were in a position to be able to build a team around Dom's vision of what his zone-blitz defense ought to be. At that time, the zone blitz was new to the National Football League. There were offenses that literally did not know how to handle it. Dom also had all of the other characteristics you want in a head coach: high-character guy, great teacher, exceptionally personable, a player's coach. He was very firm in how he wanted things done, very organized, and tremendously focused on how to build the plan and execute it.

And then the thing you can never really know—but what you sense—is that he had an innate ability to reach the whole team. We might have been four or five games into our first season and Dom was holding his customary meeting right before the Saturday-morning practice. Marv Levy and other coaches usually hold those meetings Saturday night, but Dom preferred to do it in the morning. I didn't happen to be in the meeting, but I was in the building. Don Breaux, our tight ends coach, came out of the meeting and we bumped into each other in the coffee room.

"Our guy can really reach those players," he said, pointing out that he knew Dom had connected particularly well with everybody in the room. Coming from Don, who had spent a great deal of time with Joe Gibbs, that was high praise, indeed.

Dom is extremely factual. His whole delivery was built on being rational; then he would weave in just a tad of inspiration. It was always positive, never negative, and it worked.

Thanks to the collective bargaining agreement, 1995 would be the first year of bona fide free agency. That would give us the opportunity to sign free agents in addition to veteran players we selected in the expansion draft held for us and the Jaguars to stock our rosters. It became clear to Mike McCormack, Dom Capers, and me that we were not going to get any more than a handful of good players from the expansion draft, which consisted of a pool of players left "unprotected" by the 28 other teams in the league at the time. We knew the available players would be the ones with the biggest contracts who were not performing to the level of those contracts.

Ron Wolf, the Green Bay Packers' GM at the time, was outspoken about the fact that the Jaguars and Panthers would select mostly lower-paid players in the expansion draft, and that we would have an advantage in free agency over everybody else in the league because the other teams would be saddled with players with the larger contracts. He was exactly right. We took only a handful of players with larger deals that we felt had some upside, but basically we focused on the ones with smaller contracts. Our starting fullback, Howard Griffith, was among this group.

That gave us a great deal of space under the salary cap to be aggressive in the free-agent market, which we primarily used to build our defense with veterans such as linebackers Kevin Greene, Lamar Lathon, and Sam Mills, and defensive linemen such as Mike Fox and Mike Williams to go along with Greg Kragen, a nose tackle we selected from Denver in the expansion draft. We also used free agency to get Wesley Walls, a talented tight end from the Saints, and Eric Davis, a top corner from the 49ers.

The key was acquiring those veterans to play Dom's zone-blitz scheme because it was complex and to play it you had to be a student of the game. You had to recognize formation, you had to recognize tendencies, and you had to be able to communicate.

Some people say the zone blitz originated with Dick LeBeau, when he was defensive coordinator in Cincinnati. I don't know that to be true or not true. Dick, a Hall of Fame defensive back for the

Detroit Lions, is an extremely talented coach who has put together championship-quality defenses in two stints as the Pittsburgh Steelers' defensive coordinator. I also know that Bill Cowher and Dom Capers were there at the forefront of it in Pittsburgh and that's what made Pittsburgh "Blitzburgh." It was very difficult for the offense to read, especially in the early days. You could absolutely give the offense fits in terms of how to recognize it, how to match up and who to throw it to.

The zone blitz starts with a typical 3-4 alignment, with three down linemen and four linebackers. Then, if you were going to blitz someone, the blitzer would come up close to the line of scrimmage. If he was an inside linebacker, he would come close to the line of scrimmage. If he was a safety, he would creep up close to the line of scrimmage so he could get in there quickly enough to affect the pass.

What we did was all of the above. We would bring the cornerback up, we would bring a safety up, we would bring an inside linebacker up and then one would actually rush the passer and a defensive lineman would drop off into coverage. Or two blitzers would come and a defensive lineman would drop off into a zone so the opponent wouldn't know from which side we were coming or who was coming. The key to it was that you dropped a defensive lineman in to cover a vacated zone from where a secondary person came.

At the time that had never been done before, much less with 300-pound defensive linemen. We actually had a blitz—which was our best and is still used today—called "Bullets." The nose tackle would stunt one way, the inside linebacker to the nose tackle's outside would stunt another, and the remaining inside linebacker would come right up the gut—the area vacated by the two stunters— while the two ends would drop off into coverage.

Due to the complexity of the scheme, it worked best with experienced players. So Dom and I realized that, because of this approach, we were going to get old fast on defense and that it could very well negatively impact our job security in a fairly short amount of time. But we weren't worried about that or the fact that, at least at the beginning, we were kind of patchwork quilting on the offensive side. We were ready to make that sacrifice to be competitive right away, and ready to deal with whatever the consequences were later.

You always make mistakes in player evaluation, and one of them was when, in choosing between a pair of free-agent outside linebackers, we picked Lamar Lathon, from the Houston Oilers, over Bryce Paup, from the Packers. Bryce wound up signing with the Bills, but we could have easily outbid them, and I think that Bryce wanted to come to Carolina. We took the guy who was a better athlete, which was the exact opposite of our philosophy.

Lamar played very well for us, he helped us win a division championship, but had a short career due to injury. Bryce was the better player over the long haul. So no matter how hard you work, you're always going to make these kinds of errors. You are judging human beings, and you can't be right 100 percent of the time. You're lucky if you're right 60 percent of the time.

We decided we would build the offense, finding the big-play players we needed on that side of the ball, through the draft. And that started with the quarterback. It became pretty clear early on that the quarterback derby in 1995 would come down to Kerry Collins, of Penn State, and Steve McNair, of Alcorn State, so our great personnel director, Dom Anile, and I spent that whole fall season seeing both guys live and watching all of the tape on them.

A coin flip would determine whether the Panthers or Jaguars would have the first pick of the expansion draft. The loser would get the first-overall choice in the collegiate draft. Naturally, we wanted to lose because we knew the college ranks offered us the best chance of getting the top pick with the greatest talent and most upside. We also would have the option of trading that choice for additional picks in 1995 or '96. From a value standpoint, there was no comparison.

Of course, there were people in and out of our organization who didn't understand how you could possibly not want the first pick of the expansion draft, which was an example of how little experience they had with real-world NFL competition at the time. Their competitive nature simply wouldn't allow them to accept losing to the Jaguars in any arena.

But fortunately we did "lose" the coin flip and gladly accepted the right to pick first in the college draft. Ki-Jana Carter, a running back from Penn State, was the media darling of the entire draft. But Dom Anile and I didn't think that Ki-Jana was going to be a star. We thought he was going to be a good back, just not a star. We decided not to get caught up in "Ki-Jana Fever" and focus instead on getting a quarterback.

Kerry Collins was having a great year and toward the end of the season, Penn State had a few rough games, one of which I attended, at Illinois. In terrible wind conditions, Kerry brought the Nittany Lions back from three touchdowns to win the game. It was all him.

As a pure passer, Steve McNair was like none other I have ever seen. As a runner, he was better than Doug Flutie and, I think, even better than Michael Vick. And Vick couldn't carry a candle to him as a passer. Steve was accurate, he could make every throw, he had a quick release, and he could fire the ball from any angle. He was just absolutely incredible.

Additionally, Steve had soared to prominence within the African American community in America. It was to a level that, in my career, compared only to one other person in football: Tony Dungy.

I remember going to watch Steve McNair play a game in Jackson, Mississippi, and you couldn't get a seat, you couldn't get a parking space. People came from adjoining states, far and wide, to see him play, and they certainly got their money's worth because he was just phenomenal. In early November, when Steve committed to play in the Senior Bowl, the game sold out in two hours, the earliest sellout in the game's history.

Of course, Tony was the same way. When you walked with him through an airport, it was like being with the Pied Piper. People would come out from behind the food stands, news counters, airline reception desks, and ask for an autograph or to shake his hand or take his picture and tell him what a great guy they thought he was. I always felt like I was with a rock star, and I was.

Once we got through the expansion draft, the coaches became involved with the evaluation. Joe Pendry, our offensive coordinator, looked at all of the tape and said, "Steve McNair. I've never seen anything like him." Dom Capers looked at the tape and said, "Steve McNair, only because he runs better than Kerry, but we've also got the level-of-competition issue. Steve McNair is playing at Alcorn and Kerry is playing at Penn State."

The level-of-competition issue would be settled at the Senior Bowl. That was going to be Steve McNair's coming-out party at a much higher level of competition. As it turned out, playing for the South squad, he was going to be coached by Ted Marchibroda, who was the Indianapolis Colts' coach at the time and, of course, a blood brother from the Buffalo days. Dan Reeves, who was coaching the Giants at the time, would guide the North team. One of the more valuable aspects of the Senior Bowl is that it provides the opportunity for scouts and coaches throughout the league to watch how the country's elite college players, regardless of the size of their programs, practice against each other and respond to NFL coaching.

Steve wound up doing very, very well in the game, as did Kerry for the North squad. A month later, at the Combine, I made a point of asking Teddy for his impressions of Steve from the Senior Bowl.

"It's going to be an adjustment, but he'll be fine," Teddy said. "If you're going to put him in right away it might get a little bit rocky at the start, but I think ultimately he'll be fine."

There were some scouts who said Kerry's ball placement wasn't as good as Steve's. A lot of them focused on the fact that Kerry had a "hitch," which came from his pitching motion from his days of playing baseball in high school. It was kind of a roundhouse delivery as opposed to releasing the ball from the top of the ear, which is ideal, and the way Steve threw the ball. But that didn't bother us because the hitch is only a hindrance if you don't have a strong arm, thus making passes susceptible to being intercepted or knocked down because defenders can get a good jump on them. If you have a rocket arm, as Kerry did, the hitch doesn't matter. Kerry also saw things quickly enough that he got rid of the ball on time.

We then received the psychological reports and they revealed that Steve had a learning style whereby he could not quickly process what was told to him. He had to see it in order to understand it. We asked the psychologist, who was helping us with our draft preparation, "Does this mean that if Joe gets him on the phone on the sidelines and says, 'We want to adjust this route or this particular protection against this particular front,' that he won't be able to grasp it?" And the answer was essentially, "Yes, he will have difficulty with that. You are going to have to show it to him." The psychologist went on to say, "He is going to have to see these things so he can process them and then he will be able to deal with it. Once he gets it, he gets it. But it's going to take time."

We didn't think the learning condition would ever prevent Steve from being a good quarterback. Surely, you could draw up the visuals for him and figure out ways to help him out. But when you are talking about the first player in the draft, you basically want the guy to be pristine.

Steve's workout for us at Alcorn State was incredible, prompting Joe Pendry, who was not given to hyperbole, to say, "I've never seen a workout like this in my life." At the end of the session, his mother came over to us with a picnic lunch that was out of this world. It was just a tremendous day all around.

Now, we had to make a decision between Steve and Kerry. In the end, the determining factor was who could play right away. Mr. Richardson was great in that he told us not to worry about the impact it would have on our gate; just make the football decision. And what we decided was that Steve probably was not going to play right away, that it probably would take two, maybe three, years for him to fully develop. We were also worried that, over time, Steve's body would take a tremendous beating at the NFL level given how frequently he would pull the ball down and run.

On the other hand, we thought Kerry could step in and play right away, principally because he had played at a higher level. We also thought, as a pocket passer, he would have greater longevity.

Once the decision was made, we then put into motion a plan to trade the top-overall pick because the only quarterback we would select in that spot was Steve. We knew Kerry would be available later because the hitch had become such an issue. It was typical pre-draft "noise" from the pundits; they hammered away at "the hitch, the hitch, the hitch." Everybody and his brother had an opinion on it.

A trade was our preference, so we began the process of initiating one. We had to bring in Ki-Jana Carter for a physical, just to complete the pre-draft information-gathering. We knew full well that his visit would become public knowledge in an instant. Dom Anile said, "Maybe we will scare up some trade interest if people think we are interested in him."

As it turned out, the timing couldn't have been any better for having Ki-Jana's visit become public because we were having our minicamp. We had media all over our facility covering the workouts, and then they got wind of Ki-Jana being in the building and took photos of Ki-Jana talking with me and talking with Dom Capers.

The next day, there was a headline in the newspaper that said: "It's Ki-Jana!"

About 10 days later, I received a phone call from Bengals owner Mike Brown. His team had the fifth-overall pick of the draft and he wanted Ki-Jana Carter.

"Would you be interested in moving down?" Mike said.

"Yes, we would," I said.

We discussed the parameters of the trade, whereby the Bengals would give us the fifth-overall selection and their second-round choice (36th-overall) for the top pick. I ran the deal past Mike McCormack, Mr. Richardson, Dom Capers, and Dom Anile, and they all said they were good with it. Mike Brown agreed that he was not going to take Kerry Collins, while also keeping our intention to select Kerry confidential, and we made the trade.

The Bengals took Ki-Jana Carter, Jacksonville took USC offensive tackle Tony Boselli, the Houston Oilers took Steve McNair, the Washington Redskins took Colorado wide receiver Michael Westbrook, and we took Kerry.

In the end, we wanted to get someone to be our quarterback for the long haul, but also someone who we could also put in around midseason and have them be ready to go. Kerry was actually ready to play earlier, and that was exactly what happened. Frank Reich began the season as the starter. After we went 0–3, Kerry took over and never looked back.

Sure enough, it would take Steve McNair about three years to hit his stride and through the final years of his career he was pretty beaten up because of the running. Guys who tend to run a lot are such great competitors. Some scouts have the idea that you can coach it out of them, but I just don't buy it. They're great competitors, and that's why they do it. But he did have a great career and wound up playing in a Super Bowl. Unfortunately, his life was tragically cut short.

Kerry played longer, of course. He also would play in a Super Bowl, with the Giants. When it was all said and done, their careers wound up being about equal.

I had never given any thought to what expansion would be like other than how you put the team on the field. What I never realized was how difficult it was to create a culture for an expansion team, and particularly hard to do given that the league had set up what amounted to a competition between the various cities and franchise groups to get the two franchises.

Now, from the league's perspective, that was fine. The league was going to get two cities that would be new to the league and they would get top price for the franchise and all of that made sense. But from an operational perspective, it created kind of a mind-set that the group that bid on the franchise and the skeleton group that existed before the football people ever came on board won this competition and, therefore, would win in the National Football League.

Of course, we knew that wasn't the case; one has nothing to do with the other. It was difficult to come in and have to say to people, "Look, you did a great job in getting the franchise, but now there are 29 other teams that want to beat your brains out and they are every bit as smart as we are, and many of them have more resources than we do. We don't even have a training facility. We don't have a stadium yet."

I'll be the first to admit that I can be blunt and that I'm not always the world's greatest salesman. Suzy Kolber, one of my colleagues at ESPN, calls me "Buzz Kill Bill," because someone will say, "Oh, yeah, this guy's a great player," and I'll shake my head and say, "No, he isn't."

With an expansion franchise, you have to teach everybody how to function in the National Football League: doctors, trainers, marketing people. And that's a hard job. Mike McCormick did the vast majority of the heavy lifting and was much better at it than I was. But you have to do it and it takes time and effort that you would not be used to doing had you spent your whole career as I did with an existing franchise. We didn't have an infrastructure in place. We were operating out of a floor in an office building where there were law firms and insurance firms, as far from football as you could get. It just comes with expansion.

Another strange dynamic was that the fans and the media thought that our rival was Jacksonville because they assumed our progress would naturally be measured against each other as fellow expansion teams. I kept saying, "No, we are only going to play Jacksonville once every four years, and we will be very lucky if we play them at some point in the Super Bowl, the odds of which are infinitesimal because it's never happened before. Don't focus on Jacksonville. Focus on the 49ers, focus on the Falcons, focus on the Saints, focus on St. Louis, focus on the rest of the teams in our division, the NFC West."

The fans and some media didn't want to hear that. To make matters worse, the league scheduled its annual preseason-opening game at the Pro Football Hall of Fame between us and the Jaguars. In one sense, like everything in life, there are good things and bad things. It was a blessing that we would get that game against Jacksonville out of the way, but the lead-up to it was like the Super Bowl and it drove me crazy. We were trying to build a team to just be competitive and all I was hearing was, "Are we going to beat Jacksonville? We have to beat Jacksonville. If we don't beat Jacksonville, it will be the end of the world!"

We did end up beating the Jaguars 20–14, and as happy as many of our fans might have been, it truly was not indicative of the sort of team we would have in the regular season. We went 7–9 that first year. Not surprisingly, our offense struggled, but we ranked eighth in the league in total defense and 10th in rush defense.

We made a huge jump in 1996, winning the NFC West with a 12–4 record and tying the 49ers for second-best record in the league. Thanks largely to a vastly improved secondary, we ranked second in the NFL, behind Green Bay, in total defense. We also made big strides on offense and on special teams. Michael Bates might have been as good a kickoff-returner as any I've been around. He led the NFL that year with an incredible 30.2-yard average on 33 returns.

Kerry Collins came of age in that second season. Specifically, it was the 15th week of the season when we faced the 49ers at Candlestick Park on kind of a cold and drizzly day with the division lead at stake. Here we were, this second-year franchise, and we were going to challenge the great San Francisco 49ers, with future Hall of Famer Steve Young at quarterback. It was understood that this would be a defining game for our second-year quarterback, the moment when he would prove whether he was ready to lead us to a championship.

On the bus on the way to Candlestick, Joe Pendry said to me, "We are going to put the hat on Kerry today!" That meant we were going to sink or swim on the basis of how he performed.

Joe then pointed out that Pete Carroll, the 49ers' defensive coordinator at the time, was going to play a lot of cover-two that, by design, would give Kerry the opportunity to complete passes underneath and deny him from hitting deep routes.

"He has got to get the ball in there and get the job done," Joe said. "This is it, man."

"Wow, this is only his second year," I said.

"It's time, he's got it. We are putting the hat on him. We are putting all the chips on Kerry Collins today."

Kerry responded by throwing for 327 yards and three touchdowns, with no interceptions, to lead us to a 30–24 victory.

Steve Young threw for 393 yards and three scores as well...but we intercepted him twice.

Until that game, we weren't sure if Kerry could take us to a championship because that was the next level. And there he was, leading us to victory against the 49ers in Candlestick.

We would go on to beat Dallas 26–17 in the divisional round and then lose to the Packers 30–13 in the NFC Championship Game on a bitterly cold day in Lambeau Field. But it was an amazingly fast sprint for a team in only its second year of existence.

Unfortunately, the fans and the media kind of expected that it was going to be that easy every year.

Our 7–9 finish in 1997 bore that out.

11

Tuning Out the Noise

"There are only two things that are important in this game: finding good football players and coaching them well."

—NORM POLLOM

IN 1996, MY SECOND SEASON WITH THE CAROLINA PANTHERS, there was a lot of media speculation that I wasn't happy with my role as general manager while Mike McCormack held the title of president, and that I was looking to leave the team. Nothing could have been further from the truth. We worked very well together and I was in full concurrence with Mike on all football decisions, but people assumed that I was in a subordinate position.

Mr. Richardson told me that there had been inquiries from other NFL teams about my availability. I just shrugged my shoulders and said, "That's nice. I'm happy where I am. When it's time to talk about a new contract, we will talk about that."

"Well, if at any time you're not happy here," Mr. Richardson said, "we could talk about that."

Before the season, Kevin Greene staged a very difficult holdout that I thought we could have handled better. It just became the linchpin of a lot of difficult decisions that we had to make that didn't pan out very well. Kevin's agent was Leigh Steinberg, but really it was David Dunn, Leigh's partner at the time, with whom I was doing all the talking regarding Kevin's contract. We had signed Kevin as a free agent in '96 and, with a two-year deal worth $2 million, we felt he had ostensibly gotten all there was to get in the open market at the time.

However, because Kevin led the NFL with 14½ sacks and set a league record with five consecutive multi-sack games to help us reach the '96 NFC title game, David's position to me was, "He's outperformed the contract." Steinberg also was saying that publicly. I didn't quite know what that meant other than they just wanted more money.

It became a public and private bone of contention. There were people in our organization who felt that we ought to negotiate a new deal for Kevin, and there were others that thought we should simply stonewall and let him go or sit out. I actually thought, before the holdout, that I had at least an agreement in principle with David Dunn to rework the contract to include enough in the way of incentives for an acceptable compromise. That fell through, and we ended up trading Kevin to San Francisco. It was not a good situation, particularly because we couldn't find an adequate replacement.

As if that weren't bad enough, we had a long and difficult holdout with our first-round draft pick that year, running back Tim Biakabutuka, mainly because his agents—brothers Carl and Kevin Poston—had little experience negotiating NFL contracts. Most of their work had been done in the NBA. My suspicion was that they were absolutely not going to negotiate with us, virtually under any circumstances, until the absolute last minute. My hunch was correct.

The franchise had never been through something like this in its short existence, and I'm not sure that Mr. Richardson had ever been through something like this at any time in his long business career, so it was difficult. We would eventually work out a contract, but, frankly, it wore on me.

Then, in training camp, things just continued to unravel. Kerry Collins had a terrible episode where, after having had more than a few beers, he made racist remarks that became public, which turned into a real issue, both in the locker room and in public. Kerry did very sincerely apologize, but I think there was some justified resentment toward him on the part of a small group of people.

On top of that, he got his jaw broken in about 14 places on a blind-side hit by then-Denver Broncos linebacker Bill Romanowski in a preseason game. It was one of the worst, most vicious, unconscionable and unnecessary hits I have ever seen in my career. Bill put Kerry in the hospital by smashing right into his earhole with the crown of his helmet. There was absolutely no need for it whatsoever, especially in a preseason game.

Additionally, Kerry tried to come back too soon from the injury. Steve Beuerlein was our backup and was doing a fine job, but Kerry, because he is so tough and such a competitor, wound up returning too soon. Not that we discouraged it, because we were in the race, and many people thought that we could perhaps catch Green Bay or Dallas and become NFC champions. Unfortunately, when you are in that position, you only get one chance to make that decision. We probably made it incorrectly, and most of the blame rests with me.

Kerry was not the same guy when he came back and, of course, how could he be? There still was the lingering aura of the racial remark that he made, and he was having—he would be the first to tell you—some personal difficulty and it was resulting in a little too much drinking, which became an issue. I know that we did not, and I did not, give him enough help when he needed it very badly.

He wasn't married at the time, and I don't think he had a steady girlfriend. He was living alone in a typical kind of furnished apartment, which wasn't very conducive to him having warm and fuzzy feelings about his life. It was a tough situation that, of course, would only get worse and Kerry was ultimately traded to New Orleans, where he probably hit bottom. Ultimately, he joined the Giants, went to the Super Bowl, and had a long and successful career. He also has a great family. I wish I had done more to help him, but the proof of his character is what he did to help himself.

At the fall league meeting of 1997, I ran into Jim Irsay, the Colts' owner. We had worked together as club executives on the NFL Management Council for many years to help put together a collective bargaining agreement. Jim's father, Robert Irsay—who had been the Colts' owner since 1972, when they were in Baltimore—had died earlier in the year and Jim took over the team. Jim was aware of the chatter about my uncertain future with the Panthers and said to me, "Hey, listen, if you feel like you want to move, let me know."

I told him I would.

A year after going 12–4 and competing for the NFC crown, we would fall back to 7–9. Toward the end of the season, I gave Jim a call and said, "If you're thinking about making a change, then I think you should speak with Jerry."

After Jim asked Jerry Richardson for permission to speak with me, he offered me the position of president of the Colts. Jim and Jerry then discussed what it would take to get me out of my Panthers contract, which had another season left. They agreed on compensation, which, I'm embarrassed to say, was the Colts' third-round choice in the 1998 draft. I thought it would be a fifth- or sixth-rounder at most.

I had always liked Indianapolis as a city. I had been going there for a long time both as a competitor and for the Combine. I thought it was a nice place to live and a market that, after the Colts' 3–13 finish in 1997, was rife for improvement relative to football.

I liked that I would be working for a guy that I knew pretty well and for whom I had high respect and who understood football because he had been a GM; he actually had done the job when his father owned the team. It was going to be the kind of working relationship that you long for, in the sense that you don't have to do a lot of explaining or have a lot of discussion about extraneous issues.

Jim was a "new" owner in name only. You could have a 15-minute discussion with Jim about the football team, the franchise, league rules, whatever it might be pertaining to the game that would take two hours with even a seasoned owner. New owners, in whatever sport they may be in, always try to translate their business experience to owning an NFL team, but it doesn't translate that well. A new owner thinks that the principles that operated in the business world operate in equal measure in the football world or the professional sports world. They don't. This is the entertainment business and it's a talent business and you have to understand that at the outset.

Jim did. He knew what I was saying, both from a factual standpoint and an instinctive standpoint. For example, I would say, "If we do A with this player's contract ...," he would finish the sentence and say, "Well, of course, then B and C are going to happen, and we are going to have to worry about repercussions with D down the road." He understood all of that thoroughly.

Jim grew up in the game, having been around the Colts since he was 13. He understood the culture of the locker room, he understood what coaching was about at that level, he understood players, he understood the business part of it.

In assessing why the Colts were at the very bottom of the league in '97, my immediate thought was that the team had an absolute need for discipline and focus. There were too many penalties, too many guys doing their own thing rather than playing within the offensive or defensive scheme. When you talked with people around the league and you looked at tape, those were pretty much the main issues. And the principal need was for a quarterback, the position we intended to address with the top-overall pick of the draft.

When you don't have a quarterback who can get the job done, then people lose confidence and they begin to focus on their own personal goals rather than team goals, and things tend to slide.

Before my arrival, Jim had released his general manager, Bill Tobin. I was very grateful Bill had done a very good drafting job on offense. We had some very good players on that side of the ball in running back Marshall Faulk, a Hall of Famer; wide receiver Marvin Harrison, an eventual Hall of Famer; offensive tackle Tarik Glenn; and tight end Ken Dilger. The defense wasn't anywhere near as talented. There were also some defensive guys who weren't playing anywhere near what their talent level dictated.

Jim also fired his head coach, Lindy Infante, and tasked me with finding a replacement. I interviewed a number of different candidates. Ty Willingham, who was then at Stanford, was high on my list. I admired his work. I liked his demeanor. I especially liked the fact that players who had played for Ty spoke very highly of him. But much to my surprise, Ty's agent told me that he wasn't interested in talking with us about the job. I never found out why, but was disappointed we didn't even get the chance to speak.

Jim Mora, who was available after resigning as head coach of the Saints after they started the '96 season 2–6, was high on the list of candidates from the start because I had had great respect for Jim Finks, for whom Jim Mora worked in New Orleans, and a lot of respect for Carl Peterson, for whom Jim worked with the Philadelphia Stars in the United States Football League. I also had seen what Jim's teams had done in the USFL and in the NFL. He was a proven head coach, which I thought was particularly important for our situation. I felt strongly that we had to have someone with a track record, someone who had the credentials to get the players' attention right away.

After spending the 1997 season as a television analyst for NBC's coverage of the NFL, Jim received the chance to return to coaching from us and he gladly accepted. Ultimately, it was a pretty clear-cut decision for us.

Ty would eventually make his way back to Indiana as head coach at Notre Dame, but it didn't work out well. I don't think he ever really got a chance to implement his program there. Ironically, Jim Harbaugh, the incumbent quarterback who we planned to replace with whoever the rookie was that we selected No. 1 overall, would go on to become the head coach at Stanford and wound up employing my son, Brian, as an assistant coach. Brian had also been at Notre Dame as a member of the Charlie Weis staff that took over after Ty was let go, and then Brian joined Jim at Stanford after Weis was replaced by Brian Kelly.

If that doesn't show you what the merry-go-round of a football life is all about, nothing will.

Jim Harbaugh is a feisty competitor as a coach, and that was exactly how he was as a player. He didn't take very kindly to hearing about our intentions to part ways with him. "I think I have given this franchise a lot, and I think I ought to have the right to compete," Jim told me.

"I know what kind of a competitor you are," I said. "And I know that if you compete, this competition is likely to split the team because you are such a charismatic leader and charismatic guy in the community, so I believe that it's best to just turn the keys over to the new guy for good or for ill.

"You have every right to expect to be treated well by this franchise and Mr. Irsay has instructed me to do that, and I am going to do it with every ability I have to do it. You tell me where you would like to go, and I will see to it that you get there without any impediments from the Colts whatsoever."

We wound up trading Jim to the Baltimore Ravens. Later, I got a letter from his father, Jack, who had been a college football coach for many years, in effect saying, "Thank you for the way you parted company with Jim. It was done in a professional manner and he was treated with respect, and I want you to know, as his father, I appreciate that."

I was tremendously touched by that letter. Years later, just before Jim interviewed my son, Brian, for a job on the Stanford coaching staff, I mentioned to my wife and to Brian that I hoped Jim wouldn't hold it against him that we traded Jim. Brian actually brought up the topic with Jim, and Jim said, "I'm only interested in doing what's best for Stanford. If you're the right guy for us, then you are the guy we are going to hire."

That tells you all you need to know about the Harbaugh family—classy, professional, and filled with good people.

NFL player-personnel staffs use different grading systems and language for the scouting reports they create for each player. The first thing I told the scouts in Indianapolis was to continue to use the grading system and nomenclature they had in place and that I would translate it into my way of thinking.

It would have been impossible for me, in the four months before the draft, to try to teach them an entirely new scouting system. But trying to convert one to the other was difficult. It would be as though you were trying to have a business discussion in France with a bunch of French people who have their own culture, their own language, their own idiom and you are an American trying to make a decision based upon what they're telling you. You understand that the engineering is the same whether it's in French or English, but the fact of the matter is that there are nuances and differences in language that mean a lot.

Some grading systems, such as the one we used in Buffalo, are numeric, going from 1 to 5 or 1 to 8, with decimal gradations in between. For instance, a 1.0 would be O.J. Simpson or Peyton Manning, the perfect player; a 1.5 would be a first-round/middle-of-the-second-round player, and a 5 would be a reject. The system that Dom Anile and I created in Carolina was based on rounds, so a player with a 1 designation was a first-round player, a player with a 2 designation was a second-round player, and so on.

Rather than setting up our draft board longitudinally, listing prospects 1 through 350 as we did in Buffalo, we created a horizontal grid that was arranged by round and position. We listed the rounds on the left side, longitudinally, and then broke each one out by position horizontally so that we could see who the best quarterback, running back, wide receiver, and so forth were in each round.

Then, in putting together a 250- to 300-page scouting manual that was given to each scout, we realized we had to have designations for the various characteristics of players. If we didn't—a point Dom continually harped on—we wouldn't have been able to tell the position coach, the coordinator, and the head coach what kind of player he was getting and we wouldn't have been able to differentiate between players at the same position in a round. We used letters for that, something the Dallas Cowboys had done and Bob Ferguson brought to us in Buffalo.

When we finally got the system completed, we would, for instance, have various types of wide receivers on the board. There were what we called "Clean" wide receivers; they had no letter designation because they were the requisite height, the requisite weight, and had the requisite speed by our standards. Reggie Wayne, whom we drafted in the first round from Miami in 2001, had a "Clean" designation. If a wide receiver had an "S" after his name, that meant he was speed deficient. A "B" (as in body) wide receiver was weight deficient, a "Z" wide receiver was height deficient, an "x" wide receiver had a medical problem (if it was a capital X, he would usually end up off the board), and a "C" meant he had a character problem. If he was a player who was really, really outstanding in every intangible area, he would have a gold star. And if he was someone that we had targeted, that we would trade for, that we would do everything we could to get, he would have a little Colts sticker on his card.

You could pick a player's card off the board and, if you understood our system, you would, by looking at a number and a series of letters, be able to get an absolutely clear picture of what he was all about. An example would be tight end Dallas Clark. Even if you never looked at him on film, you would know that you were getting a guy with extraordinary speed and whose body type was not ideal for the position but who had good athleticism. We actually created two types of designations for tight ends: "A," for an athletic tight end, and "B," for a blocking tight end.

Mr. Irsay got very conversant with the system and was very good at reading it, so he would come into the draft room maybe a half-hour before our pick and he would take a look at the names up there and say, "Boy oh boy, Antoine Bethea [a safety we drafted from Howard in the sixth round in 2006] is still there, huh? He's a Colt, he's a star guy."

"Yeah, he is," we would tell him. "That's who we're interested in."

But we had one other derivation and we could never find a symbol or synonym for it. When we were talking, for example, with Tony Dungy or even with Mr. Irsay, we would say, "I'm telling you, aside from all of these other things that are good about him, he's a 'Holy shit!' player. He's got magic. When you put the tape on and watch him, you go, *Holy shit!* Run that back.'" Even Tony, who never cussed, laughed.

We never could find the appropriate symbol, but we would, on those rare occasions when we saw one, refer to a "Holy shit!" player.

Examples for us would be Bob Sanders, a strong safety we drafted in the second round from Iowa in 2004; Dallas Clark, a tight end we drafted in the first round from Iowa in 2003; Robert Mathis, a defensive end we drafted in the fifth round from Alabama A&M in '03; and Dwight Freeney, a defensive end we drafted in the first round from Syracuse in 2002.

Working with Dom; my son, Chris, who was our general manager in Indianapolis; and young scouts David Caldwell and Tom Telesco—Buffalo natives who have since gone on to become general managers of the Jaguars and Chargers, respectively—we came up with a computer program that allowed a scout to enter virtually every player that he scouted into a category so that his written summation had to correspond with the categories he checked in the program. It became a fail-safe; if what a scout wrote didn't equal the number and letter categories that he checked, you knew that there was some discrepancy in the original report.

It got everybody on the same page, it got everybody speaking the same language. It took out all of the nuance you had to fight through in terms of trying to understand what a scout was saying and yet it still left room for the scout to be creative and say, "I really believe in this guy and I think he can make it." It gave you hard standards to go against and we would change those standards every year based upon trends in the game—such as the emergence of the athletic tight end versus a blocking tight end—and ultimately what the coaches wanted.

We also incorporated the idea of "video profiling," which Bill Walsh used when he was coach of the 49ers. It involved condensing several games of tape on a player to his best and worst 50 plays. Not only did that help you gauge potential, but it would also show you mistakes he was consistently making.

I had been intimately involved with preparing for the 1998 NFL Draft at Carolina, so I knew the candidates for the first pick were the two quarterbacks: Peyton Manning, of Tennessee, or Ryan Leaf, of Washington State.

Ryan Leaf had been a late riser, in the sense that he was entering his junior year, so there was less known about him than about Peyton, who had remained in school for his fourth year. Ryan had been on the horizon, but then exploded during his junior year and then, to no one's surprise, chose to enter the draft. Peyton had a great senior season and, inexplicably, was not voted the Heisman Trophy winner. It went to Michigan defensive back Charles Woodson, despite the fact Peyton had four stellar seasons and later that year won the Sullivan Award as America's top amateur athlete.

There were mixed feelings about Peyton, both in the media and among football people. Around late January or early February, I asked our scouts to submit their votes on which quarterback we should take. The result was 50/50. The interesting thing was, the people who voted for Peyton Manning didn't really dislike Ryan Leaf, but the people who voted for Ryan Leaf really disliked Peyton Manning.

The negatives commonly recited about Peyton were that he was non-athletic, had an average-to-weak arm, was a product of the system (and to this day I don't know what that necessarily meant), couldn't win the big game, and was more hype than substance. Anyone who really drilled down would find what was true about Peyton in college is still true now: he wins far more with his ability to manipulate a defense and get the ball to the right guy than he does with physical ability. He plays the position cerebrally and succeeds with good decisions, ball placement, and accuracy, rather than with pure arm strength.

Peyton understands defenses so well that he can, simply by a movement of his shoulder on a play-action pass or the slight movement of his head to one side of the field or the other, force the defense into adjusting. And then he knows immediately—not instinctively, because he has created instinct through constant study—who the open man will be when the defense reacts to his manipulation. He gets the ball there instantly and on target.

Tom Moore, our offensive coordinator at the time, and Bruce Arians, our quarterbacks coach at the time, created a system that allowed Peyton to come to the line of scrimmage and identify the defense, which really had never been done to the extent he was doing it, and then set the pass protection and the play call and the routes that would take advantage of that defense. It really allowed him to control the game on the line of scrimmage without a coach ever having to send in a play call from the sideline. Opposing defenses would try to disguise what they were doing and as time went on, they would try to create as much confusion as possible in order to bleed the play clock. They would then make a defensive change with about nine seconds left, so that it would be too late for Peyton to call an audible.

But Tom, offensive line coach Howard Mudd, and Peyton figured out a way to communicate an immediate audible, using a one- or two-word signal that told everybody on offense exactly what the snap count was, what the play was going to be, and all of the other necessary information. As Peyton led the Denver Broncos on their run to Super Bowl XLVIII, much was made of his use of the word "Omaha" before the snap. "Omaha" meant different things from game to game. One week it could be a play call, the following week it could be a pass-protection scheme, and the week after that it could mean nothing. Just as was the case with the Colts, when Peyton walks up and down the line before a play, calling various audibles, only one might be live.

We scheduled a meeting with Ryan Leaf the first night of the Combine and a session with Peyton Manning the second night. Dom Anile and I, along with Jim Mora, Tom Moore, and Bruce Arians sat in the room awaiting Ryan's arrival at the designated time. He never showed up. We checked with the people running the Combine and we called his agents, but no one seemed to know what happened to him.

As we walked back to our hotel, word began to spread that Ryan had blown us off. By the next morning, it was a major story and Jim Mora was quoted as saying he was upset about it. Leigh Steinberg put word out to the media that I had misinformed Ryan and his representatives of the day and time of the meeting. However, when some reporters sought me out for a comment, I made it clear that I had given the date and time correctly to everybody that needed it.

The next night, Peyton walked in for his meeting right on time. He sat down, opened up a briefcase, and took out a legal pad and pen. Although quarterbacks do tend to be more cerebral and more organized than most players, that scene was outside the norm even for a quarterback. What was even more striking was the fact that, on the first page of his notebook, he had about 25 questions he wanted to ask us.

Peyton inquired about our offensive system and what our approach was to offensive structure. He wanted a rundown on personnel, asking who were the people we really counted on and what our offensive line was like, and other questions along those lines. I was astonished. Of course, that was a harbinger of things to come...and the first of numerous meetings where Peyton would sit down with me with a pad filled with questions and suggestions.

All of a sudden, the horn blew to signify that our 15 minutes had expired and we said, "Well, it's been nice talking to you. We'll probably see you at your school next."

"You know, if you draft me, I'll be in the day after the draft," Peyton said.

"Whoa! You can't do that," I said. "It's against league rules. You can't come in until May 10th because you have to wait until after your class graduates before you can work out with the team that drafts you."

That was true even though Peyton had already graduated.

"No, no, no, I'm going to be in there," Peyton insisted.

"Well, the league rules prohibit it," I said.

"We'll find a way around it. I'm going to be there, and I'm going to be in the playbook and learn the offense."

"Okay, if we take you, we will figure it out."

Off Peyton went. Then, we all sort of looked at each other and said, "He just interviewed us, didn't he?"

I wouldn't say we had our minds made up at that point, but let's just say that the odds were heavily in Peyton's favor.

Not long after the Combine, I asked our video director to put together two tapes: one of every one of the 1,381 passes that Peyton Manning had thrown in his college career, and one of every one of the 880 passes that Ryan Leaf had thrown in his college career. Copies were distributed to Jim Mora, Tom Moore, Bruce Arians, and me. I asked each of the coaches to watch the tapes independently, write a report, and we would discuss what everyone saw as we went along through the process. We also asked Bill Walsh, who was out of football at the time, to look at some tapes. He was happy to help.

I would estimate that I spent roughly 500 hours just watching tape of all of those throws, while watching the passes they threw in the 1997 season twice.

The closer we got to the draft, the louder the "noise"—opinions from draft media analysts far and wide—became, until it reached a crescendo. You were hearing all of the negatives about Peyton Manning: "He's a product of the system...He's not a good athlete... He has a weak arm...He can't win the big one." On the contrary, you were hearing nothing but accolades for Ryan Leaf: "He's a natural thrower...He has a cannon arm...He can make people miss when he runs...He's the second coming of Roger Staubach." Most of that was in the media and largely, I'm sure, fueled by Steinberg, who was a master at getting favorable publicity for his clients.

I reminded myself and others in the building, "Tune out the noise! Tune out the noise!" I even delivered the same message in my public comments, saying, "We are going to ignore the noise; it's not part of the equation. We are going to make the decision based on what we believe to be sound football reasons."

Yet, there I was, on a Sunday, watching the tape of Peyton's throws and hearing all of that "noise" in my head: "He doesn't have a strong arm …He can't make the deep throws …" I began to focus on every pass in his career that traveled more than 40 yards and what I found out was that, once the ball got beyond 60 yards, he started losing accuracy.

The next morning, I got Tom Moore and Bruce Arians together, and said, "I think you have a ceiling on Manning's arm at about 60 yards."

They both look at me as if I were crazy. I could see in their eyes that they were thinking, *He's lost it. We're working with a guy who has lost his marbles and he's in charge of the franchise!*

Tom then looked up and said, dryly, "Well, then, Bill, we'll be sure not to throw any passes over 59 yards."

In late March/early April, we arranged a private workout with Peyton at Tennessee. Tom has an arm-strength drill whereby he stands the quarterback on the goal line and has a receiver facing him five yards away. The quarterback has to throw to the receiver using only his arm; he isn't allowed to step into his throw or use his feet in any way. And after each throw, the receiver moves back in five-yard increments until he eventually reaches the 50-yard line. By the time the receiver gets to the 50, you have a pretty good idea of whether the quarterback has a strong arm or not because he isn't putting anything else physically into his throws—and he already has thrown nine passes that way.

Tom put Peyton through the arm-strength drill, and his pass to the 50-yard line was on a rope. Peyton's arm was among the strongest I have seen. It maybe was not quite as strong as Jim Kelly's, but certainly strong enough. Interestingly, Peyton threw what we call a "heavy ball," meaning it has a lot of rotation on it, which was quite interesting because guys with weaker arms usually don't throw a heavy ball. When you catch a heavy ball, your hands sting because it comes out with some heat on it.

Peyton had a slam-dunk workout, as good as you could have. Not that workouts are everything, but that one served as fairly solid evidence that all of the perceived negatives—that he was a bad athlete, that he had a weak arm, etc.—were untrue.

Naturally, Phillip Fulmer, Tennessee's football coach at the time, told us nothing but the most glowing things about Peyton. He said Peyton was as prepared as any coach when the Volunteers did their game planning, that he knew as much about the upcoming opponent as any coach, that he studied film voraciously. Phillip gave us a verbal picture of what we would literally see from Peyton Manning for the next 14 years.

The next day, we went to Washington State to work out Ryan Leaf. There were actually two workouts scheduled with him—ours and one with the San Diego Chargers, who had the second-overall pick. The Chargers had been scheduled to go first, and Bobby Beathard, their general manager at the time, was walking out to the parking lot of Martin Stadium as we were walking in. Bobby smiled and said something to me like, "This guy is head and shoulders above Peyton Manning, no question about it. This was the greatest workout I have ever seen."

I knew he was joking because he had that Bobby Beathard twinkle in his eye. I laughed and said, "Okay, but we'll still work him out."

"If you're interested in trading down, give me a call."

"Okay, fair enough."

We laughed a little more and then I walked into the stadium with our group. The first thing that caught my eye was that, during the measurement and weight-lifting segments indoors, Ryan was wearing sweatpants that he never took off, even after the session began. The Washington State coaches orchestrated the entire workout; we weren't able to conduct it ourselves as we had in Tennessee.

Ryan went through all of the standard throwing drills and did okay, not great. I remember turning to Tom Moore and saying, "His arm is not as strong as Peyton's."

"I think you're right," Tom said.

Ryan didn't drive the ball quite as well as Peyton did, which, frankly, was what showed up on tape and put the lie to this idea that there was this huge gulf physically between them. And I presumed the reason Ryan wouldn't take his sweatpants off was because he didn't want us to see what kind of shape he was in.

After the workout, we met with Ryan and Mike Price, the Washington State head coach at the time. Jim Mora asked Ryan why he had missed the meeting with us at the Combine, and I thought he was being honest when he said he confused it with another appointment, or something like that. It was a plausible answer.

It should be noted that, 16 years later, Leigh Steinberg wrote in his book, *The Agent*, that he suggested to Ryan to intentionally skip his meeting with us in order to discourage us from selecting him, thus allowing him to go to where Leigh said he preferred to play: San Diego. Leigh also wrote that he cleared the idea with Bobby Beathard so the Chargers' GM wouldn't question Ryan's reliability, and added that Bobby "went along with the ruse." I seriously doubt that, because of my conversation with Bobby in the parking lot of Martin Stadium. Bobby, of course, has subsequently said that he was never approached or involved in any discussions designed to bring Ryan to the Chargers.

"Now, you know Ryan," Jim Mora said, "May 10th is the day that you can come in to work out with us, and if we draft you, we expect you there."

"Well, Coach, I can't make it," Ryan said.

Everybody's head snapped back, and that included Coach Price, who I am sure was not aware of anything that would keep his former quarterback from being on time for his first NFL practice.

"Why not?" Jim asked.

"My buddies and I have planned a trip for a year to Las Vegas, and we have to go on this trip. It's kind of a celebration of the draft and everything, and I will be in probably around the 15th of May."

That wasn't the answer any of us wanted to hear.

About a week before the draft, Peyton's father, Archie Manning —a quarterbacking icon himself who played for the Saints, Oilers, and Vikings—called me and said, "Do you have any idea when you are going to make a decision?

"Archie, I learned a long time ago from George Young, who said, 'Make no decision before it's time,'" I said. "I tend to be really slow on these things anyway. I want to dot every i and cross every t. I certainly will let you know before Draft Day, that's for sure."

I'm not sure Archie was thrilled with that, although, as always, he was polite.

Two days later, while at our facility to go through one last piece of physical data that our doctors wanted, Peyton popped into my office for a quick chat.

"You said you are going to make a decision soon before the draft," he said. "When are you going to make it?"

"I don't know," I said. "I'm sort of taking my time. I've still got to sit down with our owner. I'm about 90 percent there, but I'm not a quick decision maker, especially not when it comes to a decision with this import."

"Well, look, I have to know whether to go to New York or not," he said. "I'm scheduled to be in New York on Thursday."

"Okay, fair enough. I will let you know before you go to New York what the decision is. But please, please give me your word that you don't let it out because it's very important to Mr. Irsay that he be there and be a part of the process, and that's his right."

"Yes, you can count on me, don't worry about that. But I need to know."

"I understand and you have my word. I will call you before you leave for New York."

As he got up to leave, he turned to me and he said, "Listen, I just want to leave you with this one thought: if you draft me, I promise we will win a championship. And if you don't, I promise I will come back and kick your ass."

The next day, Jim Mora and I met and I said, "Where are you with the quarterbacks?"

"I'm with Peyton," he said.

"I'm the same way. If we believe in all the things that we both think are important for a winning football team, then it's Peyton."

"Yeah, you're right."

After that, I met with Jim Irsay.

"What's your decision?" he said.

"The decision is unanimous," I said. "It's Peyton."

Jim never let on who he wanted. I think it was Peyton, but to his credit, he never interfered with the process.

"What's the upside and the downside with both of them?" he asked.

"Here's the issue: I can't tell you if either of these guys is going to win a Super Bowl or become a Hall of Famer. We are just trying to find a quarterback that we can win with. But I'll tell you this: If we bust out with Leaf, we have busted out everything. If he busts out, we've lost. If we are wrong on Peyton Manning, the worst we have is Bernie Kosar—a really good, winning quarterback." So much for my scouting acumen.

I can't say that I envisioned everything that Peyton Manning would become, but after you have been through this process, which you trust, everything pointed to him. You hoped that he would become half of what he became, but there was no question that he would be a winning quarterback in the National Football League.

12

On Draft Day,
Let the Board Talk to You

"Just do what we do."   —Tony Dungy

Our plan from the start with the Colts was to put as much talent around Peyton Manning as we could, in addition to what was already there. Lindy Infante, who was Jim Mora's predecessor, was an offensive-oriented coach, and he and Bill Tobin, who was my predecessor, had put some very good pieces in place. We had a top-flight wide receiver in Marvin Harrison, a top-flight running back in Marshall Faulk, a very good tight end in Ken Dilger, and two top-flight tackles in Tarik Glenn and Adam Meadows.

Defense was another story. We didn't have any real difference makers there except for end Bertrand Berry, who would go to St. Louis in free agency in 2000 and spend a year in the Canadian Football League before returning to the NFL and having a few more really good years in Denver and Arizona. Looking back, I'm sorry we didn't keep him.

We finished 3-13 in 1998, but Jim Mora brought such accountability, discipline, and work ethic to the program that it was not nearly as bad a season as one would assume. By the end of the year, the arrow was pointing up significantly on Peyton, who teamed with Marvin to form the early version of the dynamic duo that they would become. One example of what led them on their path to greatness came near the end of the season, in the late stages of a 38–31 loss at Baltimore. We were in the red zone with a chance to tie the game, but Peyton and Marvin miscommunicated on a sight-adjustment route, which is what the receiver runs if he and the quarterback see a certain defensive alignment against which the originally called route won't work.

After the game, I got both of them together and said, "Listen, I don't want either of you to have your dauber down. This will never happen again because after one off-season of working together, you will be so fine-tuned and so able to communicate that you will never have a mix-up like this again. Don't even worry about it. It will never take place again, I promise you."

They both practiced in the off-season program and worked together as often as possible, year after year, until the day they no longer played together. They became two bodies in the same mind. The numbers indicate that, and they are still the greatest touchdown-making duo in NFL history. Marvin, of course, was the dominant receiver of his time in the NFL, and his induction in the Pro Football Hall of Fame is only a matter of time.

The most significant move after our first season, and a highly controversial one, was when we traded Marshall Faulk. That was quite the controversy, and I'm not sure that the story behind it has ever been fully told. Marshall, who would go on to become a Hall of

Famer, was phenomenal with the ball in his hands. He was perhaps the best route runner of any back I have ever seen.

Marshall was darn good at running the football because he had home-run speed and he could make people miss. The only thing that he couldn't do as a runner was short-yardage and goal-line power running because he wasn't that big. Also, the way that Tom Moore, our offensive coordinator, and Howard Mudd, our offensive line coach, had constructed the offensive system, there were times when the running back was a blocker, which wasn't Marshall's strong suit, either. But he was a Hall of Famer in every respect.

The problem we had with Marshall was his dissatisfaction with his contract, and I couldn't blame him. It was excessively long and bound him in ways that his agent surely regretted after it was signed. Marshall was a much, much better player than the deal had called for. But we couldn't renegotiate it because the money he wanted, or anticipated getting under the cap, would have squeezed us terribly. To Marshall's credit, he played his heart out for every single game through the '98 season. He never indicated any lack of intensity or effort on the field.

Not surprisingly, his agent approached me soon after the season to let me know there was going to be a holdout. Knowing that it was coming and that it wasn't going to be pleasant and that it would have been devastating for a young team to handle, we decided to see if we could trade Marshall, who was at the peak of his career. We were asking for a one and a two and I inferred that less than a one, with some other combination, would do it. Surprisingly, we didn't have many takers.

We finally ended up trading Marshall to the St. Louis Rams for second- and fifth-round draft choices. The trade was announced the day before the 1999 draft, and other than Jim Irsay and Jim Mora, not many people in the organization knew it was coming. When word got out about the deal, it was earth-shattering news at our facility. The building was very small by the standards of NFL team headquarters today, so I could hear some people yelling, "What? No! They can't do that!"

But that was only the first half of what would initially be seen as a very unpopular doubleheader. The next day, we used the fourth-overall pick on the lesser known of the two top running backs in the draft: Edgerrin James of the University of Miami. Ricky Williams, the Heisman Trophy winner from Texas, was the household name that most people thought we would select. Instead, the New Orleans Saints chose him with the next pick, which they acquired by trading their entire draft (plus their first- and third-round picks in 2000) to the Redskins, because that was how badly they wanted Ricky Williams.

As we were just getting ready to wrap up for the day, Dom Anile, our personnel director, tossed his car keys to Tom Telesco, one of our scouts, who is now general manager of the Chargers.

"Here, Tommy, go start my car," Dom said. We all laughed at the implications of that statement.

Despite the public outcry, Dom and I had no hesitation about our pick whatsoever. The reason media analysts and fans knew a lot less about Edgerrin than they did about Ricky was because the NCAA had placed Miami on probation and, therefore, the Hurricanes' only nationally televised game the previous season was against UCLA. In our mind, there really was no comparison between the two.

For one thing, the way Ricky carried himself, the way that he lived his life, was entirely inconsistent with being a good football player. Second, we weren't convinced that he really cared about football. Third, when you broke it down, Ricky was good, but not great, and that was what he turned out to be as a pro—good, but not great. I don't know whether or not his love of football held him back because he had great gifts, but he obviously didn't distinguish himself.

Edgerrin, on the other hand, had incredible gifts to go along with a clear love for the game and desire to excel. Although he was a scholarship player at Miami, Edgerrin had to earn his playing time. He told us that if it weren't for some bad luck for Frank Gore and Willis McGahee with injuries, he might not have ever gotten a chance to play. Edgerrin also described Frank as the most gifted running back he had ever seen, and Frank has subsequently demonstrated as much during his career with the 49ers.

Edgerrin's interview with us was tremendous, while Ricky's was the complete opposite. We decided to meet with Ricky at our facility because we were told that he really didn't like going out to restaurants. We catered a big dinner for him from St. Elmo's, the famous Indianapolis steak house, in a conference room. Ricky walked in, sat down and was essentially non-communicative.

On top of that, Ricky had done very poorly in his pre-draft workout. He ran something like a 4.75-second 40-yard dash. He certainly didn't match up with Edgerrin in terms of the numbers and that told us that he wouldn't be a good fit in our offense. We used a zone-blocking scheme, which means the blockers are moving laterally and are essentially taking defenders where they want to go. The running back has to have patience, wait to see the hole open, and then tremendous vision and acceleration to get through the hole. He has to go from a geared-down state to a hundred miles an hour.

Ricky's acceleration in the hole was average at best. He was much better suited to a power running system, where he would use all of that body mass that he had and the explosion he had to get to the hole and maybe run over people. Then, when he was out in the open, he could throw it into fourth gear.

Adding to the initial criticism we received for choosing Edgerrin over Ricky was the fact that before signing his contract, Edgerrin held out for a couple of weeks, which caused him to miss our rookie camp. We played him sparingly in the first preseason game, but he saw more extensive action in our second, at New Orleans.

I was seated in the Superdome press box with Dom and Chris. We were one booth away from the owner, so we could see Jim Irsay and Jim could see us. With the offense down in the red zone, we ran an outside stretch play to the right, and Edgerrin ripped off about a seven- or eight-yard gain. We ran the very same play again, and this time Edgerrin made two guys miss before running about 15 yards for a touchdown.

I looked over at Jim, he looked over at me and gave the thumbs up.

We wound up going 13–3 in our second season, a complete reversal of our first year and the biggest one-season turnaround in league history. After a first-round bye, we faced the Tennessee Titans in the divisional round of the playoffs at Indianapolis. As the team took the field for pregame warm-ups, I was walking with Peyton Manning and we looked up in the stands to what seemed like about 10,000 Titans fans. They were making all kinds of noise, and Peyton got upset because he knew they were going to be doing that while he was calling audibles and calling our plays at the line of scrimmage.

Something had gone wrong with the ticket-distribution scheme to allow that many tickets to get into the hands of people rooting for the other team. To this day, I don't know what it was. I have my suspicions, but I can't say for sure. And thanks to that unwanted crowd noise, I think we were a bit discombobulated on offense. We still ended up playing pretty well, but Eddie George broke the game open in the third quarter with a 68-yard run for a touchdown. The Titans won 19–16, and would go on to face the Rams in the Super Bowl, where they came up just short at the end.

We went 10–6 the next year, but lost in the playoffs again, this time to Miami in the wild-card round. That season marked the emergence of our center, Jeff Saturday, who had joined us as a free agent in 1999. Jeff had played for the University of North

Carolina while Dom Anile and I were with the Panthers. Leading up to the 1998 draft, we had seen an awful lot of Jeff because that North Carolina team had 10 guys who would be selected in the first, second, or third round. Jeff wasn't one of them. He was kind of an afterthought. He was only 6'2" and 305 pounds. He was kind of a little, round guy who didn't look as if he was much of an athlete.

But Jeff made an impression on me because he was clearly a leader, was tough as nails, and had great movement. He also had that aura about him that told you he was something special. When people asked me who he reminded me of, I said, "This is a different body, but this is Kent Hull." Jeff had everything Kent, our great center for the Bills, had: tremendous football intelligence, tremendous intelligence, physical toughness, mental toughness, and great work ethic. When you watched practice, Jeff was the guy that all of the other players gravitated to. He was the guy that you could tell was the linchpin, the spark plug.

That all said, we didn't draft Jeff. Nobody did. The Ravens signed him as a free agent after the draft. As is typical with an undrafted free agent, the Ravens only spoke with him over the phone; they didn't actually see him before agreeing to sign him. Jeff likes to joke that soon after he walked into their team facility for the first time, like hours after, the Ravens cut him; they never gave him a chance to even get on the field. Jeff actually was released a little less than a month-and-a-half later, and returned to Raleigh, North Carolina, where he took a job as a manager of an electrical-supply store.

As we began future signings for the following season, which take place usually from Thanksgiving on, I had Jeff at the top of the list of guys that we wanted to acquire, and we got him under contract. I warned Howard Mudd, "You will blanch when you see him, but give him a chance. I really think that this guy has something special going for him."

There was a part of Howard that loved developing players and loved doing things in a contrarian way. Aside from being among the best line coaches in the history of the game, Howard was a self-made player, too. He had been at Hillsdale College in Michigan, not Michigan State, and had a tremendous playing career in the National Football League, so he was open-minded when it came to guys who didn't have ideal physical attributes.

Once Howard got him on the field and saw what his gifts were—tremendous athleticism, tremendous quickness, tremendous leverage—it was obvious to him that Jeff was special. About two-thirds of the way through training camp, Howard laid out the plan: "We are going to start him out at guard, but he will be the center for the next 10 years." I always kid Howard that he was wrong by four years, because Jeff played 14 seasons. What Howard did with Jeff was a perfect example of the kind of cooperation between the coaching and scouting staffs that had so much to do with getting us to where we were for so long a time.

When Jeff became the center, you just knew that he and Peyton would connect. They were both Southern, they were both exceptionally intelligent, they were both football junkies, they were both great people on and off the field. Jeff was so smart that, just as Jim Kelly did with Kent Hull, Peyton left most of the line-blocking protection calls to Jeff. If Jeff would say, "When we run this particular play, don't use the protection that's in the playbook; let's use a different kind of protection," Peyton would never question him. As much of a detail guy as Peyton is, he would just leave it to Jeff and say, "Go ahead."

This was a relationship that really kind of revolutionized the game in many ways, because it was critical in allowing Howard to invent the silent count as a means of combating the crowd noise at stadiums throughout the league—just like the kind all those Tennessee fans generated at the playoff game. Howard had been experimenting with it, and once we signed Jeff, he had a guy who could understand it, conceptualize it, fit with Peyton and make it work.

As a member of the NFL's Competition Committee, I was part of discussions about all kinds of wild and crazy ways to try to stop crowd noise from being a problem for offenses to function. The committee was involved with it heavily because crowd noise was becoming a big issue around the league. Offenses couldn't get the ball snapped, couldn't use audibles, and there were teams that augmented crowd noise with the use of loudspeakers.

We fiddled around with the idea of using loudspeakers at the line of scrimmage. I said, "If Broadway shows can put microphones on the actors so that people in the balcony can hear them, why can't we do the same with the quarterback so people on the line of scrimmage can hear him?" That didn't go anywhere. So we wound up putting in what proved to be an unworkable rule that gave the referee the option of stopping the game if the quarterback indicated to him that there was too much noise (and the referee agreed), until the crowd quieted down. We never thought about the consequence, which was that it would rile the crowd up even more. That one died an early death.

The silent count eventually made the whole crowd-noise discussion irrelevant because now we were able to snap the ball no matter how much noise there was. When you see the quarterback lift his leg, he is telling the center, "We are going snap the ball on a predetermined count that we are silently going to count together, or you can snap it whenever you are ready, and I will be ready." It varies from game to game and even from series to series whether you have a predetermined count or not. We essentially became a silent-count team for all the time we were with the Colts.

Every time you make the playoffs, it's a good season, especially considering there hadn't been a lot of sustained success with the Colts. Still, there is no escaping the what-have-you-done-for-me-lately mentality. Not long after the playoff loss, a reporter, who was as good a guy as you could ever want to meet, hit me with a question that was totally out of character for him.

"Who is responsible for 10 and six?" he asked. "Somebody here screwed up because you were only 10 and six."

I had what others would call a "Polian Moment," when I allowed my temper to get the better of me. Maybe it was a little more than a moment.

Yelling at the top of my lungs, I said, "I will tell you who was responsible for 10 and six. *Me!* You want to blame somebody? *Blame me!* And if you don't think 10 and six is worthy of praise and you want somebody to blame, I'll take it!"

As time passed, we were able to laugh about that exchange. Every once in a while, when we would see each other, one or the other of us would say, "Who is responsible for 10 and six?"

Before the 2001 draft, our board indicated that a cornerback from Wisconsin, Jamar Fletcher, was the top-rated player for our pick, which was 22nd overall. Jim Mora and our defensive coordinator, Vic Fangio, made it pretty clear that they didn't want him, so we made a trade with the Giants to move down to the 30th spot. By the way, Jim and Vic were correct. The player never panned out.

Dom Anile would always say, "On Draft Day, let the board talk to you." A perfect example of Dom's dictum was after we moved down and that Reggie Wayne, a wide receiver from Miami, was available. The general consensus among media and fans was that we needed a defensive player, but Reggie was our top-rated player at that spot and we picked him. Media and fans were upset, saying, "The last thing they need is a wide receiver!" But it turned out to be the right thing, even though we would fall to 6–10 in the 2001 season. Reggie has gone on to have arguably a Hall of Fame career.

Peyton Manning had the worst year of his career to date in '01. To this day, I don't know why, but he did, even though our offense ranked second in the NFL. Our defense was worse, ranking next-to-last in the league in points allowed and 29th in yards allowed. On top of that, our defensive system was complex. It required us to have an abundance of experienced players, and that meant more expensive players. With the investment we knew we were going to make in the offense—where we would be re-signing Peyton Manning, Marvin Harrison, Tarik Glenn, Jeff Saturday, and Edgerrin James—it was clear we wouldn't have the salary-cap space to afford that kind of defense. It required a lot of recognition, a lot of communication, a lot of sophistication. Therefore, it would be hard to take college kids right off the campus, stick them in the lineup, and have them play with any degree of efficiency.

Now with that said, there is absolutely nothing wrong with Vic's system. To his credit, as defensive coordinator of the 49ers in 2013, he put a rookie, Eric Reid, at free safety and did very well. However, you are not always going to get those kinds of players year in and year out.

So I went to Jim Mora and said, "I think we need to change philosophy on defense largely because we are constrained by the cap; we can't help the defense by bringing in veterans. We are going to have to do it with young guys and, in that regard, I think that it's mandatory that we get a new system. We're going to have to have a defensive coordinator with a system that is relatively simple. I'm not telling you who to hire, but we need somebody who runs a system similar to the Tampa Two defense because it makes it easier to get young players on the field and it's zone-based."

Jim steadfastly refused to part ways with Vic, and that directly resulted in our parting ways with Jim. I regret that his tenure had to end that way, but it was a move that we needed to make if we were going to sustain success. To Jim's credit, he was going to be loyal to a coach who he rightly felt was competent, even when he knew it would cost him his job, and I respected that. Jim deserves a great deal of credit for instituting the discipline and work ethic that formed the bed rock of all of our Indianapolis teams.

But we felt we should cast our lot on the offensive side of the ball. We played at least 10 games a year in ideal weather in a dome and at Jacksonville and Houston. We had such a high-powered offense with very good players and our opponents had not figured it out yet. If we had been in Buffalo or Cleveland, we would not have gone that way, even with Peyton.

We had a special group of offensive players in a building and a warm-weather division, the AFC South, that was perfectly suited for them. Now that doesn't mean that we wanted to play with poor players on defense. We just had to play with young guys because of the cap.

We had a long list of candidates to replace Jim Mora, but when Tony Dungy became available—after the Tampa Bay Buccaneers released him in order to hire Jon Gruden from the Oakland Raiders—I said to Jim Irsay, "Let's go get the guy who invented the defense we want to play." He gave me the okay to interview him.

We met at the Marriott Westshore Hotel in Tampa. Ten minutes into the interview, I was sold. There was a point where I asked Tony about preparation of the team, wanting him to take me through training camp all the way to the end of the season and the playoffs, and he outlined it beautifully. About three sentences into his answer, he stopped and said, "I notice you are smiling and nodding your head. Is there something here that I said that's funny?"

"No, I apologize," I said. "But I have heard this all before almost verbatim from Marv Levy."

I knew we had the right person.

Number one, we were trying to find somebody who could teach and operate Tony's defense, and lo and behold, Tony himself became available. Second of all, we didn't have to change a thing with our high-powered offense because Tony's football mentor was Tom Moore, who had recruited Tony to the University of Minnesota as a quarterback. That went back to when Tony was 17 years of age.

Tony was more than happy to allow Tom to remain as offensive coordinator and do whatever he was going to do and had absolute trust in him.

Ironically, before I left, Tony informed me that he was going to Carolina to interview for the Panthers' vacant head-coaching job, so I told him that we would talk again in a day or two. I immediately called Jim Irsay and said, "He's our guy, without a question, but he's going to Carolina to visit, so we are just going to have to hold our breath."

Jim didn't hold his breath. He called Tony right away and said, "I want you to be our coach. You are hearing it from me as the owner of the team. The job is yours."

That certainly made an impression on Tony. He still went to Carolina, but, to our very good fortune, the next day he called me back and said, "Hey, let's do it."

You can't have it both ways in the NFL, with a dominant offense and a smothering defense. I believe to this day that you can't have it both ways. You can, for a brief time, if you're playing with a young quarterback and you don't have to pay him at the high end of the salary scale for the position. We saw that with Russell Wilson and the Seattle Seahawks, and that allowed them to be excellent on both sides of the ball on their way to winning Super Bowl XLVIII.

We were playing with a young quarterback in Peyton Manning, but he was highly paid because the league's old rookie wage scale was in place at the time. Under the new system, if you don't have to pay the quarterback a king's ransom, then you can parcel out your money basically 50/50, offense and defense. But once the quarterback gets paid, the die is cast. He is taking up 15 to 18 percent of the salary cap. That's what the salary cap was designed to do—limit the roster expenditures of good teams.

Naturally, our decision to follow the model of payroll imbalance with most of the money going to the offensive side was a source of controversy in the media in Indianapolis, but it didn't bother me because I knew that we had the right model and the right system. If you are going to be a wide-open, skill-heavy offense—which equates to the passing game—you have to be a little bit more judicious with how you spend your money on defense. Your defensive system has to accommodate that. You draft quality, young defensive players, but the system has to be simple enough to allow them to be able to get on the field right away. If the system is too complicated, then you have to uncomplicate it or change how you allocate the dollars.

Tony sat down with everybody in the personnel department, and went through, step-by-step and player-by-player, the needs and the qualities we wanted in every player and the hierarchy of where we value players in the system.

Entering the 2002 draft, we knew we were going to draft a defensive lineman. The two we thought would be available when we picked were John Henderson, a defensive tackle from Tennessee, and Dwight Freeney, a defensive end from Syracuse. Talk about a contrast in physiques. John was 6'7" and 328 pounds. Dwight was 6'1" and 268 pounds. John stopped people in their tracks, but he could not rush the passer very well and didn't have a lot of speed for pursuit. He was much more the prototypical run-stuffing defensive tackle. Dwight, on the other hand, had incredible speed and was a tremendous pass rusher.

On the morning of the draft, Tony and I were side by side on the treadmills at our facility and I said, in reference to Dwight and John, "The choice is one of these two guys—whatever you prefer is what we will do."

"Bill, given the choice, I will take speed any time," he said.

"Okay, then, we're taking Freeney."

It turned out that the Jacksonville Jaguars selected John Henderson with the ninth-overall pick, so the point became moot when Dwight Freeney was still on the board at No. 11.

Dwight had exceptional first-step quickness. He had exceptional explosion, because in that 268-pound body there was what we called a quick-twitch athlete—people who move quickly and explosively. Dwight also was an exceptionally relentless rusher; he was the Energizer bunny. He was strong enough to handle run blocks, so he could play right-handed and pick off trap-blockers and do all those kinds of things that you want a right defensive end to do.

The only thing that Dwight could not do well—and it was something that he wouldn't be asked to do in Tony's defense—was play a five technique, which is head up with the tight end. Our defensive line coach, John Teerlinck, believed the wider an end lined up, the better his chances of harassing the quarterback.

Every year after the draft in Indianapolis, we would get the personnel people together—Dom Anile, Tommy Telesco, David Caldwell, and Chis—and we would talk about trends in the game and whether we would have to change the way we evaluated players. We just kind of brainstormed and that would go on throughout training camp.

Part of that was because Dom and I decided that we were going to train these young scouts so that they were ready to take over if and when the time came. Secondly, we wanted their input because they are outstanding people and they had been in the system long enough to know it intimately. What we found was that, in selecting players, we could sacrifice height as long as every other personal quality was outstanding. In Dwight Freeney's case, he was exceptionally fast, exceptionally explosive, exceptionally strong, and he had quick twitch, which even explosive and fast people don't always have.

As time went by, we said that even if we drafted down low—and we drafted below 20 for most of the 14 years we were there—there were certain qualities in prospects that we weren't going to sacrifice. Under Tony, we were unwilling to sacrifice character and football temperament. Number two, there was no way we were going to sacrifice speed. And, three, there was no way we were going to sacrifice explosion.

We decided we could sacrifice height, and we did. To borrow a Bill Parcells phrase, we always looked like midgets getting off the bus. For whatever reason, the lack of height didn't hinder our play, but it did make them slightly more susceptible to injury. We had fairly short linebackers in Mike Peterson, who was 6'1", and Gary Brackett and Cato June, both of whom were 6'.

In 2003, we found our bookend to Dwight Freeney in Robert Mathis, a fifth-round draft pick from Alabama A&M. Robert was built similarly to Dwight—6'2" and 246 pounds. We actually traded a fourth-round pick to move up in the round to get him because we were sold on him and we felt if we left him there any longer we would lose him. In fact, Dom said, "Man, Robert is sitting there. We've got a conviction on him, we better go get him."

We all agreed and started calling everybody we could around the league looking for a team that would take our fourth-round pick in the following year in exchange for a higher spot in the fifth round.

"Wow! That's a heavy price," Tony said.

"No, not really," I said. "Look at it this way: we are getting him a year early. We are giving up a fourth next year, but we got him all this year."

"Yeah, you're right. I didn't think of it that way. Let's go make the deal."

We did, and as Dom always liked to say, "You make the deal and never look back." And we didn't. Robert proved to be an excellent player and a perfect complement to Dwight. Both were pass-rushing terrors, lining up wide and using their great speed to the fullest. If Robert said 12 paragraphs in the entire time we were together in Indianapolis, that would have been a lot. All he does is play football to the best of his ability at an All-Pro level.

One round later in '03, we selected Cato June from Michigan. The previous fall, I had watched Michigan play at Notre Dame. Cato was at strong safety. For a guy who was barely 6' tall and weighed a little more than 200 pounds, he was knocking down everybody in sight and flying all over the field.

After I got back, I told Tony, "I saw this incredible strong safety named Cato June, but he's not fast enough to be back there for us. He kind of has to play in the box [near the line of scrimmage], but he's good."

"Well, let's keep our eye on him," Tony said.

I absolutely loved the guy, but even after we picked him, I wasn't sure where we should put him. Tony said we should put him at weak-side linebacker.

"He has a lot of Derrick Brooks in him," Tony said, referring to his Hall of Fame linebacker from the Buccaneers. "He's not Derrick Brooks, but let's start him there."

We did and he remained there for a good long time. That's another example of Tony saying, "Hey, we're not married to conventional wisdom. We like this guy and he can play football, so we'll find a place for him."

The first time I saw Bob Sanders play a game in person, he was a junior at Iowa. The Hawkeyes were facing USC, and it was a battle of two of the country's top safeties: Bob and Troy Polamalu of the Trojans. I forgot who won the game, but I remember that I didn't even see anyone else on the field except those two guys.

All season, I kept telling Tony, "There is this guy from Iowa, Bob Sanders, who is tremendous. He lights people up." All he heard from me was: Bob Sanders, Bob Sanders, Bob Sanders. As far as I was concerned, he could be to our defense what John Lynch was to Tony's defense in Tampa. Chris liked to joke, "If my father had to give up one of his sons for Bob, one of us would be gone."

After the Combine, we had our medical meeting with Dr. Art Rettig, our great orthopedic surgeon and head team physician. We sat down and he opened the meeting by saying, "I should probably get this out of the way...Bob Sanders is not going to pass our physical." I didn't fall on the floor, but everybody else in the room said my face turned white—chalk white, was how it was described— and all I could say was, "Why? Why is he going to fail our physical?"

Dr. Rettig went on to say that Bob had had a plate inserted in his foot and the screw had come loose so the plate was floating around and it was going to have to be removed and a new plate put in or some sort of procedure would be required to handle this issue. It made perfect sense when you recognized how Bob played. He had a 40-yard dash time that was a legitimate 4.4, his vertical jump was off the charts, he could lift up the building. You could imagine this powerful body, which belonged to someone whose dad had been a professional boxer, putting all this stress on his joints and feet, so that a loose plate or screw would be a problem.

Our medical staff included Dr. Dave Porter, who happened to be, in my opinion, one of the best foot doctors in the country. I said to him and Dr. Rettig, "Please, guys, do me a favor and go back and revisit this. Is there any way at all, somehow, he could pass the physical?"

"All right," Dr. Porter said. "We'll go the extra mile. I'll have him in, I'll talk to the doctor who did the operation."

About a month later, we had another meeting and Dr. Porter said, "I can fix this. I have talked to the doctor at Iowa, and there is a procedure that I can do and we can fix him right after the draft and he will probably be ready, certainly for the beginning of the season, and maybe for the last half of the training camp."

That was music to my ears.

On every club with which I've ever been, including in Canada, the doctor had the final call on the drafting or signing of players with injuries (as well as on the decision on whether or not a player could practice or play). And if the doctor said no, you might come back to him and plead to see if you could get him to change his mind, but ultimately if the answer was no, it was no. I have never worked with doctors, and this was particularly true in Carolina and Indianapolis, given the tenor of the times, that didn't have great expertise and great empathy and concern for the players. In their minds the players always came first.

After Dr. Porter shared his conclusion that he could take care of Bob's foot issue, he and all of the team doctors in the league gathered in Indianapolis for their Indy 2 medical meeting, which is where they bring back the players who failed physicals or had incomplete medical evaluations. Bob was among the players receiving the once-over. Dave, who is as honest as the day is long, told me he didn't say anything to the other doctors regarding our interest in Bob.

About a week before the draft, he came into my office and said, "Listen, I'm pretty sure that Bob is going to be off half the boards in the league, based on people asking me for my opinion. I think you can probably get him in the second round. How lucky can you get?" This was Thurman Thomas all over again. For the second time in my career, a difference maker we wanted to draft had a physical question mark. For the second time in my career, a first-round talent we wanted to select would be available in the second round.

Based on that, we put word out that we planned to trade out of the first round. The phone rang and it was the Atlanta Falcons. They wanted to give us third- and fourth-round picks to move into our spot, which was 29th overall, in exchange for their second-round choice, 38th overall. Now we had a pick early in the second round, with which I felt very comfortable. The phone would ring again. We were offered another trade-down opportunity within the round.

"Great, do it," Tony said.

"Whoa! Take it easy," I said. "We might lose Bob Sanders."

"Don't worry about it. We're not going to lose him. I'm telling you, he's going to be there. Make the trade."

We made the trade and the minute we sent the paperwork to the NFL, I had buyer's remorse. I said, "Oh, my God! We're going to lose him."

"Don't worry, Tony," he said, patting me on the shoulder. "Everything is going to be fine. We're going to get him."

I was pacing back and forth like an expectant father. I later found out that someone in the room said, "If Bob Sanders gets taken by someone else, Bill is going to blow the roof off the building."

"No," someone else answered. "He'll have a heart attack."

Fortunately, Bob was there for us to take at pick No. 44.

Bob's nickname among the coaches, and some of the players as well, was "The Eraser." You might think he got that because he made ball carriers or pass receivers disappear, but that's not the case at all. He got that because he erased mistakes that other players made. If somebody went to the wrong guy in coverage or wasn't in proper position to tackle a ball-carrier, "The Eraser" would show up and make the play. He could do everything.

Bob Sanders' career wound up being far too short, but not because of that foot. He had a chronic knee problem and ruptured his biceps in two successive years.

Troy Polamalu and Ed Reed are likely to be Hall of Fame safeties from their era, but when Bob Sanders was healthy, he was right there with them.

13

No Excuses. No Explanations.
Turn the Page.

"Expect adversity. Expect more to overcome it."

—Marv Levy

THE TITLE OF THIS CHAPTER was Tony Dungy's mantra to our team during his time with the Colts. We lived by it. That doesn't mean we weren't honest or objective about ourselves in house. It did mean that we would never point fingers publicly or engage in dialogue with the media that addressed our supposed shortcomings. In order to further accentuate the point, we borrowed a phrase from Mike Krzyzewski, the magnificent Duke and USA Olympic basketball coach: "WE DEFINE OURSELVES."

Using that standard, our group with the Colts was exceptional. We set records on and off the field: 11 playoff appearances, three conference-championship game appearances, two Super Bowls and a world championship in 2006.

Jim Mora built a foundation of discipline and a work ethic that Tony Dungy was able to use as a springboard to unprecedented success, such as our record of 115 wins in 10 years. Tony, I'm certain, will take his rightful place in the Hall of Fame in time, as will, I'm sure, Marvin Harrison and Peyton Manning, the greatest passing-touchdown duo in NFL history.

Adam Vinatieri, Reggie Wayne, and Edgerrin James are, in my admittedly biased opinion, Hall of Famers as well. But don't take my opinion on it. Check the NFL statistics. You will be amazed at where they stand in the all-time rankings. Robert Mathis and Dwight Freeney deserve serious consideration as well. All except Adam were originally drafted by the Colts during our time there.

Players such as Jeff Saturday (who will also be in Hall of Fame discussions) Tarik Glenn, Ryan Diem, Dallas Clark, Marcus Pollard, Brandon Stokley, Austin Collie, Joseph Addai, Dominic Rhodes, Antoine Bethea, Gary Brackett, Donald Brown, Melvin Bullitt, Justin Snow, Jacob Tamme, David Thornton, Cato June, Rob Morris, Ryan Lilja, Kelvin Hayden, Marlin Jackson, Jake Scott, Raheem Brock, Montae Reagor, Rick DeMulling, and briefly Booger McFarland were all mainstays for us, along with many others that space precludes my mentioning. All became household names in Indianapolis and many have and many more will take their place in the Colts Ring of Honor.

That speaks to a coaching and scouting staff that was second to none in the NFL. If there were Hall of Fame spots for assistant coaches, Tom Moore and Howard Mudd—innovators in strategy, tactics, and technique—would be shoo-ins. Jim Caldwell, Bruce Arians and Leslie Frazier from our staff became head coaches. Frank Reich became an offensive coordinator with the San Diego Chargers and Pete Metzelaars, Alan Williams, Jim Bob Cooter, Devin Fitzsimmons, along with David Walker, are on NFL coaching staffs. Mike Murphy and John Teerlinck, both of whom are retired, were men who contributed mightily to our defense's success.

Our scouting staff, headed by the incomparable Dom Anile, produced three NFL general managers (David Caldwell, Tom Telesco, and Chris Polian) and will, I'm sure, will produce more, notably Tom Gamble, Kevin Kelly, and Kevin Rogers.

Thanks to Tony, Peyton, and their teammates, Lucas Oil Stadium stands as a monument to a "golden era" of Colts football. Peyton's "PeyBack Foundation" began promoting and aiding Indiana high school football from the day he arrived. Thanks to the stellar example set by our teams on and off the field, Indiana high school football thrives as never before and produces more Division I college prospects than ever before. Peyton Manning Children's Hospital will continue to contribute to the welfare of Indiana children long after No. 18 has thrown his last pass.

There is a mural, which sits atop the inner entrance to Lucas Oil Stadium, that shows scenes from our Super Bowl victory. In huge letters it proclaims, "LUCAS OIL STADIUM, BUILT BY CHAMPIONS." Yes, it was! Every one of us associated with "our era" of Colts football are very proud of that.

The ride, however, was far from smooth. Like it or not (and I don't), playoff disappointment is part of our record as well. Starting with the three-point loss to Tennessee in 1999, we had five losses in the divisional or conference round. I'll deviate from Tony's mantra a bit here. While not making any excuses—we lost—I'll offer some explanations I have never addressed at length before.

One of the defeats, of course, was against Pittsburgh in 2005 after the tragic death of Tony and Lauren's son, James. The Colts literally were a family. Jim Irsay's daughters were frequently around, and Tony made it clear that players', coaches', and staff members' children and extended family were always welcome. Saturday practice often resembled part football, part day care, and part family reunion. In addition, James spent his senior year of high school in Indianapolis, worked at training camp and was always around. He made many friends among the players and coaching staff. When tragedy struck, it wasn't an abstract news story. It was a heart-rending loss to a man and a family who embodied "family values" and to a team and staff who believed totally in them and him. "Faith, family, football" was another of Tony's mantras, and we practiced it daily.

After the tragic news, we interrupted our daily routine to have a prayer service for James and the Dungy family set up by our chaplains. Jim Caldwell, showing the mettle that made him Tony's successor, put everything in perspective for the players and talked of our obligation to Tony to live up to his standards. We practiced as we always did—professionally. Jim Irsay—showing his usual class, compassion, and care for his employees—chartered a jet and buses to take us all (the entire team and staff, including staff wives) to the funeral in Tampa. The organizers placed our entire party in a large choir rehearsal hall at the church, where Tony and Lauren spoke to us and emotionally thanked us for coming, while urging us to remember James as he was in life—with a smile. We then filed into the church to sit in a separate front section (Commissioner Tagliabue and other distinguished guests were seated behind us), Tony's football family mourning one of their own. Tony gave a beautiful eulogy, as only he could, and we left the family with their grief to return to Indy.

On the bus and on the plane, there was little talk of anything but the Dungy family. We were shaken to the core by James' passing and Tony's suffering. We were listless through most of our regular-season finale with Arizona that marked Tony's return to the team. It took a furious, fourth-quarter rally to pull out a victory in a very average performance by us.

After a week off, we hosted Pittsburgh in the divisional round. Just as in the Arizona game, we lacked our usual spark in the first half. We became our typical selves in the second half, staging a spirited rally only to fall short when we missed a 41-yard field-goal attempt.

That score would have sent a game we had begun dominating into overtime.

Might the outcome have been different but for James Dungy's tragic death? We will never know and no good comes from speculation. Pittsburgh went on to win that year's Super Bowl, and many of us believed, on paper at least, that the 2005 Colts were the deepest and most talented of all our teams.

No excuses. A brief explanation. Turn the page. We won the Super Bowl the following season.

Perhaps the most controversial of all our playoff games was the 2003 AFC Championship Game versus the New England Patriots. After ripping through Denver and Kansas City, we traveled to Foxborough to face the Pats on a nice, New England winter day. We lost, 24–14. In the fourth quarter, with the outcome very much in doubt, tight end Marcus Pollard appeared on the verge of making what looked a game-changing catch and run. However, before he could reach the ball, he was held, about nine yards into the route, by a Patriot linebacker. Marcus broke free and then was interfered with by another Pats defender. No flags. This was the culmination of a game in which Colts receivers were held and illegally contacted numerous times with no flags from referee Walt Coleman's crew.

Neither Tony nor I commented publicly on the officiating, although I must admit that I pounded the counter at which I was seated in the press box a few times, much to the glee of reporters sitting around me. Numerous media, including the game's network-television broadcasters, commented on the lack of flags. When asked about it after the game, New England coach Bill Belichick said, "Just doing business as business is done." He was correct.

At the Competition Committee in-season meeting, virtually all of the members, myself included, expressed dismay at the lack of flags for blatant grabs on receivers downfield and blatant, illegal contact far past the legal bump area within five yards of the line of scrimmage. It reached a crescendo in the playoffs with grabbing of receivers by beaten defensive backs and illegal impeding of receivers far downfield rampant. The Colts–New England game was the icing on the cake. Because it was the AFC Championship Game, it brought nationwide attention to the problem. The Colts said nothing publicly. Privately, Tony asked the Competition Committee if he could make a presentation to its members at their annual meeting in Indianapolis that February. Since he was a respected coach and former member, the committee readily agreed.

Tony made his usual intellectual, unemotional presentation while showing a video of numerous examples of uncalled defensive holding and illegal contact. At one point deep into Tony's presentation, having gotten worked up even a month after the fact, I interrupted to underscore a point. Tony said pointedly, "Bill, please let me finish." I shut up. After Tony's presentation, much discussion and tape review, the committee voted, 8-0, to make illegal contact and defensive holding "points of emphasis" in the 2004 season. That meant, in English, "Refs, throw the flags."

Naturally, flags for downfield defensive fouls skyrocketed. Defensive-minded head coaches and defensive coordinators complained. The media joined the chorus and some postulated that, "Polian stampeded the Competition Committee into doing this to help the Colts." I won't pretend I was neutral on the subject, but I don't have that much eloquence or influence. The committee saw a plethora of uncalled fouls deleteriously affecting the offense and decided to tighten things up.

Ironically, the Competition Committee did the very same thing in 2014, 10 years later, when slippage in enforcement had allowed officials to ignore blatant downfield infractions committed by defenders on receivers. Given that I was firmly ensconced in my seat at ESPN at the time, I had nothing to do with it.

Would we have beaten the Pats had the game been differently officiated? We will never know. The Pats had a great defense. What is important is that we re-learned a valuable lesson I'll bet all of us learned as youngsters in sports competition: don't give the officials an opportunity to influence the game.

Another controversial game was our 2009 Week 16 encounter with the New York Jets. We were at home, having won 14 straight games, and clinched our division championship, a first-round playoff bye, and home-field advantage.

Jim Caldwell, in his first year replacing the retired Tony Dungy, had done a phenomenal job shepherding a good but depth-challenged team to playoff nirvana. The outcome of our last two regular-season games did not affect our standing. Our goal was to get our team to the playoffs in as healthy a state as we could. Winning the Super Bowl was the only meaningful goal. Around Thanksgiving, after we had reached 9–0, with terrific wins against New England and Baltimore, our local media began to beat the drum for "going for the undefeated season." Regardless of the risk to the health of our players, we "owed it to the fans" to go for "this milestone." Pleas from the media called it a matter of civic pride.

Unbeknownst to the media, Coach Caldwell and I had met with Jim Irsay around Halloween and broached the subject of an undefeated season. We told him that both of us were in complete agreement that this team was good, but lacked depth, and health in the playoffs was paramount to our chances for success. Jim Irsay agreed completely. He knew our personnel as well as we did. When the "go-for-the-undefeated-season" crusade began, both Coach Caldwell and I were ready with a response. We said, "They don't give trophies or rings for undefeated regular seasons. Only the best shot at a playoff victory counts."

Fast forward to the Jet game. With a lead in the fourth quarter, we pulled Peyton Manning. The Jets promptly scored a defensive touchdown when backup quarterback Curtis Painter got hit cleanly on a blitz for a sack-fumble. The Jets went on to win. The pundits accused me of manipulating Jim Caldwell's decision on who to play. They said we had "cheated the fans and disgraced Indianapolis." Callers to my Monday night radio show reflected the above points in stereo. One Colts front-office employee even suggested I write a "letter of apology" to the fans.

I took none of it seriously. Both Jim Caldwell and I reminded the players that "we define ourselves" and only the Super Bowl counted.

We entered the playoffs against Baltimore hearing the usual "the Colts are small and soft and Baltimore will run the ball down their throats." Result: Colts 20, Baltimore 3. Bring on the New York Jets, who "had our number" and would "power-run us out of the building." Result: Colts 30, Jets 17. We were AFC champions, the only one of two titles that mattered.

As it turned out, in the AFC Championship Game, we lost Dwight Freeney to a severe ankle injury and Jerraud Powers, a terrific second-year cornerback, to a leg injury. Both men gave a gutsy effort in the 31–17 Super Bowl XLIV loss to New Orleans, but were not effective and we missed them. In addition, we didn't play our best game in the Super Bowl against a very tough Saints team and so ended a momentous season.

Looking back from a distance, I'm sure that most of our group would tell you we felt we were good enough to have gone to at least one or two more Super Bowls. But having a good enough team and doing it are two different things. You can't "will it to happen." Injuries, illness, life, bad matchups, and officials can get in the way.

I'm proud to have been associated with such a great group. I'm proud of all the great things we have accomplished on and off the field and I'm very proud of the way in which we did it. As Tony Dungy would say, "No excuses. No explanations. Turn the page."

• • •

As we approached the 2011 lockout of NFL players by owners after the two sides were unable to agree on a new collective bargaining agreement, I remember telling the staff, "Nothing good comes of labor disputes. They eventually get settled. The lawyers and the protagonists benefit, and almost no one else does."

Little did I know how prophetic those words would be or how events that transpired during the lockout would wind up costing a lot of really good football people their jobs.

Peyton Manning was going to become a free agent, so we placed an "exclusive" franchise tag on him, meaning no other team would be able to sign him and that he would be guaranteed a one-year contract equal to the average of the top-five-paid quarterbacks in the league (which, at the time, would have been more than $23 million).

In the meantime, we'd heard that Peyton had undergone neck surgery. Our coach, Jim Caldwell, and I never spoke directly with Peyton about it, because we were told by our club lawyer that we were to have no contact with players during the lockout. The only people within the team that players could talk with were the trainers and the doctors.

Soon after the draft, we heard, through our medical staff, there was a complication of sorts with Peyton's operation. By that time, Andy Dalton and Colin Kaepernick, quarterbacks for whom we had high regard, had been drafted by the Bengals and 49ers, respectively, with the 35th- and 36th-overall choices. Not that Anthony Castonzo, the offensive lineman we chose 22nd overall, was not a good pick; he was. But we made that choice because we weren't in the market for a quarterback...or so we thought.

The lockout ended on July 25, 2011. Not long thereafter, Peyton called me and we spoke, mainly about his contract. He had three major points he wanted to make: one, he didn't need to make as much money as Tom Brady, the Patriots' quarterback who was at the top of the pay scale for the position at the time; two, he wanted to end his career as a Colt; three, he was going to tell his agent, Tom Condon, that these were the things he wanted to get done.

"And we're going to get it done," he said, emphatically.

"No problem," I said.

I conveyed the essence of the conversation to Mr. Irsay, who was happy to hear it. Later that day, Peyton came into the facility and we sat down for another couple of hours to talk about the team, what his plans were, what my plans were, where we were going as a team, and how quickly we could get the team back to Super Bowl level. I asked him how many years he thought he could play, and he said four or five. He asked me how many years I was going to stay on the job, and I said at least a couple of years, long enough to get us back to the point where we could go to the Super Bowl and have a good chance to win it.

It was a little bit more emotional than our normal off-season conversations because we were both looking at the ends of our respective careers, and we had been so intertwined over the years.

The next day, I began negotiating with Tom Condon about a long-term deal for Peyton. We agreed on a one-year contract, followed by a four-year deal that was written in such a way that there really was no risk on the part of either party. Once we got the basics done, Tom came back to me and said, in light of the fact Peyton was convalescing from this second surgery, we needed to put a placeholder in the agreement a lump sum that, in the event that the unthinkable happened and he wasn't able to play, he would be paid after the 2011 season or he would become a free agent. I balked at it initially, but Tom had me speak with a fellow in his office who had worked for Bob Ferguson when Bob was general manager of the Broncos.

"Well, you can't be all that bad if you worked for Fergy," I said.

He explained to me that if we inserted the placeholder, number one, we'd have some cap security and, number two, in the event that something went bad, it would allow us and/or them out of the contract. So we put in a $28-million lump-sum payment as the placeholder. It was never, ever meant to be paid in toto. It was only there to allow both sides to reassess if something had gone wrong. (There would be reports that Peyton was demanding $28 million at the end of that year, but that was completely untrue. How it got misinterpreted that way, I'll never know.)

Peyton's physical status was still a mystery. No one had seen him throw. The trainers hadn't gotten their hands on him yet. And it wasn't until we got to training camp at Anderson University a short while later that we discovered he wasn't completely healthy.

We did not want to create a furor over Peyton's status in training camp, so we announced that he had undergone surgery—something we were not allowed to do during the lockout and wouldn't have been able to share the details about at that time because we didn't know them—and that he wasn't ready to practice yet and was rehabbing.

But a couple of days a week, we would watch him throw privately in the gym at Anderson. The audience would consist of only Jim Caldwell, quarterbacks coach Clyde Christensen, Tom Moore, Chris Polian, and me. It was obvious there was something wrong. There was no velocity on the ball, and it didn't improve. And he was bothered by soreness and pain. He was laboring to throw.

We had a tremendous neurosurgeon, Dr. Hank Feuer, who had not done the surgery but could offer a sound, educated opinion on Peyton's prognosis.

"This is a nerve problem," he told us. "You don't know when, but the likelihood is it will regenerate, and he'll be ready to go. Now, will he make it for opening day? I don't know."

We continued through the summer without Peyton practicing or playing in any preseason games as we prepared for our season-opener at Houston. He showed small progress, but nothing you could hang your hat on. The day after the final preseason game,

Peyton talked with Jim Caldwell and with me separately about a package of red-zone plays he had put together for the Texans game, and he wanted us to watch him run them on the practice field to get a sense of where he was physically.

After he finished, he said to me, "What do you think?"

"Well, there's good news and bad news," I said.

"What's the bad news?"

"The bad news is we can't put you out there because the velocity is not there."

"Well, what's the good news?"

"The good news is you're throwing with about as much velocity as Chad Pennington."

"Oh, no, it's that bad?"

"Yeah."

We both laughed, but Peyton was clearly upset. He very much wanted to extend his streak of 227 consecutive starts in regular-season and playoff games, but it just wasn't in the cards. As much as he is always willing to dispute anything that suggests he can't do something, he was realistic enough to know that we were right not to want to put him out there and in harm's way.

Nevertheless, we were still operating full speed ahead with the idea that the nerve would come around and he would be ready to go at some point during the season. Meanwhile, we began talking about the need for another veteran backup quarterback besides the one we had on the roster, Curtis Painter. We had no luck in the trade market and decided that we would put a trade aside while we cut down to our final 53-man roster and pick it up there when every club is in a deal-making mood.

As I gathered with our personnel staff to make the cuts, the trainer walked into the meeting room and said, "You need to talk with the doctors right now." I thought, *What the hell? Something's crazy here.* I actually began worrying if there had been some sort of medical emergency with someone in the building.

I walked into the trainer's room, and saw Dr. Feuer, Dr. Art Rettig, and Dr. Douglas Robertson, our general internist.

"I've got to show you this picture of Peyton's MRI," Dr. Feuer said.

He called it up on a computer and it indicated that there was a disc problem, which was obvious even to a layman such as me.

"He's going to have to have a spinal fusion," Dr. Feuer said, and he and Dr. Rettig proceeded to explain the serious nature of the surgery. They didn't get into any timetable on his recovery, but it was clear that this was a much bigger problem than what we thought we were dealing with up to that point. Spinal fusions are not everyday occurrences, particularly among football players.

I immediately went to Jim Caldwell to tell him the news, and we decided we would tell the coaching staff that, for now, Peyton was out and that there would be further testing and issues, but that we were going to proceed with the idea that he would not be available for the foreseeable future. It was a shock to them. It was a shock to us all.

I returned to meet with the doctors, and by then Peyton had arrived at the facility. The first thing he did have our physicians put together a list of the top spine specialists in the country to get as many opinions as possible.

Peyton was really, really down, as was everyone else.

"Hey, look," I said to him, "if this ends tomorrow, you've had a Hall of Fame career. You've got a Super Bowl ring. If they say they can't fix it, it's still been a great career. But my guess is that they're going to be able to fix it."

"Yeah, okay," he said, but he was still as low as could be.

When we returned to finalizing the 53-man roster, we kept Peyton's status as active. Then, over the next two weeks, I got together with our medical staff and we put our heads together in order to help Peyton find the appropriate surgeon for his case. Peyton's father, Archie, was involved, as was his brother, Eli, the quarterback for the Giants, and David Cutcliffe, Peyton's former offensive coordinator at Tennessee who was now the head coach at Duke. As Peyton had requested, our doctors put together a list of five specialists, and they asked each of them to review the MRI and make some suggestions. All but the doctor who had done the surgery that led to the complication agreed that a fusion was necessary.

We ended up having conference calls with Dr. Robert Watkins, a Los Angeles–based spine surgeon who would subsequently do the surgery. We asked him about the procedure, rehabilitation, and timeframe. The other surgeons basically said the same thing, but Dr. Watkins was very clear about the fact that he could fix the disc problem. He also was very straightforward about saying there was no telling when Peyton would be able to come back and play, pointing out that the nerve would regenerate at its own pace.

"It might be three months, although I don't think it will be that soon," Dr. Watkins said. "It might be six months, it might be seven months."

Peyton traveled to Los Angeles for the surgery, which was a success, and then returned to Indianapolis. If you had seen him with his shirt off afterward, you would have been shocked beyond belief because the right side of his body had atrophied to the point where there was no definition on his pectoral muscle or on his biceps or on his triceps. He looked like two people, before and after. If you didn't know all the details, you would have been shocked and frightened.

With Jim Irsay's concurrence, we decided not to put Peyton on the season-ending injured-reserve list because we felt, number one, the fact that he might be able to come back and play would be a good thing for him—it would give him something to shoot for and give him a positive outlook—and, second, for the team, the idea that he might be back would be a good thing.

Right after the surgery, Peyton wasn't allowed to do anything in the way of rehabilitation for the better part of six weeks. Then, in typical Peyton fashion, he went right at it a hundred miles an hour, but progress was slow, it was tedious, it was frustrating. But he kept working at it, kept working at it, kept working at it. He was trying like the devil to get back and play.

I was asked a million times by media, "Where is he in his recovery? Is he 85 percent? Is he 75 percent? Is he 60 percent?"

The goal was to get him to at least 85 percent, because at the outset, Dr. Feuer said to all of us in the process, including Peyton, "Who's to know what a hundred percent is in any professional football player? Who's to know what 85 percent is? Based on my long history in this game, if he can get to 85 percent of what he was, just in terms of lifting weights and doing the kinds of things he would do as a quarterback, I'd feel comfortable putting him back on the field."

Peyton would never get to that point during the season. Meanwhile, we signed Kerry Collins to be our starting quarterback, and he wound up suffering a season-ending concussion. We went back to Curtis Painter, and that didn't work out, and we ended up with Dan Orlovsky finishing the season. We lost our first 13 games in a row on the way to an NFL-worst 2–14 record.

We tried to work with Jim Caldwell to get the squad as good as we could get it, but frankly, I think there were some assistant coaches who never got over the loss of Peyton. I never once sensed that among the players. In fact, one of the things I said to everybody who asked me for a recommendation on Jim when he was being considered for head-coaching openings after the 2013 season (before the Detroit Lions would hire him) was that I thought he did his best coaching job that year because through the whole course of that awful season, that team never gave up. Jim wouldn't let them.

The only real bad loss we suffered was 62–7 at New Orleans, where we were completely outplayed defensively and they just cut us up. And great credit to Sean Payton, the Saints' coach, because the score could have been 100–7. He called the dogs off in the first series of the fourth quarter, and for that I will be forever grateful. Other than that, we were in every game. We were a fumble, an interception, one bad play away from being 8–8 or 9–7.

Even though we were 14–2 and went to the Super Bowl in Jim's first year as head coach in 2009—one of the best debut seasons for a head coach in NFL history—he did an incredible coaching job when we were 2–14. To keep those guys focused and to keep them fighting as he did was absolutely amazing. One of two back-to-back division victories we had late in the season was at our place against the Texans. And they were playing for a No. 1 seed and we kicked their butts. That tells you something about the character of the guys we had.

One day, near the very end of the season, Peyton put together kind of a mini practice after the regular practice, with Jeff Saturday and some receivers and even a couple of defensive backs. Jim Irsay and I had concerns about even having him on the field at all, for fear that something might go wrong, but the doctors felt pretty comfortable with allowing him to work within that skeleton situation.

There was clear progress in the way Peyton threw—keeping in mind that we were at ground zero in September—but not enough to where you would say, "We're going to put him on the field." We decided there was no way he was ready to play, but we ended the season with the idea that he would come back the following year. There were enough signs of forward movement that you thought he could do it.

But Jim Irsay was very concerned, and I think genuinely so, that Peyton might injure himself again and would then be in a position where he might sustain a life-altering injury.

I thought Peyton would come back without question. However, because we had no physical guarantees relative to how soon or how well he could come back, there was no question, with the first-overall pick of the 2012 draft, we were selecting a quarterback. Whether he was going to be the heir apparent and sit for a while—à la Aaron Rodgers behind Brett Favre in Green Bay—or whether he was going to take over from Day One, to me was immaterial.

Chris and I met with Mr. Irsay on the Saturday prior to the last regular-season game. By then, we had completed the vast majority of our scouting work on the top two quarterbacks in the draft—Andrew Luck, of Stanford, and Robert Griffin III, of Baylor. My, son, Brian, was an assistant coach on the Stanford staff, so I had seen Andrew up close and personal for two years, including being around him for two games during the 2011 season.

"You make the decision," I said to Mr. Irsay. "Both guys are incredibly talented. I think both are can't-miss. Andrew's bigger. He runs just as much as RG3; he just does it better because he doesn't expose himself. RG3 is far more explosive, speed-wise; he's an Olympic-class hurdler. But he does have a habit of getting in awkward positions when he's tackled.

"As far as I'm concerned, you could go with either one, assuming all of the psychological information comes back okay, which I can't believe it won't because I've talked with people at both schools. You make the decision. And then if Peyton's not ready to come back at the start of the season, the heir apparent takes the field. If he is, then the heir apparent sits for a while and we've got our quarterback for the next fifteen years."

Jim said, "I want Luck because he doesn't run as much, and running quarterbacks get hurt."

"That's fine by me," I said. "That's good logic. I agree."

That was the end of our discussion.

Two days later, I was fired, as were many others, including Jim Caldwell.

There are always things you can do better. Each year, I make a list of things I try to improve upon, which is something any executive should do. There are mistakes that you make. There are things that you should have anticipated that you didn't.

The only regret I have about any of my time in Indianapolis was that we weren't more proactive the minute we heard there was something wrong with Peyton. Lockout or no lockout, I regret not being better prepared for this catastrophe. Who's to say if our problems would have been resolved, but we might very well have ended up with Colin Kaepernick or Andy Dalton or somebody else to play quarterback and things could have turned out differently.

It's hard to live with a mistake the cost so many good people who had done so many wonderful things their jobs. But as Marv said, and Peyton proved, "Expect adversity. Expect more to overcome it."

After I was let go by the Colts, I heard from many, many players by phone. Their message basically was, "Thanks for bringing me here and helping to create an organization we're all proud of." That was heart-warming and I couldn't be prouder of them.

As I reflect on my entire career in professional football, I'm reminded of something that took place after the party Jim Kelly threw in Akron, Ohio, to celebrate his 2002 induction into the Pro Football Hall of Fame. The people organizing it on Jim's behalf put all of us who were a part of those great Bills teams into a long side room. We sat there—coaches, players, trainers, scouts, you name it—drinking beer and swapping stories and telling jokes, and just having a great old class reunion.

I'm sure I'm speaking for everybody when I say how great it was to be back with that gang again. It was a happy, happy time. It was our team, our group, our family. It was one of those moments that you'll never forget.

All of a sudden, four or five of us looked up and noticed there was a large, plate-glass window that fronted the room. And outside were people with cameras (which were still being used back then) taking photographs of all of us sitting around the table. Somebody then suggested that we should go stand on a bandstand that was outside and let people take all of the pictures they wanted rather than having them shoot through the glass. And we all said, "Yeah, that's great. Let's do it!"

Out we went to the bandstand, and people flocked to it in droves. There were so many flashbulbs going off, we couldn't even see. Jim was standing out front, with the rest of us behind him, and the crowd was cheering and singing "Shout!" It was marvelous.

Finally, it was time to leave, and as Eileen and I walked out, we ran into a couple on the street.

"Excuse me," the husband said. "Would you mind posing for a picture with us?"

"No, not at all," I said. "I'd be honored."

We took the photo and I signed an autograph. Then I said, "Let me ask you something: Why would you want a picture with me? This is Jim's night. He's the guy who went into the Hall of Fame. He's the guy who made this all possible. Why would you want my picture and autograph?"

"Because all of you gave us the happiest times of our lives."

I was just speechless. I became too emotional to have a response.

But thinking about it after so many years, what I should have said was, "No, it was the other way around."